Escape Out the Window

by Kari Lyn

Preface

Healing the wounds of any kind of abuse whether physical, psychological, or sexual is a difficult process. Nobody knows one sure way to make it all better. What is healing? How do you do it? Because of the many recent movements such as #MeToo and actions by victims of abusive sexual misconduct during 2017-18, I decided now is the time to publish this story.

Table of Contents

CHAPTER 1 - Becka's Story

I was only three the first time Momma left. I don't remember very much about her then or exactly when it happened, only that it did. Granma had a photograph of her on her bureau. I would stand on a chair pushed up against it and spend long moments gazing at her sepia-toned face to memorize how she looked. It was a wedding portrait, Momma in a teal-colored suit, an ivory blouse with a ruffle neckline, pearls, and a smart-looking felt hat that matched the suit with long feathers off to one side. Daddy wore his church-going suit, the one with little tiny stripes; he wore a hat, too.

After Momma left, Daddy and I went to live in Granma and Granpa's two-story house in Dallas. I loved my Granpa dearly and he loved me; it was a bond we had shared from the start. We both liked to play tricks on Granma, like hiding from her when she came back from the store, then jumping out and yelling "Surprise!" I could tell when he was grinning with his blue eyes twinkling that he was up to mischief, either to tease me or Granma.

One day, I was sitting at the enamel-topped kitchen table coloring in a book with new crayons. Granpa came in late for supper and Granma was angry. She always got angry when he was late. He gave her a big story about how he and his friend, Hank, had gotten off work early and gone fishing in Trinity River. The post office was right by the river so they could fish a couple of hours before dark. He told about how they had caught forty fish between them in two hours, and he marked out their enormous size with his hands, saying the game warden had shown up and taken them all away. And all because they had no license, he said. He winked at me, laughed, and smiled so hard I thought his cheeks would crack, but Granma just kept glaring at him with her steely grey eyes. Sometimes her look was so stern it hurt.

While they squabbled playfully, I sat with the crayon box to my nose, inhaling the waxy smell. When it seemed like Granma could hardly take his teasing any more, Granpa scooped her little body up in his arms, lifting her clear off the floor to nuzzle his whiskers in her neck.

"Oh, Maizy," he said, "I just love you." Granma's name was Daisy

Ann, but Granpa called her Maizy. He said that was the color of her hair, like maize. I didn't know for a long time what maize was. I could just tell that Granpa loved her and he loved me. Try as he might though, I knew he never went fishing. That's just how Granpa did things to tease.

"And you, Little Becka," he laughed as he caught my eye. He put Granma down to scoop me up next in his big, gentle hands. I ran away squealing with delight that the chase was on, a game we played every evening.

"I love to squeeze my Little Pillow, too. I'm gonna catch you and squeeze all your smiles out onto your face." I ran to hide in Granma's parlor. "I might even squeeze some giggles out too, so watch out," he called after me.

As I rounded the corner from the hallway into the parlor I ran smack into Daddy's legs and fell to the floor. He didn't pick me up or even move, just stood tall over me with an angry face. His face could be hard sometimes like Granma's.

"Rebecca Ann! How many times have I told you not to run in the house?" he scolded. Granpa came just behind me.

"Bobby, I didn't know you were here. We're just playing our game, me an' Becka. She didn't do no harm. Come on, Becka. We'll go sit on the porch swing till Granma has supper ready."

I took the big hand he had stretched toward me and followed him outside, leaving Daddy to read his books. That's how it was all the time. Granma was loving, but she was also stern. She was a church-going woman, full of Southern hospitality befitting a Dallas housewife. She would say I was just like her, always taking up the rear. I didn't think I was like her at all. Daddy was like her: hard as steel and with little to say.

When it came to my being sick Granma was full of caring. I got pneumonia when Momma left. Granma fussed over me like I was her own, nursing me back to health. First there was the medicine from the doctor, and then there were all her home remedies. She taught me their names: comfrey, licorice, garlic, golden seal, and dandelion. She tried all her teas, plasters, and soups. Nobody knew what it was that made me well.

Daddy was there in his body but he seemed far away a lot of the time, usually reading poetry books. He wore his glasses when he was reading, and they made him look so mean I would stay away from him. Other times, without his glasses, I thought he was handsome, and I loved to be with him. His deep grey eyes could look right into me, like he saw my thoughts; sometimes he looked straight through me to somewhere beyond. He had thick, dark brown hair that he combed away from his forehead in smooth waves. I would watch him comb it for many minutes at a time, twist his head this way and that. He was tall and lean, like Granpa. People said he looked like his papa, but his nose was too big and his ears stuck out more than Granpa's.

I was afraid of Daddy on his grumpy days. He grumbled to Granma or Granpa, and he rarely spoke to me. I knew he was mad at Momma for going away, so he was mad at everybody. He didn't want me near him on those days. But he was sad, too, like I was. For a long time he didn't have a job after Momma left, and then when he got one I don't think he liked it much. He worked in an office keeping books, which he said meant he would write in them. I wasn't allowed to write in books. When we were both sad and Daddy wasn't angry, I would sit on his lap quietly. Then I felt we were a comfort to each other.

My Granpa was the one who played with me and made the light shine in my heart. He had only a little hair on the top of his head, but plenty on his arms and the back of his hands. I liked to rub his arms like I was petting a soft kitten, so Granpa would purr and meow. It was his legs that made him so long, and something else that made him lean. Nobody knew what that was, because he ate plenty of Granma's chicken-fried steak, gravy, and barbecue, and he never gained an ounce. Granma swore he had hollow legs, and I couldn't figure out what she meant. I pictured them like the chocolate rabbits that I got in my Easter basket.

Summertime air was thick, clinging to my nose and hovering inside my chest. Summertime air was full of hay seed from Brown's fields just down the street, the smell weaving itself in with a chorus of cicadas. Summertime air was thick with tiny droplets that glistened on my skin and soaked my clothes. I loved all that summertime in my bedroom out on the sunporch, just off the upstairs bedrooms. Vines growing up the side of the house to my screened porch were like Jack's beanstalk, and I was sure would one day grow up higher than the clouds.

There were sweet lilacs in the spring, smelling so good I wanted to eat them. An old magnolia tree made shade and huge, fragrant blossoms, which is where I imagined the fairies lived. The fairies were just fireflies that danced on the night's dark blanket.

One day late in the afternoon the sun came through a window and beamed onto the stairs in ribbons of dust-speckled light. I lay across the front steps, moving down one step at time as the sun's rays also moved from one to another. Starry dots of dust drifted above me, then disappeared when I tried to catch them in my cupped hands. I heard Granpa talking to Daddy in the parlor, so I crept down to peek around the corner.

"You should spend more time with your daughter, Bobby. She needs you more now with her momma gone."

"I know it, Pa, but I just don't know what to do with myself any more. I still can hardly think straight since Faye left. Anyway, anybody who'd go off and leave her daughter can't be much of a momma. Becka doesn't need a momma like her."

"So, all the more reason you should spend some time with her. You been readin' your books and drinkin' too much to even notice her. Why don't you put her to bed at night and read to her; or tell her some stories, the way I used to do you when you were a boy. I play with her, but she needs you."

Granpa wasn't smiling when he talked to Daddy. His blue eyes didn't sparkle at all, and a deep trough gathered his eyebrows closer together. Mostly he only looked like that when he was lecturing Daddy. After that day Daddy started giving me my bath and putting me to bed. He didn't know any stories to tell, so I told the ones from Sunday School. Usually he was asleep soon after I started. I loved those times of being close to my daddy.

One hot, humid evening Daddy took me upstairs for my bath. Granpa happened to come in. Daddy was rubbing the washcloth and looking close between my legs when Granpa appeared at the door.

"What are you doin'?" he snarled. His brow had that trough in it, pinched up mad. "You don't need to be washin' her like that! That's not the way you do a baby. What's the matter with you, you good-for-nothin!"

Daddy rocked back on his heels, startled by Granpa's sudden entry. He dropped the washcloth, and for a moment his mouth hung open. Then he got his own hard look on his face, stood up and stomped out of the room. "Then you do it yourself, damn it," he hollered as he ran downstairs.

I heard the front door slam. I was confused about what had happened and felt sad. Granpa's face went from angry to maybe confused and sad as he stood by the bathtub looking at me. Then he smiled and said, "Come on out, Becka. Let's get you into your nightie, and I'll tell you a story before bed."

Daddy wouldn't give me my bath anymore, but sometimes he came out on my sunporch and talked to me a while. He said he didn't want to hear any more Bible stories because they put him to sleep, so I told him the stories Granpa told me. He would smile a little bit and say he remembered Granpa told him that same story when he was little. Daddy didn't have much for lips except two thin lines that were usually straight across. Sometimes when he was with me on my sunporch, the two lips would soft-en and curl on the ends, and I knew Daddy wasn't mad then.

While I told the stories, Daddy stroked me on my head and up and down my arms. And sometimes he rubbed my legs because I complained they were hurting. "Your legs always hurt at night, Rebecca Ann. Maybe it's because those legs are growing. Or maybe you just want somebody to give you attention," he would say. "I think you're just making it all up so Daddy will rub you."

When Daddy rubbed my legs, he let his fingers slide all the way under my nightie and touch the soft place between my legs. It felt good, and made me relax. After he left I thought about the rubbing and felt kind of naughty, like I had done something bad. I knew Granpa and Granma would be mad at me; and maybe God would be mad too, but I didn't know why.

Those times when Daddy came to put me to bed were special because it was about the only time I saw his lips get soft and turn to a small smile. His voice got soft and gentle too. He said I was his special little girl, and that we didn't need anybody else, just each other. He started to show his affection again, like before Momma left. Somewhere inside me was a memory of Momma and Daddy both loving me. It was a memory without any words or pictures, more like I felt it, a good feeling from the past.

Chapter 2 - Therapist's Story

Becka swayed from side to side as she made her way over
to the chair I offered her. She eased the mass of her body into the
over-sized recliner and grimaced, making it appear to be painful to
move. She had called me for an appointment in the spring of 1986,
saying she wanted hypnosis to help her lose weight. With well over a
hundred pounds to lose, I sensed a challenge ahead for both of us.

"Have you ever been able to help someone as fat as I am?"
she asked right away.

I looked at her carefully before I answered, wondering what
it was she really wanted to know. The real questions that people
want to ask are often disguised, hidden in some other questions.

"Depends on what you mean by help," I replied. "What kind
of help are you looking for?"

Becka looked at me pleasantly. She had round cheeks and
sea-green eyes that looked directly into mine. Curly dark hair circled
her face like a wooly cap, giving her the look of a rotund elf. She
sighed deeply and closed her eyes. "I need a lot of help," she said. "I
hope you can handle it."

I felt the warning in her reply. To my surprise Becka had
brought along her roommate, Gail, who also wanted to lose weight
but only about thirty pounds. Gail had the kind of sturdy, muscular
body I would expect to find in a physical therapist, as she was. She
wore her sandy hair pulled back in a braid that hung down to the
middle of her back. Both women were dressed in cotton jersey
jogging suits, Gail's a navy blue, and Becka's a deep green. But
the similarity of their jogging suits was as close as they came to
looking like one another.

Gail spoke with a drawl and I later learned she grew up in

Alabama. "We were just hoping you'll hypnotize us, say some powerful words, then wake us up skinny." She chuckled and grinned at Becka. "Right, Becka? We've tried every which way there is, and it's all just a pain in the neck. You can make it easy with hypnosis, can't you? Well, anyway, we don't really think that, huh, Becka? We know you have to do it yourself, but we're hoping you could make it a little easier."

Gail rambled on about trying to lose weight. I enjoyed hearing her accent, found it attractive. Gail was much more garrulous than Becka, who seemed all too willing to let her roommate do most of the talking. I wondered if Gail's friendly, outgoing way was ever intimidating to Becka. As we talked about the hopelessness of dieting and the possible alternative ways to lose weight, Becka kept her eyes downcast. She picked at some invisible lint fibers on the arm of the chair and dropped them onto the floor. I put my questions directly to her, but she would glance my way briefly, then answer still gazing at the arm of the chair. I felt she was guarding something or wanting to say more.

"I'm afraid I don't have a magic wand or any secret potions," I said, "but I have found some ways to help people with this. You will need patience. It could take months, even years. I do use hypnosis, which is the power of suggestion. The suggestions I give you will help you change your attitudes and desires, not only about food, but about yourselves as well. It's an approach that's very positive and reinforces self-esteem. You've got to feel good about yourself to keep the weight off permanently."

Becka looked up at me earnestly when I said self-esteem. "That's what we need, huh, Becka? Self-esteem, right?" Gail was nodding and pointing at Becka with her chin. Becka nodded back, keeping her eyes on me, waiting for me to say more.

I continued. "To me, self-esteem is at the heart of struggling with extra weight. Most people decide they will like themselves *after* they drop the weight they want to lose. Meanwhile, they lose some and gain it back, over and over, never arriving at *'liking themselves.'* I'll help you learn to feel good from the start, before you reach your goal so you'll be able to keep going."

Becka looked back down at the arm of the chair and picked at some more invisible lint. She seemed agitated, shifting her weight in the recliner. "I told you I need a lot of help," she reminded.

We spent the rest of the session covering how the hypnosis program works. I told them that they wouldn't need to come to me directly for a long time because they will listen to cassette tapes at home that will hypnotize them in my voice and keep reinforcing the attitudes they want to change. They would learn to change their lifestyle and their thinking gradually and be able to explore whether they have some unconscious payoff from overeating and having extra fat on their bodies.

I explained further, "Hypnosis is an altered state of awareness in which you are awake, in control, and able to think about what I am saying, even though your mind may wander sometimes from what I say. The common misconceptions about being hypnotized are that the hypnotist has control over the person, or that one is asleep. In fact, some people describe the trance state as one of increased or heightened awareness. People usually feel deeply relaxed, may daydream some, normally feeling refreshed afterward. Sometimes they may forget what was going on during the trance state, but more often they can remember it quite clearly. And you don't have to worry about doing something silly or dangerous under hypnosis. No one will carry out suggestions that oppose their beliefs or values."

During the second session with Becka and Gail, I learned a number of things that completely changed the course we were following. Gail started off talking right away, bubbling over with pride about Becka losing several pounds the first week.

"I'm sure it was the hypnosis tape you gave us, Kathleen. It seemed like magic, because the tape made it so easy to cut down on fats and sugar, and to eat healthier foods. We aren't able to start exercising yet though. Our tiny little apartment is just too small to set up the exercise cycle. But we'll be moving pretty soon to a bigger place, right, Becka?" Becka nodded and smiled a little at me rather than staring at the arm of the chair.

"I have a confession to make though," Gail said. "I have to admit that I'm coming to these sessions mainly to get Becka to come. I don't know if you guessed this, but she and I are lovers; and I care about her a whole lot. I'm worried for Becka's sake about her weight, but even more about her history. She's going through some problems at work, and she has a lot of other things from her past that bother her. I'd be glad to help in any way I can, like losing weight with her. But she has to do the rest."

I looked at Becka and found her staring at the arm of the chair again, plucking at the fabric. "Would you prefer individual therapy?" I asked.

Becka sighed deeply. "I don't really want to go through it again, but I know I need to. I know my weight isn't the core of the problem, but the result of it. So yes, I would."

That changed the nature of our work from their joint effort to lose weight to psychotherapy for Becka. Gail no longer attended the sessions, but she called occasionally to talk about Becka, with Becka's permission. The first week on the hypnosis program had been successful, but Becka didn't do very well following that second meeting. She was under a lot of stress and binged whenever something didn't go well. She was a registered nurse, and her position in the administration of a private nursing home was one of considerable responsibility. She told me briefly that her boss didn't like her and was making a lot of trouble for her by creating an issue out of something about which she didn't have enough information. It could result in Becka getting fired. She was also feeling discouraged about the binges and not losing any more weight.

"Why is it important to you to lose weight?" I asked.

After some thought she replied, "To have control; to be sane; to get rid of the pain in my legs and in my head; and because I want to grow up. This pain in my head is more of a psychological pain, not a physical pain."

"What do you mean by 'grow up'?" I asked.

"Oh, I can handle things in a responsible way all right, like my job. It just feels like I've missed some part of my childhood, and I need to go through it in order to be more complete. Maybe it's part of the problem I'm having with my boss, because I know I do my job well. I was in therapy for a while a few years ago, and I can tell there is still a part of me that needs to grow up. I feel stuck, needy, like I still need a mother, and stuck not being able to lose all this stupid fat."

"There must also be a part of you that doesn't want to lose the fat, or at least that doesn't want to give up eating the way you have been," I proposed. "You either want to hold on to the fat, or not change your eating habits, or both."

Becka looked puzzled. "I *do* want to lose weight."

"I'm sure you do. But don't you think that if every part of you was in agreement about doing it, then you would have?"

Becka still held her puzzled expression, so I explained further. "Think of an example of something that you really want to do, no doubt in your mind about it, and then you do it.

"Becka looked up toward the corner of the room behind me. "The only thing that comes to my mind right now is when I want to sit down in front of the TV and do nothing, after work."

"Can you picture yourself doing that?" I asked. "What is it like to know when you really want to sit down after work and watch TV?"

Becka kept looking up in the corner and said, "I just know that I am physically tired and deserve to relax after I've been on my feet all day; that's all it is."

"So at those times, no other part of you is raising any objection, and there is no conflict. But what if a part of you came home really, really hungry and part of you wanted to eat?"

"Well, I guess I couldn't relax until I did."

I went on, "Now that's an example of a time when you know with all certainty what you want. As long as there are no objections by any other part of you, you can relax. But as soon as you have some other need, there is inner conflict until you take care of it. Needing to eat is something that is easily identified, but many of our psychological needs are not."

Becka nodded as if she was following this, so I continued, "Now find an example of something you do, but you're not sure you should or want to be doing it, something you have doubts about."

Again Becka looked up toward the corner of the room, and then down at the arm of the chair. "When I eat."

"So are you saying that some part of you wants or needs to eat, yet some other part of you doesn't want to?"

Becka agreed readily. "Yes. I feel guilty about everything I put in my mouth, whether it's good for me or not. It's gotten so I don't even enjoy what I do eat. Food is almost evil."

"Then you have a part of yourself that enjoys eating, needs to eat, and another part that feels guilty about it. What happens when the part of yourself that wants to lose weight decides you will eat less or differently?"

Becka was animated now. "When I start out I do really well. I eat all the right things and keep away from fats and sweets. Then I get hungry and all hell breaks loose. Next thing I know I'm out of control and eating all the junk I had resolved not to touch."

"Would you say some other part of you took over?"

"Yes, it's like another part of me says, 'What the hell — a few more calories can't be that important;' or 'I'll lose it next week;' or 'I just don't give a damn!'"

I went on, "Let us assume that all parts of ourselves serve a useful purpose. All behavior is purposeful. And these various parts of ourselves each have their own purpose to serve; every purpose is somehow positive, even if it doesn't *appear* so on the surface. An example might be a person who drinks alcohol to cope with stress, difficulties, and pain. The useful positive purpose of alcohol for the drinker is coping. Does that make sense?"

"You're saying that I eat too much and stay fat for a good reason. It's hard to imagine wanting to stay fat. What can I do about the part that wants to be thinner?"

"That's our job," I replied. "We need to know what purposes are served by eating and by extra fat before you can actually change these things. Parts of us are very powerful. Each one takes its job seriously, and thus, change can be difficult. You can't just get rid of a part; it's not even wise to do so. But we can make it easier if we can find out how the part is serving you. We can help it find other ways to do the same job, allowing the part of you that wants to lose fat to do so."

"I know I use food to feel better," Becka said.

"There — you've identified one of the purposes for eating too much or the wrong foods. It means you have a part that has the job of finding ways to feel better."

"And my smoking is another thing I do to cheer myself up. I'd like to quit that too. Not good for a nurse to smoke."

I nodded. "And I'll bet you thought all along that this part of yourself that gets you to eat is a bad part."

"Well, it's true. It is bad. I don't want to eat poorly, and I don't want to be fat forever."

"Yes, but you see, it isn't the part that is bad, but rather the behavior that the part learned that you could call bad. The part just has the job to make you feel better, and you've agreed you want to have a part that does that. There are really no parts of us that are truly bad. They are in service of doing something for us that we actually need, but they've learned to make poor choices."

"It sounds like semantics to me," Becka said. "Word games."

"In one sense, that's true, but we are all pretty much run by words. Words are also our thoughts and a large and powerful part of our experiences of living and how we survive. Hypnosis is all about words, just words carefully chosen to create an effect, to cause a shift in thinking or feeling, or instill change. Words can manipulate and words can bring about change. Think of advertising. Change is difficult because so often we don't handle our inner conflicts and in a way that takes care of all of our needs — basic needs."

After a few more moments of thought Becka asked, "So maybe I eat to handle stress, but what possible reason could I have for wanting to keep the fat?"

"If nothing comes to mind immediately, let's go find out while you're in a trance state. The answers often come easier that way." I invited Becka to lean back in the recliner until she was comfortable and ready to let her eyes close. I spoke in a calm, soothing voice, a pitch lower than my normal voice, gradually slowing down the pace. It would become the hypnotic tone and tempo that would eventually signal immediately to Becka's unconscious that she was to relax into trance. I suggested she pay attention to how her body was beginning to relax naturally, and to notice the steady, slowing rhythm of her breathing. Then I told her that she would relax a little more deeply with each breath she took. By slowing down the pace of my words and having her think of a place that would be safe and peaceful for her, I was able to induce a deep state of relaxation. I suggested she would relax even more deeply while I counted downward from ten to one, when she would be deep asleep, yet still listening to my voice.

I asked Becka to search for reasons why any part of herself would not want her to lose her fat. The answers came readily: to keep men at bay; to have more time to grow up. It was clear that her fat was protection. When I asked if it was acceptable to her to have a part of herself that had the job of keeping her safe, she agreed. I then asked her to thank this part for trying to keep her safe for many years by keeping her fat.

"I do feel safer with the fat. I'm glad it's kept me safe, but I don't want the fat any more."

"I understand completely," I told her. "Don't forget that this part has been doing the best it knows how to do, and it might like some credit for that, even if it's not the best way to go about it. It seems it has worked to some extent. Let's propose that we begin to teach that part some other ways to keep you safe. It could still have the job of protection, but it can learn to do it in a more satisfying way that doesn't cause other problems."

"Like how?" Becka whimpered.

"For example, the part would have to learn to be assertive in general, and how to keep men at bay, to be appropriate both verbally and with body language that says no. Right now, you have a certain kind of body language that shows you are armored against men; and the fact that you are a lesbian gives you additional protection. My guess is that your size keeps more than just men at a distance." Becka made no response to this.

"Would that part of yourself be interested, even if it doesn't
know yet how to do it, in learning more satisfying ways to protect
yourself, so that the part of you that wants to be slimmer can move
forward to lose that weight?"

Becka's silence continued for a few moments. "I don't
know. I just have this pain in my chest, and I keep hearing screaming inside my head. Like a voice is screaming no."

"Whose voice is it?" I asked.

"I don't know. It's a tiny voice, like a little girl, and now
she's sobbing. It must be my voice, but it's very small. She's
scared, and she doesn't want to agree to change. She's too
scared."

"What is scaring her, Becka?"

"She's too small. She doesn't know how to say no. She
never learned how. I can see her now. She's all curled up in a fetal
position, and she's hiding under some stairs in a dark corner.

"Can you get closer to her?"

"No. She gets more frightened. She wants me to leave her
alone and not try to change anything."

"I can understand how frightened the little girl would be
that we come along and tell her we're going to change things." I
then began to drone a string of hypnotic suggestions, putting em-
phasis on certain words intended to instill some trust in her own
capacity to change and to let her know that self-demands and rigid
diets aren't necessary.

"How about if you assure her you won't make any changes
any more rapidly than you have the ability to handle those changes
. . . in a way that's acceptable to her and to other parts of yourself.
You will change when you're able to, feeling competent to do what
you need to do, . . .like an adult. . . . Yet, the little girl needs time to
grow up. You could offer her some assistance from the parts of
yourself that already know about growing up with safety. . . . You
already have some adult resources within you that you learned and
acquired over the years of your life . . and it isn't even necessary
for me to know exactly what they are . . . which can help to make it
safe for you to begin to shed a little extra fat . . . just as you devel-

op more strength to say no when you need to."

Becka had appeared to be taking in all the words, then said, "I don't remember what you just said, but the little girl looks a little more at ease. She still won't come out from under the stairs, but she's not crying now."

"Thank her for listening to us, and ask if she's willing to communicate with us again some time."

Becka was quiet. "She seems willing—."

Kathleen's Reflections

We were beginning to identify some of the deeper, underling issues for Becka to address in future meetings, as well as the surface problems with food and excess fat. Becka's need for protection was obvious, but I still needed to learn from what she was being protected. She was guarded about giving me much information and it made me curious. The appearance of the "little girl" crying under the stairs was troubling. And what was the cause that she couldn't say no, and to whom? Becka clearly had an imaginative capacity for visualizing internally, and her subconscious provided her with rich visual and auditory material with which to work. I suspected that with all the talk of "parts" of oneself, some dissociated part had shown herself as the "little girl" during the session. Such dissociation alerted me to the possibility of childhood or previous trauma, which I had come across in several other cases with obese women.

It is not unusual to find people with post-traumatic stress syndrome having flashbacks, or episodes in which they regress to an earlier stage of life, experiencing life as if they are that age. I wondered if Becka had slipped into this dissociated part prior to this hypnosis session. That might help explain her expressed desire "to grow up." I had deliberately explained to Becka my view of change and why we resist it.

I spend a lot of energy examining my own process of change, since analyzing everything is just part of my nature. Changes I had made came about through very painful experiences and mistakes. I learned to reframe mistakes as "the necessary process of gathering information about what doesn't work." By making mistakes we learn. Many people resist change to avoid the new; the new and unknown can produce anxiety or fear. Most may prefer to stick to what they can count on, rather than risk not being able to control the unknown. Yet the whole process of life and growth is full of change — constant change. As we develop, we must learn to adapt and accept. If we don't adapt we may find life more difficult to manage. And those who have the most opportunities to learn more adaptive skills do best at coping with change.

I remembered reading about research with children who live in rural vs urban areas. The rural children's social lives are more restricted, and they have far fewer circumstances requiring social problem-solving. They demonstrate less creativity, less spontaneity, and less adaptability in problem-solving tasks than urban children. All of life is dependent on a constant flow and balance of some things changing while others remain stable: people's behaviors, values, laws, social customs, all of nature itself is based on both fixed and changing experiences. Some things must remain fixed, or static, like rituals, holidays, and laws, in order to provide a structure or foundation upon which we rest and feel secure, so that we can then proceed with new and spontaneous activities.

When people don't like what's happening and want change, some of them seek out agents of change, such as myself. Becka had come to me asking for help to change. I wondered whether I would be able to help her change the quality of her life for the better. I had no idea what this venture would become, or how my efforts would assist or interfere with hers, but I knew that it would be a challenge. As with all my clients, I would strive to be genuinely myself, honest, and forthcoming whenever it was clinically appropriate. This did not mean I would talk about myself, but that I would share with her from my life experience as it might be helpful.

Chapter 3 – Becka's Story

My life seemed to turn black just before I started school even though I was very excited about it. A neighbor girl who was much older than me came to visit one afternoon. She taught me how to play school and write the letters of my name. I sat at Granma's kitchen table and practiced writing them carefully on a tablet with wide lines. "Look Granma, I can write my name," I boasted.

"Good for you, girl," Granma replied. "We'll be taking you out Friday to get you some new shoes, after Granpa gets home. He'll be coming home early with his pay and he's gonna take us shopping." The shopping trip didn't happen like Granma had planned. The night before, there was a big fight between Daddy and Granpa. I was in bed on my porch. Daddy was in my room rubbing my legs when Granpa came in. They were shouting at each other very loud, and I was frightened. Granpa grabbed Daddy by the shirt and pulled him out of my room, into the upstairs hallway. They were fighting about me but I didn't know what I had done. I curled up as tight as I could under my blanket and squeezed my eyes shut to keep the tears away.

"You goddamn sonofabitch!" Granpa growled through his teeth. I heard their bodies slamming against one another, the dull thud of fists pounding flesh, heavy breathing and grunting, and then came Granma's voice in a high pitched wail, "Dear Lord, have mercy! Please God, don't let them kill each other." Then there was a loud crash, like a body heaved against the wall; then it slumped down to the floor.

"Get out — of my — house," Granpa sputtered out. "I don't want — to see — your ugly face."

"Have mercy, Frank," Granma was begging. "Mother of God. What in heaven's name got into you? His nose is bleedin'. Why are you doin' this?"

"Just leave it be, Maizy. Bobby, I said get out of here, now." Granpa's breath came a little easier now. "Maizy, that's the end of it."

I heard Daddy groaning and Granma helping him down the stairs. I was shaking so hard I thought I might fall off my cot, but I didn't dare get up.

The rest of the night went slowly as I lay in my bed, trying to hear anything else and wondering why I had been so bad to make everyone upset.

The next morning, Daddy wasn't there at all, and Granpa had already left the house. He didn't come home early to take us shopping but when he did come, it was after dark. Granma was steely hard all day and didn't talk to me much at all. She had darkness in her eyes that told me she was brooding over what happened.

Daddy came back in the house a day later, but Granpa wouldn't talk to him. He acted like Daddy wasn't even there. Granma fussed at Granpa about the fight, but he didn't go and nuzzle her neck to make her happy. He told her again it was over and not to be talked about. And Daddy didn't come out on my sunporch to say goodnight. I wanted him to come, but thought I must have been bad to ask him to rub my legs.

Something woke me up on another night. I lay on my cot listening until I realized it was sobbing I heard. Frightened once again, I crept down the hall toward the sound. It came from Granma and Granpa's room. The door was open a few inches, casting a bluish light into the hall. I kept listening, and all I heard was weeping. It was Granma. Finally I got the courage to look inside the room. The room glowed blue. Granma was kneeling on the floor beside her bed where Granpa lay asleep. Her hands were folded like she was praying; but she just cried into the sheets, her head resting on her hands. I saw Daddy sitting on the rocking chair by the bureau. He was stiff, his long thin fingers squeezing his knees till his knuckles were white. He was staring at the floor, not looking at Granma or Granpa. The purple blotches were still there on his face from the fight, standing out from his pale skin.

I became more frightened with the confusion about what was happening. Why was Granma crying? Why was Daddy in their room? And why didn't Granpa wake up? Then Granma's crying slowed down. She hiccuped as she wiped her face and blew her nose with a handkerchief. She always had hankies in her pockets or sleeves. Slowly she turned toward Daddy.

"You did this to him," she whispered. "You killed him. I don't know what it was you two were fighting over, but you caused this to happen."

I felt like I had been struck by a lightening bolt. I didn't understand. I stared at Granpa, trying to make him out through the dim light surrounding him from the small lamp on the bedside table. He was more white than Daddy, more blue-white than white, but he looked like he was sleeping peacefully. I didn't believe he was dead.

Daddy didn't move or answer Granma. He just kept staring at the floor with his hands clenched to his knees. I waited for something else to

happen, and then started to believe I was having a bad dream. Granma
didn't say any more. She turned back to Granpa's still body and clutched his
hand. When she started moaning again, I pulled back from the door so I
couldn't see any more. I don't know how long I sat on the floor or how I got
back to my cot, but I woke up there the next morning.

I could hear strange voices in the house. Sometimes they came
from down the hall and sometimes from the kitchen below me. I waited for
Granma to come and get me. When she finally came, I was shocked to see
her face. It was haggard and swollen up from all her crying.

"Time to get up, Rebecca Ann," she said. "I want you to hurry on
up and get dressed before you come down for breakfast."

"Why?" I asked. "Why can't I have breakfast in my nightie today?"

"Never mind," she said crossly. "You're going to go to school soon,
and you have to start learning that you get dressed first."

I felt her starchily clothed body as she pulled a dress over my head
and buttoned it up the back. Her corn-colored hair was usually pulled neatly
to the back of her neck in a bun, with many rows of silken waves along the
sides of her head. But that day the hairs on the sides were sticking out every
which way, like an old broom. Following her downstairs, I hoped to see
Granpa at the kitchen table, as usual, drinking coffee and reading the paper.

"Where's my Granpa?" I asked. Granma didn't answer. "Why was
there blue light in your room last night, Granma?"

Granma just kept stirring at the stove. "Don't be asking so many
questions today, you hear?"

Daddy came into the kitchen from the parlor. "Daddy!" I exclaimed. "You didn't go to work today." I jumped up from the table and ran
to him, knocking over my orange juice. He reached out and caught my arm,
holding me an arm's length away from him.

"Now look what you've done, Rebecca Ann. I've got no happy
reasons for being home from work, and you're not helping, either. Go sit at
the table and eat your breakfast Granma is fixing for you." Daddy's face
was tired too, with nightmarish bruises and puffy bags under his eyes.

I sat at the table with my hands folded in my lap, feeling rejected
and confused. Daddy and Granma were both grumpy and not talking. She
had said in the night that Daddy killed Granpa. I didn't believe it, but I wanted somebody to tell me what was wrong. I wanted my Granpa to come right
then and lift me up and tell me everything was all right.

Later Daddy drove Granpa's car and took me and Granma somewhere like a church, dark and hollow-sounding. It smelled like too sweet
flowers, and there were candles everywhere, but not lit.

The organ in the back corner of the room made me think it must be a church. This place had blue light, too. I could just barely see. A man with a round face and very red cheeks led us into another room beside the church-like one. Daddy and Granma talked to the man for a long time. Then we went to Granma's church and talked to the priest, but we went to a different room than usual. After the priest and Granma talked a while, she began to whimper, and Daddy got very stiff again. The priest put his arm around Granma, and she cried louder. He tilted his head down, looked over the top of the glasses, and saw me by myself. I pulled my legs up and hid my face against my knees. The priest came and sat beside me, touching my arm lightly.

"RebeccaAnn. Look at me." I obeyed. "Has anyone told you where your grandfather is?" I shook my head. He spoke softly, almost in a whisper. "Your grandfather has gone to be with God. The angels came last night and took him to live most happily with the Lord. I know you'll miss him, but it's God's will that he go to be with Him."

My head spun. I didn't see any angels in the night. I didn't believe my Granpa was gone. "Is he coming back?" I asked.

"No, my child. I'm sorry." The priest looked sad. He went back to Granma who was still sobbing. I looked at Daddy and he just kept staring down at the floor.

Going home in the car I asked her,"When is Granpa coming home?"

Granma looked at me through her puffy, reddened eyes, still wet with tears. "He won't be comin' home again, Rebecca Ann. He's gone with the angels to heaven."

"Did Granpa want to go there, Granma?"

Granma began to whimper again and squeezed me closer to her. That was the last of the hugging from her that I can remember getting. Some of Granma must have gone with Granpa.

The day of the funeral, I asked Daddy if my Granpa wanted to go to heaven with the angels to be with God. Daddy said he did. "How did they get to heaven? Did they fly out the window?"

"Yeah, girl, they flew out the window to heaven. And Granpa's not coming back."

I was angry with Granpa for leaving me. He never told me he wanted to go live in heaven, and he didn't take me with him. I wanted to go where Granpa was, but they told me that only God decides when you go to heaven.

It was then that I got pneumonia again. My throat and chest hurt real fierce, and I knew God was punishing me for the all the bad inside me, bad to Daddy and Granma, and so bad that both Momma and Granpa went away. I remember choking for air, sucking at my lips to draw in what I could without so much pain. When the fever came, I had dreams that I was flying with the angels to find my Granpa. My body tried to give up the fight and shook hard to be set free. The nurses in their white dresses were like angels caring for me. They did something to me until I fell into a dark hole, down, down deep. Could this be going to my Granpa? But everything just stopped, and that was all I knew.

I only went to school in the morning. When I got home I would have my lunch on the back steps where I pretended that the angels came to take me to Granpa. I felt swallowed up by emptiness and it made me miss my Momma even more. I tried to fill the void with Granma's home-baked bread, apple pie, and chocolate chip cookies.

Granma took a job and was always working now when I got home from school, but Daddy was home from his job. Soon I needed to find a new haven, because Daddy ruined my sunporch. It didn't feel right anymore. It happened when he came and sat on my cot to talk a little. It started out real nice, with Daddy being so interested in me. "I see you sure like school, Rebecca Ann. What do you like best?"

"I like when Miss Burke reads to us. Some children fall asleep, but I never do because I love stories."

"I'll tell you a story, Rebecca Ann," Daddy offered. "You sit on my lap and I'll tell you about a little girl who loved her daddy very, very much. She loved him so much that she would do anything he wanted her to do. Her daddy had a fortune in gold and jewels. He had everything they ever could want. And the daddy let the little girl have whatever she wanted, as long as she did what he asked."

I imagined a princess and a king, even though Daddy didn't say that was who they were. Caught up in the story, I begged him to continue. While he talked, he stroked my legs, letting his fingers slide under my dress to my panties. I got that warm, relaxed feeling and leaned back against his chest. He continued telling the story, touching me, and soon his hard warmth pushed against my thigh. He reached under me to press on it, stroking it up and down. It was happening again, like the night Granpa hit Daddy.

"Rebecca Ann, you can do this with your hand," he said as he opened his zipper. I was afraid. "Rub up and down right here." His penis bulged out through his underwear, and he pushed my hand against it. He told me to keep rubbing until he said to stop. He grew more warm and sweated. The feeling of his body against mine, sticky, pulsing, and his heavy breathing frightened me more. When my arm grew tired of rubbing, I quit; but he took my hand in his and kept pushing it, groaning quietly, until the wetness spread out on his trousers at the end of the throbbing, and the hardness eased off. I felt sick and ashamed. Somehow I knew it wasn't right.

Many nights I cried myself to sleep and dreamt about Granpa hitting me or beating on Daddy. I awakened in a sweat with my heart pounding, then cried some more that my dear Granpa would hurt me. Other times I dreamt of heaven with Granpa, or of Momma, coming to me like an angel to take me away.

Daddy's story was always about the king's daughter who would do anything the king asked her to do because she loved him so much. There was always a demon that lived in a cave that would try to ruin their happiness. Something bad was happening inside me. A demon lived inside me, with snarling teeth, foaming mouth, and feet with sharp, tearing claws. I knew I was very bad. I was the demon, the bad child that didn't deserve a Momma, that made her Granpa go away because he hated what he knew. The demon came out to punish me and make me bad. I couldn't make it go away. I couldn't stop it and I had to escape, and the only way I knew how was go out the window, the way Granpa had gone.

Chapter 4 - Therapist's Story

Becka came into the office moving very slowly, as if she were weak and in a lot of pain. Her face was pale and aged from the week before. Her eyes didn't look their usual blue-green, now color-less and empty. She had lost more weight and said she was glad about the loss, but that was all she felt good about. Aside from this success, Becka was very angry. The problems with her supervisor had grown more grave, and with the growing conviction that she might be fired, she had resigned. Her previous therapist had been on her mind quite often, and she felt there was something left unfin-ished with her. Becka professed that she had had suicidal thoughts. Gail was planning a trip to visit friends in Memphis without her, friends that Becka didn't know. The prospect of being alone for ten days was upsetting her beyond reason.

"There's a lot of crazy talk going on in my head, Kathleen," Becka said. "A lot of it is negative self-talk. Mumbling that seems to be saying it's not worth it. Life is too shitty to bother to keep putting up with all this. I have a bladder infection. It's painful, and I was trying to treat it with natural diuretics, like cranberry juice, but it got so bad I had to get an antibiotic. One voice says it's because I de-serve it. It's always like this. One thing after another piles up on me and I just don't have the strength to tolerate it any more."

I just listened as Becka heaped the problems into my lap before I had a chance to congratulate her for the weight that had come off. She clearly had reasons to be disheartened. "You know, Becka, you need to see a doctor about taking an antidepressant. The medication may lift you enough to keep you going."

Becka sighed deeply and kept her eyes lowered on the

arm of the chair. "I've been feeling so low that life doesn't seem worth bothering about. I can't take it much more, but I really don't want to take drugs. I know there can be all kinds of problems with medications for depression. I'm so scared Gail is going to Memphis to rekindle her feelings for a former lover. She says it isn't so, but all that fear of abandonment is keeping me depressed."

"And your rage keeps you depressed. You said that you're still angry with your previous therapist?"

Becka looked quizzical, but continued. "Yes. She left me too. I stopped therapy was because she moved away, not because I wanted to. I trusted her. I wish I could tell her off. Everyone I love leaves me."

"So there's all this anger about abandonment, especially women who leave you— your mother, your therapist, your lover, and even in some sense your boss."

"Yes. And then I hear this voice inside me that says I'm crazy to trust another therapist, only to be left again."

"Is that what you think— that I'll leave you too? Or that I might reject you?"

"I suppose so. Kathleen, I just can't take any more losses. I lost my grandmother three years ago too. But I'm already hooked with you. I like you, and I believe you can help me do the work I want to do to grow up. I couldn't leave now even if I thought I should."

"So you have conflict there, too. Part of you is scared of abandonment by me, but another part of you wants to stay and get through the growth that needs to happen."

"Gail is leaving on Friday. Kathleen, I don't know what I'm going to do." She looked at me pleadingly. "I'm terrified of being alone. The worst time of day is from four o'clock on. That's when he used to come home and . . . ."

She closed her eyes tightly and clenched her fists. I asked, "When who used to come home, Becka? — and what?"

She sat with her face pinched into a pained expression, as if tears would flow, but they didn't. After a few more minutes of si-lence and gentle coaxing from me, she whispered, "My father. He came home from work then. That's when it usually hap— happened." After another pause she said angrily through clenched teeth, "Why am I still dealing with this crap! How long does it take to get through it?"

"Did your father abuse you sexually, Becka?"

"Yes. And physically, too. I already went through therapy over it with Myra."

Becka's hands were squeezed into two doughy balls, no evidence of knuckles. Her anger had bolstered her strength. "I had forgotten it all. A few years ago it came back to me— the things that happened. Then Myra moved away, so I figured I had done enough screaming and crying over it." She sat silent once more.

"For some people, incest takes a lot of time to get worked through. Is that where you want to start— giving me some more of your history?" I asked.

Becka seemed to pull herself together, still squeezing her fingernails into her palms and gave a big sigh. "I'm sure it would be easier for you if I start at the beginning. I was born in Dallas. My mother left me and my father when I was about three, so my grandparents helped my father raise me for a few years until she came back. They had gotten a divorce, but when she came back my parents got married again. I don't know why they did. I suppose it was because she was pregnant with my brother, and they had to do the 'proper' thing.

"My mother lived and breathed for men, and she still does — just so they can use her for whatever needs they have. She can't see how she lays herself down like a doormat and lets them walk all over her. She takes care of her latest husband now, a bedridden invalid, like there was nothing else in life to do. She works at her job all day, then goes home and puts up with his whining and complaining. It isn't enough but maybe Joe wants her to pee and shit for him, too."

I made notes as Becka talked. "She left again when I was eleven. I was six years older than my brother, so I had to take care of him and myself. My father was useless. He depended on me all the time to look after Roy. I was a child-mother when I hadn't even had much of one to show me how to do it. Even when she did come back and got herself pregnant, she expected me to help take care of the house and cooking. Then she left to marry some other guy. She was some kind of whore. She was never there when I needed her, and she still isn't. I guess I'm still looking for a mother."

"The issue of looking for a mother is important," I said, "and we'll come back to it. Let's keep going with the history for now."

"The best time was when Granpa was alive. We were very close. He knew Daddy was touching me. I believe if he'd lived I never would have gone through the hell that I did.His love for me is what made life worthwhile. He died when I was five and part of me died with him."

I noticed that she pronounced the names 'Gran-pa' and 'Gran-ma,' with a distinct fondness in tone.

"My mother has been married eight times, twice to my father.

I found out when I was a teenager that I had a half-sister. My mother had her before she married my father the first time. Linda committed suicide when she was thirty. Gassed herself in the garage. Left a husband and two little kids. And nobody could believe it was suicide. They couldn't see any reason for it, but I could. I knew she was unhappy because her husband was beating her, and he was verbally very abusive. Linda was married three times herself, heading in the same direction as our mother.

"My brother Roy has become a lunatic member of the Ku Klux Klan, so that tells you something about him. He is in a world completely foreign to me now, and I loved him so much. I really tried to take good care of him, but I was just a kid myself. I have nothing to do with him anymore. For that matter, with any of my family."

"And they all still live in Texas?" I asked.

"Yes, my mother's mother, too. Grams Kirkwood is still kicking at 83, can't see a blessed thing, but can still tell everybody how to mind their business. Except my mother. She never could tell my mother anything, to this day."

"And where is your father now?" I asked.

Becka's expression became cloudy. "He's in Dallas, too."
"When did you see him last?"

After another long silence and study of the arm of the chair.

Becka replied, "At Granma's funeral about three years ago. And that's the last time I ever will see him, if I have anything to say about it."

I waited for more about why that was so, but let her choose her own time to talk about it. She went on, "History: I got through high school, the last of it at Ursuline Academy for Girls, thanks to Granma. I went on to college and eventually became a nurse."

"So you're a registered nurse. When did you know you were a lesbian?" I asked.

"I always knew I was a lesbian," she stated emphatically.

"It's one of those things you know and never have any doubt about. At least for me it was. I always had a crush on my current teacher, but I fell in love with Miss Windemere when I was thirteen. She taught French. She had beautiful hands, kind hands..." Becka's pupils dilated in a far-away look. Some of the anger dissolved from her face, allowing a bit of a smile. "That was just puppy love. I really fell in love with another student in college, Leslie, who turned my life around. It was my first true relationship. We were together for eighteen years."

I felt startled at this. "You lived together that long?" "Eighteen years is a long time. I thought it was for life." "What happened? How did it end?"

"I met Gail, whom you know, and my world of security came crashing down around me. Everything I thought I knew about love was shattered and in question. I eventually left Leslie for Gail. I still have some guilt, I think, but I'm glad I did it."

"Tell me about your relationship with Leslie," I requested.

"It became very dull, routine. We'd work, come home, maybe watch TV together. It was secure. We believed we would stay together forever. I really cared for her, and she loved me. We grew apart without even knowing it was happening. But the sex part of it wasn't very satisfying. It wasn't until I met Gail that I knew what good sex could be. With Leslie it was always me giving her gratification. I wanted it that way, actually. I was afraid to feel good, and it made me happy to make her happy. We were both immature and didn't know anything. One difference was Leslie didn't know she was a lesbian. I brought her out. I sought her from the start. And I ended it. The end came really hard for Leslie. That was a difficult time."

"And did you and Gail live together after you left Leslie?"

"Yes. We stayed in Dallas for a while, but it got to be too difficult with Leslie nearby. We all had some of the same friends in common. Gail and I moved here to Denver several months ago. I got the job in the nursing home, and she's been building her physical therapy business."

I wondered aloud how the counselling she had gotten fit into this timing. Becka's eyes darkened, and I waited while she thought about what to say next.

"I went to counselling after Granma died, three years ago. Myra dragged it out of me about Dad. I had forgotten all of it until then, but she wouldn't let up on me. First she got me painting pictures, and then she tried to get me on the floor to pound on pillows, but I just couldn't do it. She pushed me too hard, and once I almost hit her. I was afraid I'd kill her. Finally I smashed out the window to keep from hitting her."

"You broke the window in her office?" I clarified.

"I had to get some air! I couldn't breathe in there. I ended up crouched in a corner, just begging her to let me be. I felt like I was going crazy." Becka leaned her head back and closed her eyes as tears began to stream slowly down her cheeks and onto her jersey shirt. "I had just been to my Granma's funeral, and that sonofabitch actually had the balls to try it with me again. Can you believe it? My fat was no protection. That's when the memories started, and I had to go for therapy. I spent four months curled up in a corner every day from four o'clock on through the night. Myra wanted me to do some kind of role-playing and beat on pillows, but I couldn't take it. I begged her not to make me. Oh, Kathleen, you're not going to make me get on the floor, are you?" Becka beseeched me with her eyes, and her voice became small. "I can't.

He had me on the floor. I just can't . . ."

I had pulled my chair closer to Becka's. She took my hand and clung to it. I stroked the back of her hand, assuring her in my hypnotic droning voice that she would not have to get on the floor. After she calmed down I invited her to lean back in the recliner and guided her into a deep hypnotic state.

"You can tell me what your experience is, yet remain very relaxed," I told her. "What is going on right now?"

Becka replied, "All I see is a deep, frightening black hole."

"Usually black holes are pretty frightening. But you're safe now, sitting here in this big comfortable chair, here in my office. You're here with me, and you can see the black hole. Can you make it far away from you, where it's not so frightening?"

Becka could do that, so I continued, "Would you be willing to look into that black hole with X-ray vision and see what's there, from far away?" She was still holding my hand and squeezed it harder when I said this. "It's okay. You're safe."

After some silence Becka said, "Little Becka is in there.

She's a little brat." Her squeeze on my hand got harder still. "I want to bash her!"

"What is that all about, Becka?"

"I want to bang her head against a wall and knock her brains out. She ruins everything in my life. She's mean, vicious."

"You can see her in the black hole. What is she doing?"
"She's making ugly faces."

"Is she the same little girl you talked to last time?"

"No. She looks like me. Spoiled Little Becka, not fat yet, about five years old. I want to bash her."

I wanted Becka to explore this figure further, but with less animosity. "Let's consider for a moment she may be there with an important message to give you, Becka, and not just to be bashed out of your awareness. Perhaps you can acknowledge that Little Becka is there to communicate something you need to learn, or know. Can you invite her to tell you what purpose she serves?"

This was a new thought for Becka. She remained still. "She just taunts me. 'It's for me to know and you to find out,' she says."

"That's right," I said. "It is for you to find out, Becka. Ask her what it would take for her to tell you why she is there."

"It's obvious that she is all the evil and venom inside me. She's everything dark, painful, mean, thoughtless, grotesque, self-ish, and cruel. She thinks the world revolves around her; nobody needs like she does. Always wanting attention, touching— love."

"Do you believe that's true of you, Becka? Do you have parts of you that are mean, thoughtless, and grotesque?"

"Yes. It's Little Becka. She is all that— and worse."

"How does she know that she's all those things?" "Her Daddy told her so. He said it all the time."

"So you have been believing it was true all these years, and when you were a little girl you didn't know that a daddy could be wrong— that your daddy was all wrong about you. He said and did things that he shouldn't have done. Now, as an adult, you know that even fathers make terrible mistakes— that your father made some terrible mistakes and did some pretty awful things, didn't he? He even lied to you about who you are. And somehow the stronger adult part of you is going to have to help Little Becka come to find peace over what happened when you were young."

I chose words to reframe her perceptions of herself and implant positive suggestions. I would soon have to bring Becka back from this altered state, and I wanted her to return with strength to cope with all this negative darkness. I asked her to think what would have to happen to transform the energy of this Spoiled Little Becka into a part that was more positive. She lay quietly be-fore answering, "I have to get rid of her."

I protested, "But she's a part of you, and my experience has been that parts won't leave just because we want them to. Think about what positive traits Little Becka has that could actually be helpful to you?"

"She's got guts— spit and vinegar. She persists and doesn't give up. She's got power."

"Power could be very useful, couldn't it?" I asked.

"I don't want that black power she has, but perseverance could be helpful." Becky continued, "How can I get what's positive without the venom?"

"You might start by thanking her for taking care of your
need to persist, for the spit and vinegar when you need it. Besides,
didn't you say this is the part of you that wants attention, touching,
and love? Is there anything wrong with having a part that wants
those things?"

Becka's grip on my hand loosened a little. "I guess it's
okay. . . . It worked. She kind of changed and got a little color in
her, instead of being just black and grays. She doesn't look quite as
nasty."

I began to drone on in my trance voice, "And I wonder just
how much of that perseverance will be useful to you this week
while Gail is away . . . to keep yourself occupied with things you've
been putting off, reading, letters to write, bills to pay, handwork
you've been wanting to do . . . perhaps now bringing you some
feelings of accomplishment to get things done . . . touching some
other important needs you have, and managing your life with all the
spit and vinegar that it takes to hold strong on your own . . . And
then, too, how quickly you discover the hands of the clock have
already passed through the afternoon and evening . . . hardly taking the time at all to notice what might as well be left forgotten, until
you deliberately choose to recall . . . and then only with the strength
that comes from that adult part of yourself that is strong."

I eased Becka back from her trance state with phrases that
were paced a little faster, gradually increasing in volume. She sat
up, looking transformed from the person who had first come into
my office, dark, angry and in a panic over Gail leaving.

"I feel so much better," she said.

"You can feel wide awake and alert now, too." Becka
looked at our hands, still clasped, and realized she had been
squeezing mine the whole time. She opened my fingers to find little
red arcs that her fingernails had pressed into my palm.

"Oh! Kathleen, I'm so sorry," she exclaimed. "I didn't mean
to hurt you. See how thoughtless and selfish I am."

I assured her it didn't hurt, and I was so caught up in the
trance-work that I hadn't even noticed it myself.

"Can I have a hug?" Becka requested.

The feeling of Becka's soft, fleshy arms wrapped around me, pressed so close to her large body, came as a surprise. It was very gentle, nurturing. There was some sense of her neediness, but more than anything I felt her gratitude, and I was getting rather than giving a hug. I knew she needed a lot of reassurance after being so vulnerable, and she needed modelling in the form of an accepting, caring, and non-rejecting mother-figure. There would be time later to explore this with her.

Kathleen's Reflections

Becka's history had established a pattern of abandonment that was repeating itself, involving feelings of helplessness, futility, and a serious lack of worth. I was concerned about the intensity of her anger with the dissociated part of herself that had appeared in trance, having re-directed that anger and blame from her parents to herself. Her most pressing current problems related to coping with Gail's taking a trip without her, the loss of employment, albeit by resignation, and obtaining new employment soon. I was concerned that she would not consider taking an antidepressant.

I was drawn to Becka and drawn to her story. When I first met her, I had no idea how much her life would become intertwined with my own, how much she would teach me, or that we would someday talk of writing her story together. I found her passionate, inventive, and far more durable than she gave herself credit for.

In the course of one's work as a therapist there are bound to be conflicts or life events of the client that resemble one's own. I had spotted a few with Becka. The first was the simple fact that we were the same age, within two days. Just as Becka's early years were fraught with her mother coming and going from her life, my own mother was also absent a great deal, in her case due to illness and being hospitalized. We were going through similar life experi-ences at the same time: absent mothers, living with relatives, struggling to be good little girls, and praying to have our mothers back. We both wound up in service professions, caring for sick people and trying to make things right. I could relate to Becka's need to please and pacify people to gain acceptance and be liked. Indeed, it would become apparent that it was an Achilles heal for both of us. The parallels I would find over the years could serve to guide me to help Becka make the changes she wanted to make, and at the same time, if I weren't careful, could interfere with her growth. My hope was to use these parallels, any counter-transference, to Becka's advantage.

Becka believed that her mother left her because she was bad, and the same when her grandfather died. Adults seldom realize that children have an unfortunate misconception about how powerful they are. Children can assume themselves responsible for a multitude of events through magical thinking, or infantile narcissism. It is natural in the development of the child, and normally outgrown. So, when unfortunate things happened to Becka, she believed she had caused them. It seemed that her child-mind beliefs had served as a powerful fortress of psychological protection that played well into her adult life, due to emotional stress, and these beliefs had made her the victim in many of her relationships.

I would have to take care to separate which issues were Becka's and which were mine. Knowing myself as I did, she and I were headed into something quite intense, our life threads inextricably woven together by the common and the uncommon of two separate lives. I was about four years old when my mother first became ill. She had a seizure when I was alone in the house with her. I believed that I had caused it, and was very frightened. It happened when she was playing the piano, a classical piece; she was a talented musician and singer. I kept whining at her to give me a cookie, even though she had told me to be still and wait until she finished her piece. I continued to make a pest of myself by interrupting her. Suddenly she started to shake, her whole body convulsing, her right leg banging against the base of the piano. She shook for what seemed to me forever, as I stood watching in horror, immobilized by fear. I thought she was having an angry fit about me being a pesky little brat.

Finally she gasped some words to me: "Go get Mrs. John-

son!" Then the shaking subsided, she passed out and fell over backwards off the piano bench. Relieved to be told what to do, I ran out the front door, down the sidewalk, and down the hill to Mrs. Johnson's house. I thought that my mother was dying. My short legs couldn't carry me as fast as I wanted to go, and I nearly fell forward onto my face. Nothing else existed but the thought that Mrs. Johnson would have to save my mother.

The next part I recall was that my father and a doctor were standing over my mother, now stretched out on the sofa. They talked to each other, but nobody talked to me. I couldn't understand the big words they used, which added to my confusion and guilt about what had taken place.

That was the beginning. My mother had those seizures many more times, but that was the only time she fainted. At first her doctor thought it was epilepsy, but the symptoms were peculiar to her right side, and from then on she remained conscious during the seizures. She would moan and mumble while her right arm and leg shook and contorted, her twisted face silently screaming out the pain she was feeling. It was dreadful to behold, traumatizing my unknowing child-mind.

I carried the guilt of that first incident and her illness with me, believing that being naughty was the cause of it. There was no comfort for me, perhaps because nobody knew what I had experienced, or what I was thinking. That belief helped to shape my personality by my desire to be as good as I could possibly be, because when you make someone angry you can make them sick — or crazy. My brothers and I were told much later that she had multiple-sclerosis, but they didn't really know for sure. People with the diagnosis of multiple-sclerosis don't end up in a state mental institution, and their behavior isn't usually so eccentric or psychotic as hers became. But the diagnosis helped to shield me from the stigma about mental illness that was much worse around 1950 than it is now. Even now it isn't good.

The years my mother spent in a mental institution and the ways she acted so crazy influenced my interest in psychology and the choice to become a therapist. I was very intrigued by human

Chapter 5 – Becka's Story

There's a photograph of Momma in a family album that must have been taken on Granma's front porch the day she came back. Most of my early memories were kept alive because of that family album. She came back near the end of the summer, just before I turned six and went to first grade. Without any warning, I remember she just showed up on Daddy's arm. He glowed like a firefly, he was so happy. I couldn't take my eyes off her, nor could I seem to talk. She wore a soft, flowered sundress with a deep v-neck and a cameo pendant I wanted very much to reach out and touch her, but didn't dare. Shoulder pads under her dress gave her a proud, queenly look. She had on silk stockings and low pumps of woven straw. Her clothes probably came from Neiman-Marcus, where she worked as a sales lady.

When Momma saw me, she hugged me and wanted me to sit on her lap, but I felt too shy. After nearly three years of absence, she was a stranger to me. My only memory of her had been from the wedding picture on Granma's bureau, where she looked very beautiful, but, somehow, I never thought of her as my mother. Momma was an angel in white chiffon, with flowers in her hair. Momma would come and sweep me away to a safe and beautiful place, like heaven maybe, where Granpa was. I recall sitting on the front porch, playing jacks and pretending I'm busy, but secretly watching Daddy and Momma together on the porch swing. They sound like pigeons cooing softly and holding hands. Sometimes Daddy gets louder, like he's gonna get angry, but he holds it back. Sometimes he says, "Aw, come on, Faye, we can do it." He keeps saying, "It will be different. I promise."

I figure they are making up, Daddy courting her all over again. Momma finally gets up from the swing, Daddy still holding her hand. She says, "Give me a little more time, Bobby. I need to think it out." She pulls her hand away gently and comes to sit beside me on the step.

We sit quietly, and Daddy doesn't move. I want her there, close, where I can feel her without touching. I can smell her cologne, hear her breathing, feel her eyes watching me. All of a sudden I want to cling to her body, want her to hug me, want to hear her voice say my name. And as quickly as I want it, it happens. She reaches out to me, and we both burst into tears and heave deep sobs of joy and sadness, of pain and relief. The crying lasts a long time, until we have used up Momma's handkerchief and the one Daddy has in his pocket. Both of us are sopping wet. Daddy brings us more tissues and then walks around to the back of the house.

I curl up in Momma's arms now and pray it will never end, that she won't go away again. A perfect moment: sun filtering through brand-new leaves on the poplar trees in the front yard; the sweet smell of roses mixed with Momma's salt and cologne; the feeling of my body fitting perfectly against hers, safe, so right. I feel the softness of her breasts against my cheeks. I am filled with an urge to bury my face in them, but I don't.

"Let's take a little walk, Rebecca Ann," Momma says. "I'll tell your daddy that we're gonna spend some time together. I'll buy you a treat down at Schriver's Drug Store. How is that?"

I remember sucking a chocolate soda through a straw while Momma told me that she and Daddy were talking of living together again. We would go to our own house and not live with Granma any more. She told me I would go to a different school and make some new friends. I was sad to have to leave Granma's house and my school, but I wanted desperately to be with Momma, so it didn't matter so much. I begged her to take me with her that same day, but she said it might happen soon.

We moved to a different house and everything was different. Daddy was different. For a long time he seemed happier; you could tell because sometimes he read his poetry out loud to Momma and me, and he smiled a lot. Momma was pregnant then and kept her job at Neiman-Marcus until she got really big. When my brother was born, I felt like he was my baby, not Momma's. I wanted to do every- thing myself— feed him, diaper him, make the formula.

It must have been around the time we moved to our own duplex that I got sick again, and the doctor found I had a thyroid problem. He gave me medicine for it, and I started getting fat. I was hungry all the time, even then. Momma didn't like to cook, so she would tell me what to do in the kitchen. Most of what I learned came about by reading cookbooks and fig- uring out how to do it myself. I must have eaten a lot while cooking. Life was good most of the time for me and Roy, once Momma and Daddy were together. I don't recall much of what Momma and Daddy were like with each other. The few memories that stayed with me of those several years were mainly about taking care of Roy and housekeeping, and later, of my French teacher.

One event stands out from all the rest because it involved the whole family. We went to see the Fourth of July parade when Roy was about five years old. There is another photograph in the album of Momma, Roy, and me, probably taken by Daddy. Roy and I are holding little flags, and we look hot and sweaty. Momma is wearing shorts and a halter top and is holding a broad brimmed hat in her hand, which I remember wanting for myself, but she wouldn't let me have it. Roy is wearing shorts, too, but I have on blue dungarees and a striped tee-shirt. I think the stripes were red and white for the holiday, but the photograph is not in color.

Daddy told me to take Roy through the crowd and up front so he could see the parade better, and Momma and Daddy stayed further back. I took Roy's hand and we pushed our way through. Roy waved and shouted as the parade passed, and we both were having a wonderful time. Suddenly I noticed that Roy was no longer beside me, nor anywhere in sight. My heart pulsed with fear. I had to find him, but I didn't know which way to look. Momma and Daddy were frightened and angry. I knew it was my fault.

We all searched for a long time and then went to the police station. I knew the monster in me was making it happen. Suddenly I heard Roy's voice. He came in the door with a policeman and relief swept over me.

Late that evening, I heard Momma and Daddy having an argument in their room. I didn't know what it was about, but they had been fighting more lately. All the feelings of joy that we were a real family that day were drained away. The arguing was a warning of real trouble to come, but I had no idea that Momma would leave us again.

Chapter 6 - Therapist's Story

Becka missed her next appointment when Gail was away because she had contracted bronchitis. It seems they had argued several times before Gail left, and Becka was dealing with flashbacks of childhood experiences with pneumonia and convulsions. She had gotten seriously ill both times her mother left, after her grandfather died, and when she broke up with Leslie. I noticed how inevitably her health decompensated when she was stressed and depressed. Bronchitis appeared this time, illness attacking her body at its weakest point.

"Gail's anger reminds me of the convulsions I had with fever when I got pneumonia," Becka told me. "She gets out of control. Her body contorts, her face is red; she looks like a freak in a circus."

"It sounds like your arguments with Gail get pretty scary," I remarked.

"I honestly believe that Gail is psychic, or possessed, or something strange. She can be hot and cold, sweet as pie or a wild tempest. When she has a wild hair across her butt about something, she goes pretty crazy. She's been depressed since our last fight and doesn't even want me to touch her. I need to touch— and be touched. I wish she'd deal with her depression."

"Deal with it how?" I asked.

"I think she needs therapy herself. I've talked to her about coming to see you, but she says she can handle it. It's affecting me, making me more depressed."

"Why do you think she is psychic?" I wondered.

"Because when she was young she saw events happening before they actually did. She tried to tell her parents about it, but

they ignored her. I think she's extremely intelligent, too. As a teenager, she had a nervous breakdown and was hospitalized for a month
or so. She was having lots of visions and freaked out."

I was concerned that Becka's home life was so unstable, at
a time when she was on very rocky ground herself. She was unable
to take another job because her license was temporarily suspended
in a dispute with the nursing home she had just left. And without an
income, she considered not continuing the therapy that was critical
to her survival. In an effort to ground her with something positive, I
asked her to consider the previous work she had done in therapy,
her present status, and to tell me what issues or themes she felt she
needed to work on now. She listed many things:

Coping with separations from people close to her.
Coping with that time of emptiness, after four p.m.
Jealousy: jealousy of her mother's husbands, lovers.
Having to be a peacemaker. Keeping everyone happy.
Being willing to accept hurt.
Food.
Being the exact image of her maternal grandmother: fat.
Not sleeping.
Wanting to commit suicide.
Submitting to sexual abuse.

That was the order she named them, but not necessarily the
order of their importance. I wanted her to focus on the resources she
had for handling these things. It's easy to conjure up what is wrong
with life and to wallow in it all, but more constructive to consider how
to handle it.

"What would you say, Becka, if you had to be honest, are
your greatest strengths? . . . all the positive things someone who
knows you well would say about you?"

This could be tricky. If she were in a very low spot, she might
tell me there's nothing positive about her at all. But it worked. She
named quite a few resources.

"I would say my ability to develop relationships; to be
touched; to evaluate, sit and work things through; to know when I

need help. I'm loving, caring, understanding, compassionate, industrious, organized, fair. I try to communicate clearly. I learn fast. I have a pretty good memory, and common sense."

She took time to think in between some of these, but I was impressed with the degree of ease with which she came up with them. It indicated that she had enough ego strength to give her some hope, and possibly avoid any suicidal gestures at this time.

"How about if we go to work on some of these while in a trance," I suggested. "You can simply lean back and get comfortable in that chair . . . ."

After assisting her into trance I suggested Becka tell me how she felt or what she noticed.

"I have that heaviness in my chest again. It almost feels like a huge hole, but it's heavy. And empty at the same time."

"Those frightening holes again," I said.

"Spoiled Little Becka is back. She's smiling and full of the devil. She can't take it when things are tough, though. She runs and hides so she won't get hurt."

"You say that like she shouldn't want to protect herself. What would you have her do?"

"She's supposed to be full of piss and vinegar; stick things out." I made an interpretation. "That's another aspect of who she is, isn't it? Spoiled Little Becka isn't bad, but she was taught to think she is, when really all she is trying to do is survive. She gets feisty sometimes, and she runs away scared sometimes, but she's just doing the best she can under the circumstances. Maybe she should have a different name than 'Spoiled' . . . something that more fully describes her."

"Hmmm. Maybe Feisty Becka," said Becka. "What is Feisty Becka hiding from now?"

Becka was quiet, then, "She can't take it when Gail gets so crazy. She wants to hide."

"She's pretty scared of Gail. What is she afraid Gail will do?"
"Kill me. Kill herself."

"Don't you find it reasonable that she would be scared if that were going to happen?" I asked.

"It could happen— Gail gets crazy enough to do it."

"What does Feisty Becka need in order not to be so scared of Gail?"

Becka couldn't come up with an answer from that place of the little girl in her. I asked her to contact the part of herself that has all those resources that she had named a while ago. "You have an adult self, too, Becka. I think it's time to start to reorganize the various parts of yourself, and put the one in charge that's best at handling problems; that adult part might be the nurse and administrator. Would that be the part?"

"Yes. I do have that part. She's definitely an organizer."
"Okay. Let's ask that organizer part of you if she would be willing to give some assistance to the younger, less able parts of you, at handling the things that get to be so frightening and overwhelming. And if she is willing, ask that part what needs to happen for Feisty Becka to feel safer."

Again Becka was silent as she retrieved the information I had asked her to get. "The organizer part is telling Feisty Becka to stick close to her and she'll keep things sane. She'll keep order in my head, remind me what is real, be objective. She tells Feisty Becka not to listen to crazy people. That's what she's been doing, listening to Gail, and that gets her all balled up. She just gets hurt. People take advantage of her. The organizer part says she'll help."

"Ask her, specifically, what she is going to have you do so that you can handle things," I suggested.

"I can write in my journal, make lists; that helps me stay organized. When I write, I can sort out what Gail says and throw out the craziness. And I can look forward to coming here. It seems like I get some of the tangles out of the messes I'm in, and I can see things more clearly."

I urged Becka to continue, "And what else can the organizer part of you offer as help to the scared Feisty Becka?"

"If I can make myself stay busy . . . but there's a lot of time on my hands right now, waiting for this license thing to get resolved. I worry about that, too. I'm trying to do a little gardening, and my organizer part likes doing that. And I can organize myself to meet other friends for lunch and get away from Gail for a while."

"So how does it feel to be organizing these ideas, especially to Feisty Becka?"

"It's strange. I can see her hunched up with a stubborn look on her face, but she's not arguing, yet not quite accepting— sort of pouting. But I don't feel so much like smashing her like I did before. She wants to wait and see how well I can do this. She knows she can always take off on me."

"Okay, Becka. Just relax now as you listen, and let the sound of my voice relax you more and more deeply the more I talk. . . . Let yourself sink deeply into the chair, becoming more at ease with the sound of my voice, as you listen to hear the importance of these words . . . perhaps the same words you've heard so many times before, yet words heard not quite the same way as so many times before, just to listen and relax. ... Accepting the relaxation . . . accepting the sound of the words . . . accepting your own abilities to relax and to handle your life as an adult . . . to take charge by organizing yourself each day, being able to handle things with all the many things you've already learned through the years of your adult life. . . . And you have so many positive resources already within you, . . . the strengths it takes to be in charge, to make it feel secure . . . simply knowing how many ways you have handled problems before . . . trusting your adult self to make it safe to relax and live your life in the best way you know how. . . . And you can do this, Becka; you already know how . . . you have managed to succeed so many times before."I continued to drone positive suggestions a while longer, observing that Becka had become very deeply relaxed. Then I roused her gently in the usual way, and when she was fully awake, we scheduled an appointment for the following week.

Kathleen's Reflections

My mother continued to have convulsions, so Dad took her to the Mayo Brothers Clinic for tests. My brothers and I stayed with families who were friends of Mom and Dad's. My brothers stayed together with a family who had two boys about their age, but I stayed with "Uncle Herb and Aunt Lillian," who were not true relatives of ours. I arrived at their house on a day of icy Boston winter, so I was wearing a snowsuit, which I refused to have removed. I must have been five years old.

I cried and clung to my father's legs so he couldn't leave without me. Dad peeled me off of him, closed the big front door, and Uncle Herb locked it. I wailed and sobbed by the door, refusing to be touched or to speak. Uncle Herb and Aunt Lillian let me sit there, having tried to get me to come to the dinner table. I sulked and sniffled in my snowsuit for hours. I barely knew these people and didn't want to stay alone in their strange house. I don't remember how I got from the front door to a big stuffed chair in their living room, but that's where I finally fell asleep after they had gone to bed.

The next morning I awoke in a strange bed, famished and somewhat ready to behave better than the night before. I had already shown them I was good at pouting, and when Uncle Herb discovered how much I liked prunes for breakfast, he nicknamed me "Pruneface." It was traumatic to be left with strangers at such a young age, but they took good care of me. The underlying tension and anxiety surrounding my mother's mysterious illness probably made it more difficult than it had to be, in addition to being separated from my brothers.

The Mayo Brothers Clinic put my mother on anti-convulsant and sedating medications, which kept her drugged in bed all day — until the evening when she usually perked up. Like Becka's, our happy family life rapidly deteriorated. Dad worked all day as a test pilot. Before leaving each morning, he got us ready for school and made our brown-bag lunches. When we came home, Mom was usually still asleep, and all Dad could do was pray we would be all right. Eventually, he had to hire housekeepers to be there after school, but few people would stay around our crazy mother when she would yell at them that she didn't need their help.

As time passed, things didn't get any better, and tough circumstances pushed Dad into a corner. He had to leave his job in Massachusetts and move us to Upper Michigan where other family members could help care for us. Initially, we all lived with his mother, except Mom, who was hospitalized. Medical bills and her wild spending sprees on credit in Filene's Basement had put Dad in such financial difficulty that he had to declare bankruptcy. We were left with almost no worldly goods, no home, and a mother committed to the state hospital. Her behavior was too out of control for her to be at home any longer. To make matters worse, my father, who was trained in very specialized work, was unable to find a job in Upper Michigan, other than as a minimum wage laborer in a lumber mill. After a few months the mill shut down, and he was left with no alternative but to seek work outside the area. He eventually found a job, moved to Wisconsin by himself, and left my brothers and me temporarily in separate foster homes. I was along again.

A few months later we moved again to live with relatives. I lived with an aunt and uncle and my three cousins, while my brothers lived with Mom's parents. My brothers were only sixteen months apart, so I guess it was natural for them to stay together. Nobody wanted to keep all three of us. I was now abandoned by my mother, my father, and my two brothers.

I recall the aching loneliness, too, the many nights I prayed for a miracle that God would make my mother well, and we would be a family again. I cried and I prayed for three and a half years. Then one day it seemed there was a miracle. The doctors were permitting Mom come home from the hospital to take care of the three of us in our own apartment. I was then eleven years old, going on to sixth grade. The next year and a half with my mother was in many ways a happy time. She was loving and affectionate when her thinking was clear. I still missed my dad and was uncertain why he couldn't come and be with us, too, but at least I could be with Mom again. I've always been grateful that she was the one to tell me the facts of life. The day it came about, my brothers were getting ready to go camping with the Thompson twins. They were going to ride their bicycles into the woods and pitch a tent somewhere. I desperately wanted to go along, but of course I wasn't wanted. My mother wouldn't have let me go even if my brothers did allow it. She told me she had a surprise for me after they left, and it was just for "us girls."

The surprise was nothing I could have imagined. She sat

down with me and held me close to her. She said that I was soon to become a young woman — that it was time for me to change from being a tomboy, always trying to keep up with my brothers. She explained how my body was changing: I would develop breasts and shapely hips; and also some changes were happening that I couldn't see which would make my body capable of having a baby someday. She explained about my uterus, and eventually got to the part about how women become impregnated.

This was the first honest explanation of where babies come from that I had ever heard. Before that I was told, and believed, that the seed is planted in the woman's body by God, when He deems that the woman and her husband are ready to have a child. I was shocked and horrified at her description of lovemaking, of the husband inserting his penis into the wife's vagina. She seemed so delighted, even romantic, in her description of this process, telling me that it is a wondrous union of love being shared by the couple. In disbelief, I had to ask her for verification that, indeed, my father had done this to her at least three times. She laughed and said it had actually happened many times, because couples find it a very pleasurable way to show their love for one another. Further, there are only certain times of the month when a woman's egg is ready to be fertilized, so every act of love-making doesn't end in a pregnancy. I had difficulty digesting this shocking news.

My mother seemed so pleased about it all, as if she were telling me about a great vacation we were going to take. Instead, she went on to describe menstruation and suggested we go shopping for the "special items" I was going to need, once I began having my periods. She said when that happened, it would mean that I had changed from being a little girl to a young woman. It was years later before I could truly appreciate the wonderful way that my mother handled that important step in my development. She celebrated my first menses as a passage of joy, which gave me the clear impression that sex, menstruation, and having children are positive experiences, not something to fear or dread. She had told me how she found out about this life change, and had vowed not to do the same thing to her daughter as her mother had done.

My mother was never told anything about sex or that she would eventually have normal, regular menstrual cycles. She started bleeding one day and was terrified. She was too frightened to go to her mother, so she wadded up toilet paper and secured it inside her underpants. When the bleeding didn't stop readily, she told her older sister. Gertrude explained that it was supposed to happen, and taught her how to use the special rags that she and their mother used. Gertrude thought it was funny that my mother didn't even figure out what all those rags were always hanging in the basement to dry. Maybe she was afraid to know.

The happiness with Mom had lasted about a year when she began to slip back into her former behaviors. She gradually stopped cooking for us, so we fed ourselves and did the dishes. My fourteen-year-old brother vacuumed the apartment and went to the grocery store in a taxi, with a shopping list if he was lucky. Mom slept during the day and stayed up much of the night watching TV or listening to the radio. Sometimes she said strange things, ranting in long, senseless tirades. She claimed that the police had a special watch on our house because somebody was stalking her.

That summer while my brothers were both away at Bible Camp, she staged a robbery in our apartment. The police were there when I came home from playing with a friend. She said that someone had stolen all her jewels, her silver, and her good clothes. I was frightened and confused. Later my grandmother told me that the police didn't find any evidence of a robbery and thought she had strewn things about the apartment herself. Maybe she even did it in anger and then forgot about it, later thinking that someone had broken in. She didn't own anything of value— no jewels or silver, only costume jewelry.

After a year and a half, Mom went back to the hospital, and the three of us were homeless again. The relatives who had cared for us the first time weren't prepared to take us in again. Dad was changing jobs and about to relocate to California, so he needed another six to eight months before he would be ready to take us. Lucky for Dad, a close friend of his from high school offered to care for us for several months. This required that we move to yet another town and start at another school, only to have to move again in nine months when we went to California to join Dad.

Chapter 7 – Becka's Story

I always remembered when Momma left the second time; I was eleven. I stood at the kitchen window and saw her coming home early from work one day, walking really fast and looking upset; her face showed trouble. She wore a navy blue suit and felt hat, stylish like the one in her wedding picture, but more for work. I was puzzled that she was home early.

"Rebecca Ann, sweetie, I have a lot to do. Can you help me by going next door to get Roy John from Mrs. Andrews? You're such a good girl. When you come back, give him some graham crackers and milk, and then keep an eye on him for me, would you?"

I did what she asked, but then, I usually did anyway. Roy was in kindergarten in the morning, and the neighbor took care of him until I came home from school to fetch him. Daddy usually got home soon after I did, and then Momma came after five. I felt like I was Roy's momma myself after helping with him so long. Momma always gave me a lot of responsibility when it came to Roy.

Momma kept busy in her bedroom for a long time. When I tried to talk with her through the door, she seemed impatient and told me to wait until she was finished. Finally she came out dressed in a casual, rose print dress. "Rebecca Ann, I need to talk to you." She had a very serious face. "I have to go out. I want you to warm up the leftovers in the ice box for supper, and make sure Roy John gets a bath and put to bed by eight o'clock. If you need help with your homework, ask Daddy."

She held my cheeks between her hands and looked right into my eyes. "Rebecca Ann, I don't know when I'll be back. But you keep on being a good girl, and do what you're told and everything will be all right, you hear? I want you to keep on being such a good, smart girl, do you understand?" I stared back into her eyes, reading between the lines; her words sounded like the distant rumble of springtime thunder. I knew she was leaving us, like before. I wanted to wrap my arms around her tight to keep her from leaving, but I was frozen. I wanted to beg her, to cry, to scream no you can't go, but my mouth wouldn't move.

Momma squeezed me real tight for about a minute; it wasn't long enough. Then she went into the sitting room where Roy was playing and hugged him, too. I could see her eyes filled with tears, and she took out a tissue and wiped them quickly. A horn sounded outside on the street. She went to her room and took the two suitcases she had packed, struggling with them to the door. After she had opened the door and passed them through, she turned to me and said, "I love you, Rebecca Ann." She didn't look back again.

I watched from the front door as she put her things into the taxi that took her away. Then the tears and the sound did finally come: "NO, MOMMA! Don't go, please don't go!"

That's what I remembered for years, that she left and Daddy was in a rage that day when he came home and found her gone. He drank all that evening and into the night. She had left a note that I found later and saved. It had been crumpled into a wad, then smoothed out again, all kinds of dirty spots on it, like he had maybe cried and got it wet. It read:

Take care of the children. Don't come looking for me. You won't never find me. I don't never want to see you no more. I can't take no more of your cruelty. Faye.

I managed to take care of Roy, and then spent the rest of the evening in my room. I cried myself to sleep after hours of listening to him throwing things around the kitchen, like the chairs. He banged a pan on the counter top, shouting one word with each slam, "God … damn … you. .. Faye! I'll . . . kill … you."

Oooh, he comes into my room— it's maybe two in the morning. I am jerked upright into his face, his hands grasping my shoulders, hard and painful. The stink of whiskey on his breath goes up my nostrils, so strong I almost retch. His teeth are clenched tight as he talks to me.

"She thinks she can just walk out on us, just like that. Runs off with some no-good. She thinks she's so smart. I'll show that whore what she can do. And I'll show you what this is all about."

Daddy drops me back against my pillow, kneeling on the edge of my bed, and opens his trousers. Then he pushes my nightie up and comes down on top of me, squirming to get himself in place.

"Don't you make a sound, you little bitch," he whispers. "You don't have no say in this, so just be quiet, or I'll smack your fat little face."

He fumbles with his penis, trying to force it into me, but it won't go, so he shifts his weight over to one elbow and jerks at it a while. He stinks so bad— his sweat and whiskey— I feel the retching start again; but

I fight it back. Everything he does hurts— every place where he touches me
to keep me still— my arms, my shoulders, my legs. His body is ugly, dead
weight on me. I stay quiet like he said, waiting and praying for him to leave
me alone.

When he finally pushes it in, there comes first a flash of memory
that it happened before, and then I don't feel anything at all. But I tell myself I have to keep my eyes on the window so I won't feel it. I have to go, I
have to escape out the window! His body goes up and down against me—
up and down, his butt in the air as he jams his thing into the hardly-ever-
virgin place between my legs. In my mind, I leave my body and go out the
window. I pray for Mom- ma to come back and stop what is happening.

I got pneumonia again, soon after Momma left. This time I stayed
in the hospital for days in an oxygen tent. I just wanted to die there and kept
dreaming that maybe I would go to be with Granpa. I had nightmares and
hallucinations from the fever, but I got over it.

Nobody knew where Momma was, though Daddy had tried to find
her. He came into my room another night, half drunk and crying, and sat on
the edge of my bed, facing me and stroking my hair. He wanted to talk
about her.

"I love her, Rebecca Ann. I've got to get her back— and I will," he
said. "And I love you, too. You need your momma, like any kid does. I'm
gonna make you a promise that I'll find her and bring her home. It'll be like
it was when you were born. We were so happy, Rebecca Ann . . . so happy.
I was the luckiest man in all of Dallas to get her for my wife. I was proud to
be with her wherever we went— she looked so good. And any man who
took a second look at her was taking a risk. Trouble is, she was always
looking back. Tramp is what she is."

I thought he was going to fall asleep, but he kept talking, his
words all running together and his breath so foul. "She's got me all torn up
inside, you see, honey? She's done this to me before— run off. Some no-
good jerk. Why did she leave, honey? What's this guy got that I don't? I
take care of her and you kids. She can't find a better husband. If I could find
him, I'd kill him. I can't let some creep have her; and if I can't have her,
nobody will — I promise." He lay his head on my lap, circling my waist
with his arms, and cried.

Then he fell asleep. I tried to make him go to his own room, but he
wouldn't wake up. Finally, I just pushed him off my bed onto the floor and
covered him with the blanket from his bed. Other times, he was so mad
about Momma leaving him that he blamed me, calling me thoughtless and
inconsiderate, a burden on him for always getting sick. He got his sex from

me at those times, being hurtful and mean. I begged him to leave me alone, but all he did was threaten that if I ever told anyone what he was doing, he'd beat up Roy. He said he knew how much I loved him, and I wouldn't want Roy to get hurt. He even said sometimes that he would kill Roy. I believed him when he said it, because he was so angry. I felt sure I did something to deserve what happened.

I was only fourteen when I got pregnant. Daddy had done it. He was planning to take me to a doctor for an abortion and told me to keep it secret from Granma and everyone else. Nobody could tell, he said, if we did the abortion soon enough. But the day before he was to take me to somebody to do it, my body took care of it. I think my fear caused it to abort.

I got home from school with really bad cramps. Then, during the evening, I started bleeding. I thought my whole insides were coming out of that place. I no sooner got a Kotex on than it was soaked clear through, so I just sat on the toilet and bled. I sobbed and thanked God that Daddy wasn't home. The cramps became severe for a while, and then it was over. The little fetus plopped out into the toilet bowl. It was an incredible sight — all the little tiny fingers and toes on its hands and feet— a complete baby, and so tiny I didn't think anything that small could be human. It was a girl. The sight of it put me into a rage, a fury inside that ripped me apart from my head right down through my heart and into all my female parts, a fury I didn't think I would survive. Humiliation and shame made me want to die. I thought about killing myself right then, and maybe I should have— to save myself from the grief still to come.

The razor blades were right there in the cabinet— a cut to the wrist, blood everywhere anyway— why not? Fantasizing an end to all the painful emotions brought sheer relief, at least for a few moments. When I flushed the little baby away, I let out a shriek of anguish so loud I thought Mrs. Andrews would hear and come running over from next door. I must have sat in the bathroom sobbing for another hour before I brought myself to clean up the mess and crawl to bed. Roy had been pounding on the door for me to get out of the bathroom and let him in there; otherwise I would have stayed on the floor all night.

Sometimes I wondered if Granma knew what Daddy was doing to me. Once in a while I had a bruise where she could surely see it, but most of the time the bruises didn't show, and she never asked about them. She always had us over for dinner on Sundays, and one day she had decided I should go to Ursuline Academy for Girls. She announced her plan over her chicken fried steak and gravy, and then she and Daddy had an argument.

She said she was going to pay for my schooling and make all the arrangements— that it wasn't right I wasn't getting the kind of education I needed.
I didn't think she had much money, but she said something about Granpa's
trust. She said I would come home on weekends, that Roy John was old
enough now and he didn't need me all the time.

Granma said he could come to her house after school, since she
worked at home, sewing for Neiman-Marcus. There was no point in Daddy
arguing with her. Once she had her mind made up, she was immovable. I
guess if there was any way I was like her, that was it.

I loved the Academy and the classes. I worked hard, made good
grades, and even made some friends. The time passed much faster when I
was busy, and there were fewer occasions when Daddy could get to me. I
struggled to lose some weight, but the starchy food in the dining hall was
very gratifying. It seemed to fill up some of the empty holes that I had
throughout my body— in my stomach, in my heart— everywhere. I kept
chocolate and cookies and other pastries hidden in my room for after lights
out. I had to share them with my roommate to keep her from squealing on
me, because we didn't like each other much.

Momma was simply gone from my life. I was angry with her for a
long time but always found myself rationalizing she must have hated Daddy
so much that she had to run away. I just excused her actions or blamed myself for them. I couldn't understand why she didn't take Roy and me with
her and decided it must have been because I was too fat and unlovable.

Chapter 8 - Therapist's Story

"I am concerned about the difficulty you seem to have with coping when Gail leaves for a while," I said to Becka at our next session. "I believe you need to do some work on finishing old business."

"What do you mean?" she asked. "You have a pattern of abandonment running through your life that keeps repeating. That could mean that you may somehow set yourself up for abandonment, such as with Gail leaving, and then respond to it in the same unsatisfying way each time you are left. There is a saying in the therapeutic community: *Incomplete endings interfere with new beginnings.* Things weren't well resolved or handled properly when you were first abandoned, so you find yourself unable to get on with your life in a more gratifying way. It's like being caught in a loop. Your earliest abandonment was by your mother, and then by your grandfather. Both of those instances occurred so early in life that you are trying to resolve them through your relationships with people like Gail, Myra, and even your former supervisor. Does that make sense?

"Yes. It feels like all the leavings are unresolved."

"What about when you left Leslie? That was a time which you chose to leave rather than that you were left by someone."

Becka thought about my question a moment. "That actually does feel finished. I have some regrets about hurting her, but I feel it was over and that I ended it pretty well."

"What was it like when it was ending?"

"We had quite a few long talks about it over a period of a few weeks. We both cried and screamed at each other, said a lot of things that hurt, then apologized and had some more talks about it. It was all very painful, but by the time I left we weren't screaming any more."

"So it was a parting that got talked about, explanations and apologies were made, and goodbye was said. That sounds like a fairly complete ending, showing you have adequate adult resources to do that. How does that compare with the partings with your mother and grandfather; and also Myra, your therapist?"

"There were no explanations or apologies. The second time my mother left she said goodbye, but she didn't tell me that she wasn't coming back. And I never had a chance to say goodbye to Granpa. With Myra — she gave me an explanation, and I suppose an apology that she was leaving, but I didn't like hearing it."

"Did you ever tell her how angry you were that she would leave you?" I asked.

"Of course not. How can you be mad at somebody you care about, who has done so much to help you, when she says she is going to get on with her life and get a PhD? I was happy for her."

"And angry for yourself. That's normal. So you never shared your true feelings with Myra about her leaving, nor did you ever get to do that with either your grandfather or your mother. Are you ready to finish business with them?"

Becka sighed deeply. "I feel like I can handle it with Myra,but I'm not ready yet to do it with the other two."

"Fine. That's a good place to start. Let's use the trance state.I think you'll find it quite helpful. Just lean back in the chair."

Becka tilted the recliner back and adjusted herself to get more comfortable. "I'm scared.

"Of? " I asked.

"Just nervous that this will be hard. Can you hold my hand?"

"Sure. But I don't think it will be as hard as you think." I took Becka into a deep trance state, which, by this time, she was able to attain quickly. She was a willing subject in spite of her fears about doing the work. I asked her to focus on Myra, to remember her, and to see what she found as she did this.

Becka began, "It's that nasty Feisty Becka again. She is the one who is mad at Myra. The selfish little brat."

"What does she have to say to Myra?"

"That she should have smashed her that day instead of the window. Myra just kept pushing her until she felt trapped. There wasn't any way to escape her, and the door and windows were locked, so she had to break the glass. She made it feel like when

Daddy locked her in the closet — no way to get out— couldn't breathe."

Becka's fingers were squeezing my hand much harder now.

I said, "You can tell Myra anything you want to, Feisty Becka. It's safe to do that now. No one will hurt you."

"You can't make me tell! I won't!" Becka's voice changed slightly, sounding a bit more childlike. "I won't talk about it. I can't tell, so leave me alone!"

"You're telling Myra to leave you alone and not try to make you tell. And does she leave you alone?"

"Yes. She stops for now. She isn't mad at me for breaking the window. I said I was sorry."

"You were mad at Myra, but you didn't tell her, did you?" "No. I just broke the window."

"And you were mad at her again later, weren't you? But you didn't tell her then either. Tell her now, Feisty Becka. Why are you mad at her?"

"You can't just go off and leave me, you whore. You just take what you want from me and then you go and leave whenever you want to, without so much as a care about what I need." Becka almost shouted this and then broke into sobbing.

"Keep talking to her, Becka."

"You're so selfish. You're mean. You don't care about me. I hate you!" She just cried then, for a few minutes. I handed her tissues when her face became wet with tears and her nose was full of mucous.

After she settled down a bit I asked, "Who else might you be talking to, Becka?"

"My mother. I could say the same things to her. But I don't mean them. I don't hate her or Myra. I just said that because I was so hurt. It was wrong for me to say that."

"No, it wasn't, Becka. That's the way most people respond when they are so deeply hurt. They say things they don't mean, just the way you and Leslie did when you had those fights. And remember how you apologized to each other — how you didn't really mean all the things you said? And you made up. And that's what people do who care for each other. That is who Feisty Becka is, feeling the anger in you that is very real, even normal People all get angry, they make up afterwards, and they still love each other. Is there anything else you would like to say to Myra now?"

Becka blew her nose again and regained some of her composure. Her voice changed from the childlike tone to something older, yet there was still something different about it, not Becka's usual adult voice. "I see Myra. She is standing at the door of her office where I last saw her, holding the figurine of an eagle that I gave her. She looks so confident, so strong. I admire her confidence, envy it."

"Myra . . . it hurts that you're leaving me. I don't want to let you go. It's tearing me apart inside. You have opened me up, and now you're leaving, and I feel all exposed, raw. You made me bring the memories back, and now that's all I have are these ugly, horrid memories floating around in my head. I can't push them away. And you are leaving me with them to fend for myself."

"So you can tell her you're upset being left so vulnerable with your memories," I said.

"Yes. I am angry that you are leaving. And I know you have to leave. I know you have your own life. I just wish you hadn't opened Pandora's box and now you're leaving me alone with it."

"How old do you feel now, talking to Myra?"

Becka thought. "I feel like I'm about sixteen."

"Okay. Do you have anything else you wish you had said to Myra before she left?" I asked.

"I thanked her for helping me. I just couldn't tell her how angry I was."

"Now she knows. Do you still see her at her office? How does she look, now that you've told her?"

"She hugs me and says it is okay and she is sorry." "Do you believe she is sorry?"

"Yes," said Becka. "I know she is. She had to go."

"Do you feel like you can say goodbye to her now and feel really finished with her, or is there something else?"

Becka reflected quietly. "It feels finished."

I asked Becka to relax again and to let herself drift back into a peaceful state once more. I gave her suggestions that she would continue to heal from this past hurt, that it would generalize to other losses and let her unconscious mind know how to feel more resolved about those as well. I said she would feel strengthened to be acquiring new adult-like resources that would allow her to express her anger appropriately in any future situation, rather than bury her feelings inside. I tied that in with having the resource of not having to use food or fat to bury the unpleasant feelings that are normal for people to have, and I reinforced that she could safely continue to lose extra fat from her body. Then I began to end the session.

"I'm going to have to give you an appointment for ten days from now," I said, "because I'm going to be out of town for a few days next week, and that will be during our usual time."

Becka's peaceful-looking face began to tighten as I said this.

She looked down at the arm of the chair, indicating she was struggling with something.

"Where are you going? . . . Or do you mind my asking? I suppose it's really none of my business."

"No, I don't mind telling you. I'll be going to a conference for a few days in Philadelphia. If you need to reach me I'll be checking with my answering service daily. This is an opportunity to find out how you handle another short-term loss. And it is short-term."

"I hope you enjoy the conference. Is it one you're looking forward to, or one of those have-to-go types?"

I replied, "Oh, I'm very much looking forward to it. So I'll see you on Friday then, same time."

Becka rose slowly from the chair and steadied herself, still quite relaxed from being in a trance state. She asked for a hug again, and whispered to me, "Kathleen, you mean so much to me. You're like a breath of life. Thank you."

Kathleen's Reflections

California! What a strangely wonderful place. I hated it at first, the whole first year, mostly because it was such a contrast to where I had grown up and was so far away from all the people I knew and loved. I was shy and reserved as a teenager. I went to a summer school where three quarters of the students were black. I was in the minority and very uncomfortable. In Marquette, Michigan, there had been almost no black people at all. When my brothers and I first got off the jet in Los Angeles, I was bedazzled by the look of newness everywhere— clean brightness. Buildings were modern stucco with colored lights shining against them at night. There were many fountains, fragrant flowers and lush vegetation everywhere. The ocean seemed exotic, and we were taken to a seafood restau-rant where waves crashed against the windows, a restaurant where we were told movie stars came often. It was all completely different from Upper Michigan. We felt like we were celebrities ourselves.

Dad drove us to our new home. The apartment building looked like a wealthy person's estate. The front had huge palms, bird of paradise, and ivy growing alongside the sidewalks. The colored spotlights played against the white walls and the sign that read "California Palms." I learned that many apartment buildings in California had names. We entered a courtyard through a wrought iron gate, bringing us to more lush gardens and a swimming pool. A swimming pool! also lit up with colored lights. All of the apartments entered into this courtyard for privacy and safety. This was a new concept for me. Little walk lights lit the paths to each door, and beside them was a small patio, privately enclosed by shrubbery. We entered our apartment, and I was once again stunned with its modern, clean and rich-looking appearance. There was light tan carpeting, wall-to-wall, and the walls were stark white. Each room had new draperies and contemporary light fixtures. The kitchenette had a dishwasher, stove, and refrigerator. I thought my father must have become a wealthy man.

That first year I was terribly homesick for my mother and friends. The next summer, Dad put me on a train back to Michigan for a visit. Mom was still there in the same state hospital, and seeing her was very painful all over again. She wanted to live with us, and was angry that her husband had left there and taken her children so far away. I returned to Dad and my brothers, confused and sad about the direction of our unfortunate lives.

A call came from my grandmother some months later, telling us that Mom's seizures had increased, and she had undergone some new tests. The results showed that a tumor had been growing slowly throughout the left hemisphere of her brain. The surgeons would attempt to remove some of it, but the prognosis was poor. In the early fifties, there were no CAT scans or ultrasound, no chemotherapy or radiology treatments as we have now.

The surgery rendered Mom paralyzed on her right side and unable to speak. Because we now lived thousands of miles away, and we would not able to see her. Perhaps it was best that way, not to see her further debilitated. Some months passed, showing a slight remission of her symptoms, and then the cancer took over and swiftly swept through her body. My grandmother called again and said this time she didn't think Mom had long to live. Dad and I took the train to Michigan, leaving my brothers at home because they couldn't afford to miss so much school. We stayed about a week, but she held on to *life.*

Comatose, wasted to about 70 pounds, and shriveled like an ancient old woman, she lay there, day in and day out. Her skin was transparent white, and her brown hair was now dulled and speckled with grey at 39 years old. Dad and I stood at her bedside for days, talking to her, stroking her, not knowing for certain if she heard us. I wanted to believe she did, and looked for any sign that she knew. Only her slow breathing, an occasional rattling in her throat, or grimaces of pain told us she was alive. Finally, she opened her eyes and looked at me as if she was truly seeing me. Her mouth opened and her lips moved a little, but she was unable to speak. Only her eyes gave me assurance she knew me. My beautiful mother was dying, leaving me at the age of thirteen.

I wept for her suffering as much as my own. I could never understand why her life was disrupted, just when it had begun. She was a young, talented, happy mother with three children when her symptoms first appeared. She had a successful husband whom she loved. We were a family, post World War II, and my father was fortunate to have an excellent job, paying more money than anyone else in our family had ever made. We had a new house and a dog in the suburbs of Boston, and we did nice family things. Then she began having inexplicable and non-diagnosable seizures.

After what I have come to know of schizophrenia, perhaps she was lucky it was a brain tumor and not that dread illness. The tumor caused her craziness and her suffering, but then she was relieved of suffering after eleven years, while schizophrenia would have dragged on a lifetime. There are no cures for tumors such as hers, and no cures for schizophrenia, but to live through either must be a kind of hell on earth.

It isn't fair that children lose their parents. As a child, I thought nobody else understood what I felt. Other children around me had their parents. I prayed to God for a miracle to make Mom well. When she died, I was disappointed in God at first. Eventually, I reasoned that he took her because he knew what was best, and I had to trust his will.

My Christian beliefs in heaven and immortality with God were an antidote to that terrible pain when no answers were forthcoming. I found comfort in believing I would someday be reunited with my mother, that her spirit lived on, watching over me. It would take many years before I would come to better terms with death— to be nearly free of the fear of it.

I was well aware of what Becka faced with some of her un-finished business. Losing my mother was the ultimate loss and abandonment. Like Becka, my child-mind could comprehend only so much during the early years that Mom was ill, and the adults who were in my life did their best to explain and apologize. While I felt deep down that I was the cause of Mom's illness, I was always aware that I was loved. I believed Mom loved and missed me, being locked up in the hospital. I believed Dad loved me, even though he had to leave me behind with family in order to make money and support us. And I knew I was loved by my various aunts, uncles, and grandparents. But there is nothing like being with one's own parents on an every-day basis. I felt my mother's love, both before she be-came ill and even during those years of separation— her love from a distance, and it made a great difference for me that Becka did not have. We were both separated from our mothers and had to grow up quickly. She had missed knowing she was loved by her mother. But a far more critical difference in our lives was that I hadn't suf-fered the traumas of sexual and physical abuse. My black hole wasn't as deep or bottomless as hers.

Chapter 9 – Becka's Story

Journal Entry to Kathleen: July 18, 1986 – 23:20

I used to write everything whirling around in my mind and it seemed to help. I don't know what else to try. Your voice on the tapes only makes me cry. I don't think anybody really knows or understands all I'm feeling — not even me. I can't seem to talk and tell you. Maybe I can write. I'm so tired of even breathing and my heartbeat seems to only tire me more. There's a hole in my chest, jagged edges. I'm teetering on the edge of it. I used to be so sure of death— warmth and light and peace. Now there are doubts. Everything I've read says suicide is not the same as just dying, and I need the peace. I'm too tired to fight. What little I was is being torn to shreds and it's ceaseless harshment. There's no peace even at home. The only thing I ever did well or that gave me merit is gone. I'm useless. It's gone.

I've used every last bit of strength to do it the past one and a half years, and everybody is tearing at the sham, showing me what I am. Nothing. Make believe, sheer will, and now no will at all. Everything I believed in and believed of myself is gone. All my dreams for the nursing home have ended up a scandal, a joke, an unsalvageable situation, an endless "to do" list.

Since before I could remember there's been a part of me so tired rest could never reach it — a bloodless part with no life. Now it seems to be dominoing through the rest of me, all the pieces struggling to survive, with no direction, no strength in numbers, falling one after the other into the pit.

It was that shitty Feisty Little Becka that called you, always wanting, needing, always grasping and clambering for more, never enough. Nobody else in the world needs anything except for her, just ask her. Nobody is as important as her. Watch her, she's already got you on the hook. If she sets it she'll use you up, run you off. Nobody can withstand her, her sweet poison, her web. She's clever and malicious and she kills. I almost killed her today but she called you, pulled you in. I sat with a vial of poison and felt it and heard all its promises, felt the sharpness of the needle, imagined the burning in my arm, then my chest, my whole body screamed for that peace, but she had made me read stuff that put up doubts. I must at least do my death right. As for my life, the one good and beautiful part of it is Gail, and I destroy that a little more each day with the craziness. I try to work with it and it just tidal-waves and washes my efforts away.

The confusion is stronger than me. It has beaten me down. I want to hold onto your hands so tight. I wonder if you know what you've done by offering them. Myra knew better. She always pulled away. If you can sense the depth of my need you must be very strong. I wonder if you know.

I really want this trip for you, Kathleen— me, not her— yet I'm so afraid. You give me hope, despite the tiredness, heaviness and confusion. Please, Please, Please, do not give up on me. I need somebody so desperately that can stay near but not be manipulated or consumed. When I gave up today, you stayed with me and didn't give up or bully me. You helped me come back. I just don't know if I can stay. The craziness is so close, it's like a second skin. If I move, it gains control, takes away parts of me and they never come back the same or as strong. This will be the last battle I'll fight for and there are no draws. I need strength. There seems to be none in me. I sense great strength and courage in you. If you choose to continue to stand and face the craziness in me, I dare not take and you dare not give your resources. Yet I cannot do this alone. My life is not worth the death of anyone or anything else.

Letter to Kathleen: July 18, 1986 – 22:45

I'm not calling you, but I feel really shaky. I have no control nor any right to control your comings and goings, but how can I tell you how it affects me when you leave? I don't even know why it affects me but it does at the deepest levels. The time you're gone is like an eternity between one free breath and the next. I know in the real world, anything could happen to you at any time, yet your leaving— putting distance between me and you— exaggerates the fears. I warned you in the beginning about my attachment. It's almost symbiotic in its intensity. The need to have the assurance of you comes from my very core, something deep and nameless and needy. Something that seems as if it must come from someone else but never has. Something I have been seeking in others since the beginning. The need of it when I contact it, or should I say, when it overwhelms me, is a maddening, incessant pain that controls and directs despite my sense of pride or property. It's primeval — help me —it's endless longing, hunger and quenchless thirst. It is so overwhelming I do not know how to deal with it. It comes and goes — ebbs and flows, barely conscious of it consuming me. There is no way I

could deal with it very long without breaking into infinitesimal pieces —
imploding or exploding, I'm not sure, but definitely coming apart. If Friday
ever comes, you'll help me be free of the pain. Because of this I know Friday will never come.

Chapter 10 - Therapist's Story

I put Becka's journal-letter down and looked at her. She sat with her shoulders hunched up and her fists squeezed between her thighs and the arms of the chair. Her eyes seemed to be tracing the patterns on the oriental rug. She appeared a bit disheveled in her usual snug-fitting pants and blouse, as if she might have slept in her clothes.

"So you made it to Friday, but it seems you've had a difficult time doing so," I said.

Becka just nodded.

"How are you doing today?"

"Better, now that you're back and I'm here. I've had a little re-play of the bronchitis, and I may have a kidney infection. I told you to watch out for my attachment."

"Yes, you warned me. I can handle it, because you seem to be eager and willing to work on it, to change. I think we should continue today with the issue of unfinished business. Being left by people to whom you have strong ties still proves to be a challenge."

"I told you that everyone I love leaves me," said Becka. "Significant people have left you before, but now you're handicapped by feelings of abandonment even when they go away for a few days to a couple of weeks. It shows your dependence is stronger than it should be for your own good. Do you feel ready to work on the losses of the people closest to you as a child?"

"I guess I've got no choice but to keep going. I'm not really ready to work on my parents, but I think I can handle Granpa."

"Good," I said. "Let's get to work then." In the usual way, I took Becka into trance, getting her to become deeply relaxed and then offering some imagery in which to say goodbye to her grandfather. I asked her to imagine that she was standing with Granpa on a vast open plain, like a mesa where she had been in the Southwest. I knew she loved the desert and felt at home in that setting. I suggested she look out over the expanse of never-ending space and time with him, and tell him the things she had never had a chance to say.

"Granpa's there, but he's not alone," Becka said, sounding surprised. "Feisty Becka is there, too."

"And what are they doing?"

"He's beckoning to Feisty Becka to come to him, but she won't go. He wants to talk to her, but she's afraid he is angry with her."

"And where are you, the adult Becka?"

"I'm there too, but they don't see me. I'm watching like a fly on the wall."

"Would Feisty Becka be more likely to talk to him if she knew you were there with her and offered to help?"

"Maybe. Yes — she's letting me hold her hand. It's the first time she's ever let me get this close."

"Before you both go talk to him, what can you tell Feisty Becka that will help her?"

Becka was silent while she appeared to be running a sequence of thoughts. "I tell her not to be afraid of Granpa because he always loved her, no matter what. He never hurt her. He wanted to save her from the hurt. That made her cry." Becka was quiet again, then, "Granpa comes closer and takes her two hands in his. He asks why she is crying. Feisty Becka says she is sorry that she was bad and made him go away. She didn't mean to make him mad. He says no; he went away with a broken heart because his son was bad. Feisty Becka cries some more, and now she is saying she is mad at him for going away and leaving her to handle her problems alone. If he hadn't gone away, then Daddy wouldn't have done those bad things to her. Granpa cries, too, and says he is sorry he had to leave. He did not want the bad things to happen to her. Feisty Becka says she has been a mean, selfish little girl and she is sorry. Granpa says no — she's not selfish. He loves her and she is not bad."

Becka had been relating this story from the position of the adult in her, observing her inner child's conversation with her grandfather. Her voice was calm and steady, even as tears rolled slowly down her cheeks.

"Is there anything that the adult part of you wants to say to your Granpa, Becka, here on the mesa?"

"Yes . . . I love you, Granpa, for being the one person in my childhood who gave me so much, who loved me so much. If it hadn't been for your love, I don't know how I could have survived. I was only five when you died, but I learned a lot from you in that little time. Forgive me for ever having one bad thought about you. Please be with me always — I need you still."

"And what is happening now?" I asked.

"Granpa is holding Feisty Becka and hugging her for a long time. He hugs me, too, and then he slowly begins to fade away. He says, I am here, always."

In the months that followed, Becka continued to bring up the black holes she saw whenever she went into trance. She had re-peated encounters with the frightened little girl and Feisty Becka, two parts of herself that had seemingly split off during childhood. Becka did not have a split personality disorder by the clinical definition, but she did employ dissociation to cope with certain kinds of stress. She also found there was a teenage part of herself that seemed to be developmentally stuck in time. I tried to bring her back gently during trance to specific memories of her father, but all she would find were the black holes, and she was quite terrified by them.

On numerous occasions I got phone calls at home from Becka. It was usually late in the evening when she was restless and too frightened to sleep. Her voice would sound very small and help-less, and she would beg me to do something to take away the fear. It seemed that the only time the frightened little girl part had a voice was over the telephone. It wasn't exactly a whisper, just very far away. I would talk her through those times by trying to evoke the re-sourceful parts of herself, giving her the constant message that she had a strong adult self on which she could rely to remove the fear.

She believed that just hearing my voice was what would get her through, so I had suggested she listen to my tapes until she could sleep.

One time she called me and said that Gail was in a very bad

temper and talking about committing suicide. Becka didn't know what to say to her and couldn't talk her out of it because she felt what Gail was saying made so much sense. She had agreed with Gail that life was so full of frustrations and constant road blocks, it wasn't worth trying to keep overcoming them. I realized Becka's identification with Gail was so strong that she was suicidal as well, and I had to work especially hard to lead her back to a thread of hope to which she could cling.

Her own circumstances were very tenuous. She had no sooner gotten her license cleared over the nursing home problem (and had found an excellent job as a visiting nurse) than the nursing home matter was brought up again with a potential law suit. She regained several pounds, and lost even more self esteem. After the incident seemed to be cleared up, she was offered a promotion at her three-month review. Just as she was beginning to perk up, Gail became suicidal and brought her down again. Two more months passed, she was losing weight, and the legal matter was re-opened a third time. I knew Becka was on very thin ice then, because Gail had sold her physical therapy practice and was planning her own suicide for the spring. It seemed that every time Becka got up, she was knocked down again. I could hardly minimize the problems she faced, since they involved matters central to her existence.

Spring came, and Gail made a plan to return to Memphis, thinking it might help her depression and take her mind off suicide. This put Becka into another tailspin, accompanied by a case of kidney stones and low-grade fever. Meanwhile, I continued to work with her on resolving old unfinished business. My goal was to help her integrate the split off parts of herself by delving deeper into the black holes. I felt certain that these holes were where she kept her painful memories buried, but she didn't have the strength to pull them into the light. When uncovering the past persistently failed, we worked on boosting her self-esteem to be able to confront the memories later.

The constant battle up and down in her life circumstances made the process of ego-strengthening very slow.

A month after Gail had taken her second trip to Memphis, Becka came to her session exuberant and more alive than I had seen her. Normally a sedentary person, on this day she got up out of the recliner soon after she sat down and walked around the office as she talked. She was too excited about recent events to settle down.

"Gail is going to manage an apartment building in Loveland, and we're going to live in one of the apartments. She doesn't want to do physical therapy anymore, and she figures she can take care of the building full-time. I'm going to apply for a job at the hospital there, but until I get one, I'll have to commute from here. I guess the trip to Memphis did her a lot of good; she has been just high ever since she came back."

I was surprised and cautious. "It sounds like it could be rather risky, don't you think?"

"Not really. She's been unhappy about her career for a long time. She's even taken those aptitude tests to try and figure out something that's more suited to her. She's very excited about maintaining and renting apartments."

"Does she know anything about being a handy person?" I asked.

"Not much, but she'll learn. She's quick. I'm just glad the depression is over. She's been a much nicer person to be around, more loving. Intimacy has kind of gotten back to normal. She was really sweet last night, and had a nice dinner ready for me when I got home from work— candles, flowers, the works."

Becka's manner softened and she seemed to be calming down. She sat down in the recliner and continued what appeared to be the beginning of a farewell message. "I think the work we've been doing on my lost parts and unfinished business is having a positive effect. The past couple of sessions on Granma, Leslie, and my supervisor have brought a deep sense of peace. I've been sleeping well, and I lost four pounds this week — haven't done any binge eating. I think I'll be ready to stop having therapy when we move to Loveland."

The following week Becka reported a profound sense of well-being. She said that the void was gone, there were no more black holes, and she felt more at peace than she had in years. I wondered if she had convinced herself that all was well, since a break from therapy with me was inevitable. Time would tell.

Kathleen's Reflections

I felt triumphant for Becka, yet was uneasy about her claim that the black holes were gone. I knew there was more to the holes, more hidden in them— her father, and her mother, too. All the rage she buried beneath her protective covering still dwelt, unexpressed, inside her. I would have to trust her own psyche to know what she was able to handle, and assumed that this would be a time of integration and rest. Our efforts to build her self-esteem had helped to some extent, and there seemed to be some relief from the roller coaster of life circumstances occasioned by the move to Loveland.

Another factor worried me more. Becka had related several stories about Gail which gave me the uneasy sense that Gail was having both manic and clinically depressed episodes. Becka seemed to go along with whatever happened in their lives just to keep Gail happy, such as moving to Loveland and finding another job because Gail wanted to do it. Their relationship fit the pattern of Becka and her father, in which she was victimized by Gail's out-of- control behavior in order to keep peace at home. She couldn't begin to break the pattern if she didn't recognize it.

To change requires first seeing what needs to change. It isn't as simple as telling a client what needs to be changed, or even telling how to go about making the change. Seeing is the most difficult part. There is an intellectual knowing, and that is what the therapist can offer, complete with explanations or theories about how the problem came about, if that's even something the client asks for. But truly seeing comes from a visceral experience which is rather profound, an "Aha!" experience. When that light bulb comes on, hopefully it stays on long enough to integrate the full impact of what needs come about. At that point, a true desire for change evolves, and one of two things happens: either the change happens effortlessly, with the clearest vision of the problem, and all the resistance falls away; or the client must make an act of will to bring it about. The willful act must overcome the remaining resistance to the change, involving the fear, and other needs that would be affected by the change. Change requires skills for coping with the unknown.

Chapter 11 – Becka's Story

I remember the day I met Leslie at college, my first true love, like it just happened. She was sitting on a stool in the biology lab, leaning on her elbows at the table where we would spend hours together doing our lab experiments. She was sitting in a shaft of sunlight, gazing out the high windows along one side of the room. I loved her soft blue eyes, framed by long dark lashes. She was wearing a powder blue sweater that intensified her eyes. Her blond hair was cut short, and very thick with curls that bounced lightly when she moved. I would learn later that she hated those curls, but I loved them. I had always wished for naturally curly hair myself, and was attracted to people with blond hair, dark lashes, and blue eyes.

When Leslie turned and looked at me for the first time, I felt my heart fling itself at the inner wall of my chest. It seemed like we had looked at each other thousands of times before, like we had known each other forever. She smiled at me and my heart leaped again.

"Hello. You must be Becka. I'm Leslie, your lab partner. I remember you from the first lecture. Weren't you sitting up close, about the second or third row?"

I was surprised that she had noticed me. I didn't remember seeing her at the lecture. There were about ninety people in the class.

"Yes, I can tell you're going to be a great lab partner," I said.

"Oh, how is that?"

"You're so observant. I can count on you for help already." We both laughed and started talking about the class and our first lab assignment. Leslie was bright and had a perkiness that magnetized me. Instantly I wanted to be with her more and get to know her. Luckily, she seemed to feel the same way, and we soon became friends. I wasn't sure whether she was attracted to me in the way that I was to her, but I was in no hurry to find out and just wanted to let things happen naturally.

Life began as if I had never really seen what was going on in the real world. My father had kept me so close to home that I had become pathetically naive. With the intense relief to be away from him, I was soon swallowed by complete amnesia for what he had done to me. During high school I had read a lot, but I didn't go to movies or watch much television. I read the newspaper just to get through current events class, and that was the extent of my knowledge of the world. I had been living in some kind of fantasy world, just trying to avoid him and what I thought life was about.

I went to plays and poetry readings, sang in the chorus, and enjoyed my classes, especially the small seminar discussions on western civilization and anthropology, which I really wanted to major in, but knew promised no future. Other students went to dances and pep rallies and football games, but I was happier in the library or studying in my room. The hours of learning fully absorbed my attention during the first two years. I must have been overly concerned with studying and trying to achieve, because I eventually found myself in the infirmary being given medication for too much stress. I had become depressed and didn't really know anything was wrong until the medical staff told me. Many years later that I realized that the depression was related to suppressing the memories of my father's actions.

They claimed I had crawled out onto a ledge of the physical sciences building, three stories up, and was screaming that I was going to jump. I had no memory of doing that. The doctor wanted to keep me in the infirmary for a few days, and I told him I would cooperate only if he would not call my father. I'm not sure if he kept his part of the bargain, but Dad never came and he never mentioned it. That was my first encounter with a psychiatrist. He tried to get me to talk about what was bothering me. I was afraid he could see right inside my mind and would know everything about me. I bluffed my way through every meeting with him and eventually quit going to the weekly appointments and quit taking the medicine. I didn't even need it after I met Leslie.

That was the sixties, full of talk of "free love and peace and human rights." Gay people weren't coming out too readily at that time, but a large university was probably the best place for a lesbian to be. I wanted to open up to Leslie about my feelings, but for a long time I wasn't sure how she would take it. I felt I would burst with joy every time I saw her and she smiled at me with those soft, blue eyes. I couldn't concentrate on my work.

I couldn't remember a fibula from a tibia. I dreamt about her at night and all day, too. I found myself making doodles that turned out to be her curls, and then I would try to capture the shape of her eyes.

My obsession with Leslie was delightfully fulfilling and achingly painful at the same time. Sometimes I wanted to not think about her for a while, but I couldn't stop— couldn't sleep. My feeling for her was so fragile that if it were even named as love, I feared it could be engulfed in an instant and lost forever to some un-embodied entity, irretrievable, unknowable as something that had once been mine.

Leslie and I loved the same things: poetry, music, serious talks about life, and hot fudge sundaes. She was big, but not as big as I was. I weighed around 200 pounds throughout college, and she was about 160. We didn't talk about our size the first several months, until after we had started living together, and then we joked about it. It didn't seem important to either one of us. I was eating better and feeling better, so that was all that mattered.

Leslie didn't know it, or do it on purpose, but she saved my life. She gave me a reason to live, to feel that what I did mattered. I found a renewed interest in my studies and felt for the first time that becoming a nurse was worthwhile. All my previous efforts at studies had been mainly an escape from my lack of self-worth and lack of meaning.

It was late one evening, after we had been in the library for hours and were on our way to our rooms when I finally found out where I stood with Leslie. We had been studying at our favorite big oak table way in the back, stacks of books built up around us to make a private fortress. There had been many moments of looking into each other's eyes, reading the un-named friendship that had been growing between us. Under the table we had kicked off our shoes, sometimes giggling quietly as we let our feet rub and poke. I had dared only dream of, yet never hope for such tenderness, such playfulness as Leslie and I had shared then. It was almost intoxicating to know it was real. She was there, lovingly attentive, and just for me.

Leaving the library, we found the mid-winter air cold, the sky clear and star-filled. We walked briskly to stay warm, and I linked my arm through hers. This close together, I felt completely warmed. She gave me a shy smile, and then her brow arched down and toward the middle, the look she had when she was about to say something.

"What?" I asked.

"Let's go to my room and talk." "Talk about what?

"About us."

My heart was racing. It was finally going to happen, and Leslie would bring it up. I had waited patiently, hadn't pushed, let her take the initiative. When we got to her room, she made some hot water in an old percolator so we could have tea. Then we curled up crosswise on her bed with our mugs, facing each other with our knees touching, and I waited.

"I don't get what's happening to me," Leslie said. "Tell me."

She held the mug of tea under her face and let the steam warm her. "I feel so attracted to you, Becka. I love being with you. And I know we need to talk about it, because I know you're attract- ed to me, too."

She had said it, and almost all of it. I was more than just attracted to her, but I was still afraid to call it anything else. I just looked into her blue eyes and smiled, not knowing what else to say without scaring her.

"Well, you are, aren't you?" She started to look nervous. "Yes! I'm very strongly attracted to you. And it's wonderful." "Doesn't it scare you though?"

"No. I'm not scared at all. I've always known I'm a lesbian, so it feels natural to me. What scares you about it?" Leslie sipped her tea and stared into the cup. Her face was flushed a bright pink.

"It's just that … well, I don't know. I never thought much about liking another girl or, woman— before. I actually never felt much for any-body before now. Boys were always an enigma to me, but I just figured it would come when the time was right, or maybe since no men have been interested in me, it just seemed easiest not to bother about it. I've never felt this way at all, in any shape or form. Have you?"

"Not like this," I said. "When I was little, I had a crush on my French teacher and I was in puppy love with her. Then throughout high school I had crushes on a few older women, and I knew that meant I was a lesbian. I never told anyone until two years ago, when I went out with somebody a few times. It didn't work out."

"So this isn't as new to you as it is to me," she said. "Then you're going to have to help me with it. I've been thinking about it so much that I'm worn out wondering how to handle it. Mostly I don't know what I would tell anyone if we were to act on it openly. Do we keep it a secret? Do we hide?"

"If you're not comfortable about it showing, let's take our time.

There's no hurry. If things work out between us, and if you want to later, we can go to a lesbian group meeting where gay women talk about how they handle it."

"Just talking to you about it feels like such a relief," said Leslie. "I could hardly stand it any longer, not knowing if I was crazy and imagining it all. You just feel so comfortable to be with."

I soaked in the sweetness of Leslie's face as we gazed at each other. Then she leaned across our tea mugs and kissed me on the mouth with warm, tender lips, her eyes closed. I wanted to see her eyes and wished she would keep them open, but since she didn't, I closed mine, too. When I did I became dizzy, as if lifted up and spinning in a tornado with her, both of us going around and around, holding each other tightly, swept up in a new and unknown dimension of life. It was the beginning of the best years of my life.

Chapter 12 - Therapist's Story

Becka appeared to have completed her unfinished business with Leslie, judging by the way they had said their goodbyes and parted on fairly friendly terms. But she was now headed straight into the matter of losing significant people again by making her move to Loveland with Gail. Rather than leave any more unfinished business behind, I encouraged her to find closure with the friends and people at work that mattered most to her. I suggested she clear up unpleasant problems, as well as give any positive feedback she had to offer. She was fortunate to find employment quickly at a local hospital, and gave two-week notice to the clinic where she had been working.

Then she spent her spare time packing and meeting with friends for one last visit. She felt quite good about the way her life was going; having made progress toward her goal of growing up, Becka decided not to continue treatment, with me or anyone else. She also cited the commute from Loveland to Denver as something she preferred not to make.

We spent the final weeks of our sessions summarizing what Becka had accomplished in therapy and planning how she would proceed on her own. She was reluctant to say that she would not see me again, and talked of continuing counselling with me at a later time. I assured her that I would conceivably be available to her, but for now we would have to go on the premise that we were saying goodbye permanently ... and mean it. I reminded her of her unfinished business with Myra when they parted, and we would avoid anything like that happening again. I asked her to tell me about the things she felt had been good about from therapy, as well as what hadn't gone the way she might have liked, including any negative feelings she may have toward me. She was unable to come up with anything negative at the time. I knew we did not achieve the goal of a clean termination.

Several months after Becka moved, I received her registration for a workshop that I would be teaching on stress management and self-hypnosis. She and Gail were both planning to attend. I looked forward to seeing them again, curious to know how they had fared in their new life. During the workshop, Becka appeared depressed. She made very little eye contact with me throughout the entire weekend and spoke to me even less. There were several informal opportunities during breaks and following the working sessions when I visited with various people attending the workshop, including Gail. But Becka hung back behind Gail and didn't participate in the conversations. When I asked her questions, she returned with minimal and sullen responses. About a week later I received a letter from Gail:

Dear Kathleen,

Becka dreamt of you the night after the workshop. In the dream, she beat you to a pulp with the "valve" of the outside water spigot. And she commented that you "fucked" with her mind and that the damage is probably beyond repair. She feels that you don't love her, that you only care about the money she gave you— that, in essence, you used her much as her father used her for his needs and desires (fucking). And her typical reaction to anger is to "shut it off" because she's afraid she would hurt someone. Becka doesn't know what to do with the anger. From her point of view, she doesn't know any other way to keep you from abusing her except to not give you what you want: money. She feels that you took advantage of her weakness for your own gain, as when she was a child and her father took advantage of the situation. She's gained even more weight since she stopped seeing you. Yours truly, Gail

I was deeply saddened by the letter. My assessment was that the bond Becka had formed with me made it too difficult for her to accept having to "share" me with other people, like in sibling rivalry, as with the other people attending the workshop. Yet, her de-

pressed demeanor signaled even more reason for concern. I knew
she was still very angry with her mother, and the issue of her father
fucking her still needed to be brought to the surface and resolved. I
felt helpless to get her back into therapy, since it was her choice.

While I was thinking about calling her on some pretense, the
matter took care of itself. She called me and asked for an appointment.

Becka was in a frail state of mind, as if the frightened little
girl part of her had motivated her to come. She could not afford to
resume therapy at the time. She had come this once, primarily for
reassurance of my concern for her. Becka told me about her dream
and said she felt terribly guilty. I said that the dream was a symbol of
yet unfinished business with her parents, and in the dream I represented the mother who had rejected her, by attending to the others
in the workshop the way her mother attended to her husbands and
boyfriends.

"See if you think this fits: the past is repeating itself," I said.
"You feel anger toward the person you love, you have some mean
thoughts about that person, and then you feel guilt and shame for
being so bad to think that way. Once you reach that stage, you can
no longer connect to the anger you felt initially. The subsequent guilt
you are feeling is the result of your child-mind believing that you will
lose your mother permanently by having those bad, blaming
thoughts. In fact, your childhood seems to bear this out, since your
mother abandoned, returned, and then left again. And so you came
today to make sure I still care for you and will not abandon you.

Becka was listening to my interpretation carefully. "Yes . . .
that feels right as you describe it. Oh, Kathleen, what shall I do? I
feel like there is no bottom to this pit of longing for a mother. No matter how much you care for me, or Gail —or anyone— it never seems
enough. I know I keep trying to fill it with food, and that's the worst of
it. Food pales compared to the real thing I want."

"And that is?" I asked.

"Unconditional mother-love." Becka sighed, picking at the
arm of the chair in her habitual way. "My mother. I want to be a baby
in her arms again. I want to feel safe, and warm, and content. I want
her to look into my eyes so that I can feel all her love. I want her to

feed me and sing me to sleep, and to never let me go, just hold me
forever. Pretty stupid, huh?"

"Not realistic, perhaps, but nevertheless very real, human
feelings. But it shows you believe someone else is responsible for all
your needs. You keep waiting for someone else to fulfill you."

A few more months passed and Becka phoned again. At first
she didn't speak at all. Somehow, as I listened to the silence, I recognized something that told me who it was. When she finally answered my question of who was calling, her voice was very weak, in
a tone I had never heard before, like a frightened little girl.

"This is Becka. Gail is going to kill me today. Then she is
going to kill herself."

"What is going on, Becka?" I tried to sound calm.

"She has the gun loaded. She is going to blow our brains
out."

"Where is she? Is she holding the gun now?"

"She's not here. She took the animals to the animal shelter.
Everything is planned."

"Why? What is going on that she is doing this, Becka?"

There was a long silence. "I just wanted to hear your voice
again."

"Becka, you must do something. Call the police. Get out of
there right now and get some help. Go to a neighbor and call." I
heard a faint "goodbye" and a click as the line was disconnected. I
stared at the receiver in my hand, not knowing what to think. I found
her phone number and dialed, only to get a busy signal. After waiting
a few minutes I dialed again, still unable to get through, nor did I on
the next several tries. I tried to locate her address, since all I had
was a post office box and no idea where she lived. I tried the hospital where she worked but they refused to give her address, even
though I said her life could be in danger. Then I called the police in
Loveland and told them what little I knew. For the rest of the day,
every time I dialed her the line remained busy, and no one called
me.

That evening Becka called me at home. This time it sounded
like Feisty Becka. "I just called to tell you Gail didn't do it, because
when she got to the animal shelter it was closed for the lunch hour,

and she decided that meant today is not the day to do it. I'm sorry about upsetting you."

"What?" I was stunned. "How can you put up with this nonsense, Becka? You have got to get some help for yourself and for Gail. You cannot go on with the kind of fear you've been experiencing. Can't you see that?"

Becka remained silent.

"Why did you call me today? Didn't you realize that I would call for help, after what you told me was happening?"

"I just wanted to say goodbye to you, that's all. I know Gail means it, and she is still going to do it. She wants us to die together— for both of us to be out of our misery."

"Becka, I want you to come and see me. You need to be in counselling again, and so does Gail. The adult part of you knows that what Gail does and says is really twisted and sick. You know it isn't healthy to live this way."

"Well the adult part of me knows I can't afford therapy right now, and I can't afford to be driving all the way to the city to get it. It's that simple."

"Not quite that simple. You need to go see somebody. I insist that you find some counselling there in Loveland that you can afford, and have that therapist contact me. Please, Becka."

After another long silence Becka whispered, "Okay. I'll call you soon. And thanks."

I waited a week, and when I didn't hear from Becka or anyone else, I called her. She said that Gail had settled down and things were going all right, so she did not go to a counselor. She did not want to start telling her story all over with someone new and preferred to wait until she could resume therapy with me. There was nothing more I could do. It would be another several months before I would hear from Becka again, a lapse of a full year and a half for her without counselling and living with Gail's insanity.

Kathleen's Reflections

Like Becka, I thought I had found my true love when I was in college. I later realized that I was attracted to the man more for qualities represented by his family than just himself: stability, playfulness, humor, Christian faith, and togetherness. It was all of the things I felt I should have had and missed. I married a Rock of Gibraltar, someone who could make a family with me and give me security. I was utterly convinced that I was mature enough to make such a decision as marriage at the age of 19, during my second year of college. By the end of the first year of marriage I wanted to have a child, even though I was still in college working on my degree.

Any similarities in this part of my story to Becka's stop at the point of falling for someone at the same age as her, out of desperation to find security. Becka was a lesbian; I was not. She stayed with her lover for eighteen years; my marriage was coming apart after three children and only seven years. The glue that bound us both in relationship was security, and that lasted for Becka for a long time. I did a lot of growing after becoming a parent and discovered that I had not been ready at all to make such an important choice as a mate for the rest of my life. I doubt, actually, that anyone has enough wisdom to make such a choice. Some just get lucky.

Divorce was never in my plans or dreams. I had bought the ultimate fairy tale of living life happily ever after. My prince was the one in Cinderella who rescued the weary, maiden from a life of being second-rate to stepsisters, in a broken family not quite her own. When I found myself unhappy and unfulfilled, I tried having an affair to complete something. It was my own black hole, that only later would I realize was like Becka's, a longing to have a mother's love, always a sense of being incomplete. I sought completion in my relationships with men, but none of them ever gave me that longed-for, unconditional love.

I was selfish to choose the path of having an affair, as if I didn't care what would become of my children. But at the time it seemed like the best alternative. I felt I could handle the adversity it would bring, and I did. But it didn't make me proud of myself. I did the best I could, given what I had to work with, and in the process created loss and pain for my children, not unlike what I had suffered myself as a child. Perhaps my early childhood experiences of loss and separation contributed to the poor choices I made as a young adult, through unfinished business and the repetition of patterns.

Curious how the more poor choices one makes, the more likely one is to make poor choices. It's as if I spent my young adult life seeking to make up for the losses of my childhood, and the later years waking up to it and being baffled about how stupid I was to think one could do such a thing. Kierkegaard wrote:

"Life can only be understood backwards; but it must be lived forwards."

There seems to be no way to forewarn young people about the consequences of their youthful and inappropriate choices. The adults in my life tried to tell me I was too young to get married. Wait a while, they said. There's plenty of time for that. Naturally, I thought I knew better, because my life so far had matured me. I wonder what would have happened if I had waited. If only . . . if only . . . if only.

Chapter 13 – Becka's Story

Journal Entry: July 22, 1989 – 23:5

I am terrified of going home after work — of what I am going to find. Maybe Gail will be dead. Maybe she will be singing and smiling, with dinner ready for us both. Maybe she will be gone — or maybe she will never leave. I know I am being punished for leaving Leslie. I deserve this. I asked for it.

I pushed the key into the lock and turned it, like I had many times before, but it wouldn't turn. After trying a few more times, I rang the bell and waited for Gail to answer. Seconds felt like minutes as I stood on the dark doorstep. I pounded on the door and called out to her. After more waiting, I heard her moving around on the other side.

"Gail! What's taking you so long? Please open the damned door. My key won't work."

Gail answered in a sing-song voice, "Your key won't work, honey, because I changed the lock, that's why."

"Why did you do that? Gail, let me in— NOW."

"I'll let you in, but just make sure nobody else is out there." "What are you talking about? I'm the only one here. And I'm tired. Open up."

I heard her slide the chain across and turn the dead bolt. When she opened the door, she looked out past me and to both sides, pulling my sleeve to drag me in quickly. She was wearing shorts and a halter top, and even though it was a hot summer evening, she had rarely ever dressed that way. It was also strange that she had put on a lot of makeup, making her face appear plastic and unreal. Gail never wore makeup, and often criticized women who did. I didn't think she even owned any makeup. I knew there was going to be trouble that night.

"I had to change the lock because somebody has a key and tried to get in here. I know somebody is trying to get ahold of my plans. But they're not getting anything from me. Anybody who comes in here that doesn't belong, I'll shoot their head off."

Then I saw the gun on the living room table. Gail picked it up and paced around the room, waving it in the air and talking constantly. Her voice kept getting louder as she ranted on about her "plans" and how she wasn't going to let anyone near them or us. I was exhausted from a double shift at the hospital and just wanted a bath and to go tobed.

While the tub was filling, I went to the kitchen and made a cup of tea, then returned to the bathroom. I heard Gail continue her ravings out loud in the living room, and every now and then she yelled to me, "Right, Becka?"

I just yelled back at her, "That's right, Gail." As I soaked in the soothing heat of the tub water, I heard other noises coming from the living room, as if Gail were throwing things. It sounded like books and magazines. Then she appeared in the doorway with the gun in her hand. Her face was flushed and her make-up was now smeared, as if she had wiped her arm across her face.

"Are you even listening to me?" she screamed.

"Yes, I'm listening. I'm just tired, Gail. Go ahead . . . I"m listening."

She paced around the kitchen just outside the bathroom door, sometimes looking in to see if I was listening. None of it made much sense, and I was hoping she would run out of steam and let up on it soon. But she didn't. She came into the bathroom and sat on the edge of the tub. She laid the gun on the counter.

"Becka, you and I have to stay together in this. You know that. We're in this together. The world is so totally screwed up there's just no way anybody can stay sane. Nobody can fix this mess we're in. People are just greedy. Morals are corrupted. There's no end to it, is there? We can't change the way people are, Becka. They're just going to have to find out for themselves how badly everything has gotten out of hand. Remember what Kathleen said in that workshop: that the way to get other people to change is first to change yourself. That's what we're going to do. I have the plan almost complete.

We're going to change so that others will have to change. The plan is totally brilliant. I've been writing it all down, and I can't show it to you until it's done, but you'll be impressed, Becka."

When I was ready to get out of the tub, I tried to move past Gail, but she pushed my shoulder and told me to wait. She wanted to talk some more. She went on about her plan and the world being messed up, and every time I said I wanted to get out of the bathtub, she refused to let me.

She became more agitated when I tried the fourth time, and pushed me forcefully back into the tub.

"You can get out when I tell you to get out." She raised her voice and kept ranting until her face was red. The water got cold, and I must have stayed shivering in that bathtub for nearly an hour. She finally let me get out and started getting romantic.

"Let's get into bed and I'll warm you up," she said.

I tried to tell her I was too tired and needed to sleep, but she wouldn't listen. She pushed me into the bedroom and down onto the bed, a mean smile on her face. I knew it was going to be another of those nightmare lovemakings. She was out of control by this time, and I was too scared to resist her. I wanted to cry and scream but was terrified she would become even more abusive. Gail hurt me, and she got more excited when I begged her to stop, squeezing my arms hard to keep me down. She even bit my breasts and told me that I loved it. It was all familiar somehow. When Gail got in a crazy state like this, all I could do was leave my body. I looked up at the window in our bedroom. All I could see was diffused light coming from a street lamp outside, enough to pull me out toward it, so I left my body. I told myself I must deserve it.

Journal Entry: November 14, 1989 – 22:30

Strangely wonderful to find Chris back in my life again. It's amazing to have run into her again here in Loveland, after we worked together at the nursing home. I'm seeing her in a different light this time. She keeps popping into my mind out of the blue, and into my dreams, too. Being around Chris is like swinging easy in a hammock on a mellow summer's afternoon. She moves like a bird, slowly drifting on air waves, maybe an eagle. I have become captivated by her winsome ways— her honeyed, silken voice, and her boyish grin.

Chris is not generous with her smiles. She bestows them as gifts, and when I receive one I feel uniquely fortunate. She is a rogue. Shy and taciturn, yes, but she is barely a woman at all. I see her like the rogue elephant that leaves the herd, determined to do things her own way. I see her cocooned in a cave, living out a life of hermitry. I see her like the ascetic, clothed in a simple robe tied at the waist with rope, climbing interminably upward. She is intriguing; she is beyond the pale; she is "wondrous strange."

Journal Entries: November 22, 1989 - 04:20

when am I going to wake up from this nightmare it is living hell to be with Gail we have shared so much now she is crazy she won't take the medication I wish I could fix it all I can't even fix myself

December 2, 1989 – 22:2

Today is Chris' birthday, so some of us at work took her out to lunch. Sitting next to her, I tried to inhale her quiescence and let it soak in through my blood. I prayed for it to quell the fires that are raging inside. By some magical osmosis, perhaps I can be healed, just being with her.

****

Gail is still not helping herself. She has gone to homeopaths, acupuncturists, chiropractors, and even conventional doctors, but she is not getting better. I have begged her to take the lithium. They believe she has manic depression, and that's probably the only thing that will help. She has tried herbs and homeopathic remedies, and antidepressants that she said made her feel worse. She doesn't trust Western medicine or psychiatry. She thinks she can fix it herself. Sometimes I start to believe everything she says. I have to keep reminding myself that it's crazy talk.

We talk about what suicide means. Gail believes that people who take their lives will create karma that they will have to pay for in another life. She would rather work it out at another time than have to put up with life the way it is now. My religious upbringing tells me that it is a sin, and my soul will burn eternally in hell if I kill myself, but I don't believe there is a hell.

God is loving and tries to help us cope with life, as long as we try to help ourselves. It is wrong to kill though, whether there is hell for it or not. Gail keeps telling me that our souls are guided by God and His teachings, but He wants us to make choices and learn from our mistakes. We have to go on living many lives until we learn everything we need to know about being mortal— the good side and the bad.

Apart from religious teachings, I read what the supporters of the Hemlock Society say about suicide. They talk about terminal illness and physical pain being justification for medically assisted suicide, or self-inflicted death through the least intrusive means. They don't accept mental and emotional suffering as cause for suicide.

Gail says they don't know what it is like to be sane and intelligent, and then go mad, or become chronically depressed. She says they don't know that in some ways it is far greater torture than physical pain.

I don't know what to believe any more. It was much simpler before I started to think about things myself, when I just accepted what I was taught, like a good little sheep. If I'm not supposed to think and decide for myself, why did God ever give me the capacity to question, to even comprehend, to wonder? Why does science exist, when all it does is create doubts about what God is all about? I don't believe in hell or the devil. I do believe there is right and wrong, with many shades of grey. I believe God has presented us with all the shades to make it challenging to evolve, to give us opportunities to make many mistakes, learn, and go back and try again. Maybe Gail is right, that we do it over many lifetimes. Or maybe everything that happens to us is just coincidence.

At least thinking about Chris has become a stabilizing force. When I talk to her I feel sane. Strange … how I've known her for a long time, and how she ended up here, too. Or is it strange? Maybe it is destiny. Maybe there is a plan for all of us, a massively intricate design of many dimensions, crossing in and out of time, space, and matter on many levels. I never thought we would end up working together, but here she is, back in my life and even more of a magnet for me as she was four years ago when I first met her.

Chapter 14 - Therapist's Story

It was just after the holidays in January of 1990 when Becka returned to therapy. She had seen a doctor in Loveland about her depression and was given a prescription for Prozac, a controversial antidepressant that had been making news for its dramatic palliative effects for some patients. It was also proving to affect others in potentially dangerous ways, like increased suicidal tendencies or weight loss, and inciting agitated or aggressive behavior. I was alerted right away to the possibility that Becka was not doing very well on this medication.

During her first hour with me, she vacillated between states of elation and confidence, then moderate despondence and insecurity.

"I'm just going to have to put up with the long drive to see you," Becka said. "There is so much going on, I just don't think I can handle it anymore by myself. The doctor wants me to be in therapy, and since she's a gynecologist, not a psychiatrist, I can't see her.

Besides, I don't want to start with someone new."

"Well, I'm glad you're coming back. I've been really concerned about you, you know. Things haven't been good for you at home for a long time, so fill me in on all that's going on."

"Most important is that I feel much better on Prozac. I have energy for the first time in a long while. I'm exercising three times a week. I have little appetite, and I've lost thirty pounds in the past six weeks. I feel depressed at times, but it isn't as deep, and I have periods of feeling wonderful, which make the depressed times more bearable."

"Gail has been going in and out of depressed and manic states now since I was last coming to therapy, even longer. She has tried a few antidepressants and didn't like the way she felt taking them. She reads about the side effects and decides before she's even tried them that they won't help her. The doctor I'm seeing says Gail has manic-depressive disorder and needs lithium, but she won't take it because it causes weight gain, and she has to have her blood level checked regularly. I'm just about at the end of my capacity to cope with her. And then there's Chris. She's in administration at the hospital."

Becka's face and manner changed when she started to talk about Chris, someone who's name I had never heard her mention before. She had been talking at a rapid rate, picking nervously at the lint on the arm of the chair, erratic in her emotional demeanor. Now she smiled serenely, her pupils dilated dreamily, and her speech slowed down as she spoke, almost in a whisper.

"If it weren't for finding Chris, I don't think I could have sur-vived these past several months. It was so good to see a familiar face there. I first met her a few years ago at the nursing home where we both worked, and then we both end up moving to the same hos-pital. Now is that just coincidence?"

I didn't answer, just raised my eyebrows, and Becka contin-ued. "I was attracted to her then, but I didn't think much about it be-cause things were so good between me and Gail. Something about her really got my attention and the attraction is still there, I have to admit."

"She is a lesbian, I presume?" Becka nodded in the affirma-tive.

"And are you saying that you're having an affair with her, or just that you're attracted to her?"

"No! Not an affair. She's been a good friend. I haven't told her about Gail being crazy, but she knows we're not getting along well. But it doesn't matter because Chris has made it clear that she is very happy living alone and plans to keep it that way. She's a true, self-professed hermit. Still, she has a lover that she spends time with when she feels like it, and I guess both of them like their own space. It seems they've been lovers for a long time, maybe nine or ten years. I don't even see potential there for a relationship."

I wasn't convinced. "But you might wish to have it work out that way. Am I correct?"

Becka glanced at me and then down at the floor. "No, it's not going to happen. I have to deal with Gail right now, and that is my priority."

"And what does 'deal with Gail right now' mean?"

In a matter of seconds Becka's face began to lose color, tension drew around her eyes, and she began to sob. She buried her face in her hands, crying and unable to talk for a few minutes. She regained her composure and said, "I'm going to have to end our relationship. I have to throw Gail out of the house. I've been supporting her for two years, and she's not doing enough to help herself. I've known for a long time that I should not put up with all her crap, but I've kept hoping she would do something and be the old Gail I fell in love with. I know I have to do it if I'm going to have a life of my own."

I had pulled my chair up next to hers and held her when she cried. She clung to my hands as she talked. "I think you've done all you can, Becka. You do need to let go of her."

"You know how terrified I am of being alone, Kathleen. Can you help me go through with this? I can't do it alone. I'm afraid she'll sweet-talk me and I'll back down. It's happened so many times that way. She has a way of manipulating me that I have to get by."

"That's what I'm here for, to stand by you in doing what you need to do," I said.

She looked at me imploringly. "Do you think it's the right thing to do? She's sick. How can I be so cruel to throw a sick person out on the street? I must be terribly selfish."

"So that's what you've been thinking that keeps you there?" "How can I hurt her? We've been lovers for so long. She's sick, and it's not her fault that she is."

"And it's not your fault, either, is it? You've always been an expert at taking the blame though."

"I worry about what will happen to her. If anything does, then I'm going to feel responsible."

"Yes, and you're going to need a lot of support for a while as you go through this process. You're going to need to do reality checks with me, and I'll encourage you to keep taking care of yourself as best you can. That means reinforcing that you are not responsible for Gail's illness, or problems, or her life. You are responsible for yours, and if you're letting your life be destroyed, then it's even more irresponsible of you to let two lives go down the drain.

Gail has family and she has friends. But even more important, Gail has enough intelligence to know that her life is her responsibility. She hasn't lost it so much that she doesn't know that. She knows her options with medication and therapies, and only she can decide to take advantage of them, just like you."

Becka looked at me. "What about me? I'm taking medication."

"You have finally elected to take medication and return to therapy. My position for the past year has been the same as yours. A year and a half ago you were in therapy with me, working out some important issues from the past and getting some resolution. Then you moved with Gail so far away that you couldn't continue. Gail became really disturbed and threatened your life, on more than one occasion. You were still quite depressed, and you let me know what insanity you were having to put up with. But you did not get counselling or any help for months. In the meantime, I knew that Gail might kill you, or maybe you would kill yourself. What could I do? Nothing. I believed you were in danger, as you did. I would have wanted both of you committed to the hospital when Gail was planning to kill both of you, if I could have found you. I couldn't make you or Gail get help. I couldn't require you to take medication for depression. Only you could decide to do that. And only Gail can do those things for herself. Love, caring, compassion . . . even begging won't do it."

"I've really put you through a lot of worry, haven't I? I'm sorry."

"Becka, the point is not me or to get you to apologize. And you see the point I made. I can only do so much for you, and you can only do so much for Gail. You already went way beyond what is reasonable, I think."

"What about living alone? What if I can't handle it? I've never lived alone, and it's scaring me half to death to even imagine it."

"Well, imagine it, and practice that a lot," I said. "Imagining is the place to start. But when you're making pictures of how life is going to be when you're by yourself, you've got to make very bright

pictures. You need think of yourself enjoying your apartment, arrang-
ing things in it to suit your own style; enjoying the discoveries of how
to plan your spare time with satisfaction and creativity; learning new
ways to look at life and friends and potential new relationships; playing and working and getting some of the goodies life has to offer
you. You deserve them, you know. You can turn this into the most
positive step in your growth that you've ever taken. Are you willing to
approach it that way?"

"I'll try. But I'm going to need your help. Don't let me back
down."

"I want to ask you something: do you feel motivated to
make Gail leave because of your attraction to Chris?"

"No. I'm going to do it because I know I need to. There's no
chance with Chris. I told you."

"I know you said that, Becka, but I also know that love is
blind, and it makes us do things we don't think we'd ever do. I've
been there myself a few times. I just want you to stay clear about
what motivates you, what is realistic, and what gives you strength.
Love— especially new love, is very powerful. It can give us strength,
and it can weaken our resolve. And I think you're falling in love with
Chris by the way you talk about her."

"I can't deny it. I think I am, too. But I want to get my own life
together and do for myself, not because of something that has only a
snowball's chance in hell."

"Most of all, I want to see you doing things motivated by
what is best for Becka, and nobody else. Let's work to keep Chris
out of the Gail problem." I paused to make some notes. "There's
something else I want to discuss. When was the last time you talked
to your doctor, since you started taking Prozac?"

"It's been a few weeks. I have an appointment the day after
tomorrow."

"I'm concerned about the rapidity of your weight loss and the
reduced appetite. I know you think it's great to be losing weight, but
this is much too fast. I'm sure your doctor will notice it. She'll weigh
you. Also, I'm concerned about the instability of your moods; even in
the short time today you have fluctuated rapidly between different
states. I want you to tell her that, too. This may not be the best med-

ication for you. Let's be cautious, and tell the doctor everything you notice."

Within a few weeks after Becka returned to therapy, I received another letter from Gail:

Dear Kathleen:

I love Becka more than anyone or anything else in the world. I never thought it humanly possible to love someone this much. And because I love her, I want for her the best and most life has to offer. I want for her love, laughter, happiness, all the good sex she can handle, money, security, all good things. If someone could promise me that if I subjected myself to the most painful thing in the world, that Becka would have all the good things her heart desires, I would do it without hesitation. Letting her go is the most painful thing I can imagine and am currently experiencing.

I can't offer her all those good things, except love, and in fact, can only foresee just the opposite. I love her too much for that. Please help her to let go of me, to seek out the good things in life that are a reflection of who she is and what she deserves. Help her to be free, to choose a healthier, balanced partner, and a good relationship.

It's sad to say, but this is the only gift I can give anyone, most of all Becka. I know it's not going to be easy, but it will be a relatively short period of pain compared to a lifetime with me.

As always, Gail
P.S. Please do not tell her about this letter, ever.

Kathleen's Reflections

I was dismayed to learn of Becka's interest in another woman, mainly because it was someone who was intimately unavailable to her: the mother who was never available. Neither of these women could be there for Becka, whose goal in life was to have unconditional mother-love. Not that Chris, or any lover, should be the one to fulfill that need, but Becka had chosen, unconsciously, I'm sure, to attach herself to someone who, by description, had no love to offer. Here again was another pattern: Becka's choice of Chris was a repeat of the pattern with her mother, while Gail had been a pattern like her father.

I was pleased that she was finding the strength to extricate herself from an unhealthy life with Gail, and I understood how difficult it was going to be to abandon her when the chips were down. The time ahead would be a challenge for Becka and for me to help her get through it. She had built up a negative concept of living alone, which I would try to convince her did not have to be so.

Becka had convinced herself, and formed a belief, that life without a lover is no life at all. She had never lived alone, so it was an unknown prospect. But there was more to it than that. It was the ultimate aloneness every person must face and which creates the pain that she feared most. It begins during birth, during that shocking separation from the warmth and security of the mother's womb. From that moment onward, life means separating from the mother, more and more. Fusion, being part of the mother once again, is a subconscious wish, even though we know it is impossible. We become more alone as we grow into, or are forced into, independence. Healthy means to be well adjusted to coping independently, dealing with life experiences and being alone.

Becka's life experience had driven her toward fusion with a loved object, while mine had driven me into greater independence, only after fusion had failed. Both of us were abandoned as children, yet our trials were quite different. And then there was intrinsic nature, which was also a difference between us. What I call intrinsic nature is the core personality we have at birth, aspects of personality that sustain unchanged. I believe that core personality affects the beliefs we each adopt, but beliefs are malleable and can be changed.Most beliefs and values are taught by the families and social groups that rear us; they influence the choices we make, or even whether we make choices. Beliefs are added to personality over time, but influenced by core personality. Most young people begin thinking for themselves about how things are and ought to be. In my late teens, I changed my belief about why God didn't cure my mother, to the extent that I discarded many beliefs with which I had been raised. Unconsciously, I still held the child-mind belief that I could cure my mother with love, by being especially good to everybody.

Becka had developed beliefs about her life and the quality of it, one of them hinging on a necessity for fusion with a mother love-object. (To be fused with another means to be safe, never alone, constantly satisfied and nurtured, and perhaps to feel so safe that even death can be escaped.) She could not easily discard or change that belief without something to replace it that would have reduced her anxiety equally well. In adulthood, Becka's lovers became the mother love-object.

Becka was paying a price for fusing, or trying to, with her lovers. She was unable to reflect upon herself, to see herself as an individual, or consciously choose to change. Self-awareness breeds anxiety, along with a sense of one's aloneness. By being in love, she could avoid self-reflection and avoid taking responsibility for sepa-rateness. She could reduce the anxiety, but had to pay for it by miss-ing out on individuation. I noted the fact that Becka did not separate herself from Gail until she had fallen in love with Chris. Her struggle for Chris' love and attention would eventually become the driving force for her actions, all in service of the part of self that fights to ward off existential pain.

I had similarly come to see my own process of repeating or recreating history as variations on a theme of fusion for security. After my first marriage fell apart, I spent several years as a single parent, yet making certain my children stayed closely involved with their father. In time I met a man with whom I fell in love, this time seemingly much more at a soul level than the attraction to someone's good history and personal integrity. My first husband was a good man; the notion of goodness has always been a strong value I have held. A good man, or a good woman, is someone who is honest in all dealings, truly thoughtful, respectful and polite toward others, and abides by a code of ethics not unlike the Golden Rule.

Vince, the new man in my life, had a depth for philosophical issues and interests that more closely resembled mine. I knew I could learn from him, and yet I could teach him as well. My first husband had projected an attitude that only I could learn from him, and not the reverse (or so it seemed to me). There followed several years in which my relationship with Vince grew and evolved. That evolution came about through experiences of sharing and communication, but also through difficult arguments, struggling through misunderstandings and differences in thinking. We both enjoyed a period of valuable personal growth.

One thing which had never existed in our partnership was security. I could not trust that Vince's presence was for the rest of our lives; it seemed always tenuous, not least because he made it clear this was so. He believed that people should have multiple partners, even simultaneously at times. I never knew whether he might already have an alternate partner. He chided me at any suggestion that we would grow old together, or for entertaining the notion we would grow old at all. Vince seldom could say the words "I love you," because it led to an intellectual analysis of the words' meaning. I knew the love was there, but he believed the words would dilute, perhaps dissolve, his feelings if they were spoken.

Finding that Vince would not take responsibility for filling in my black hole for me, I had to face it out in the open. Fusion was not possible, and I became stronger. Rather than grow old and co-dependent, Vince and I each grew along our individual paths, which sometimes crossed and sometimes paralleled, and we gave each other the gifts that we had to offer. When the time came that Vince found a different partner, I wasn't ready to let go. Actually, he was not either. He wanted to keep both relationships. He wanted time to explore why he had allowed this new person into his life and what she meant to him. He still loved me and didn't want to lose me, yet he was so strongly pulled toward the other person he couldn't resist the force of the attraction. I chose to bone up and consented to give him time.

We lived apart, but saw each other often. He continued to profess his deep connection to me, and I continued to wonder if I was losing my mind. I found myself alone once again, acutely aware of all the early issues of abandonment and feeling unworthy of a gratifying love relationship. My patterns were repeating, and surely I had to be the only one responsible for finding myself there. I had to discover what it was I was to learn and to change, what I was to accept in order to go on. Acceptance of what I cannot change was the lesson. Individuation was the lesson. That we are all ultimately alone was the lesson. Fulfillment in life does not come from another person; it comes from within was the lesson. Balance and flow was the lesson. Harmony and discord are both necessary forces of life was the lesson. For every action there is an equal and opposite reaction (what goes around comes around) was the lesson. Not swimming up the river was the lesson. Yin and yang. The balancing forces of the Tao.

I was the one to make the break with Vince a reality, when repeated attempts to make him choose between me and the other woman had failed. By now my sons were in high school, soon to be off to college and on their own. Their time was divided between two sets of parents, but at least in one school and community. It was difficult for them, as for children of any split family, but they were more fortunate than most. They had two sets of parents who loved them and spent a great deal of time with them. Each one in the family had sacrificed something, so the burden of loss had not fallen on any one of us in particular.

I had felt highly successful, given the divorce, in our joint efforts to raise our children. But the price I had paid and the sacrifices I had made took their toll and added to the general theme of my life: abandonment, loss, an unworthiness for secured love. Plus I knew everyone in the family had made sacrifices. These were the lessons I had been learning, and was still integrating, when Becka had entered my life. I saw the similarities between us and wished to impart to her whatever wisdom I could that might help her learn, too. There was a gross assumption that what I had learned fit some general category of "Truth."

Chapter 15 – Becka's Story

Journal Entries: February 16, 1990 – 04:00

When am I going to stop and think? What am I doing? The love is there— where is the coping? Is loneliness, aloneness, talking to myself and no one to touch or be touched by, no sharing— are all of the losses worth the gain? And what is the gain? Independence?

February 24, 1990 – 01:00

she's going to kill me it's just a matter of when I know how I'll make her angry enough it'll be quick— no more torture I hate her she's probably gone and I'm glad but how do I get the terrors out of my mind

She even took my crystal

March 3, 1990 – 02:30

Priorities concerning Gail:
1. Tell her it's completely over. Tell her I don't want to see her or be around her again, maybe forever
2. The rages are not part of depression. Her mental problems are much worse than that.
3. I care for her and will help— from a distance, when I can, as I can, i.e. half the tax money.
4. There is no hope for any further relationship, probably not even as friends.
5. I enjoy my aloneness— I need it like breath and a pulse.
6. I am packing up her stuff on my next days off.
7. I don't want her coming to the house to get it. This is my space. Options: storage, ship to her family, someone else coming after it.
8. I'm changing the locks.I can't and won't talk to her on the phone. Her illness has made her "homeless," not me. I am very clear that these decisions are for me and mine and nobody else's.
9. I regret that these decisions leave her in the state of limbo she is in. If I had been clearer and stronger, it would not have come to this in

this way. I will die if it drags on.

10. Another possible relationship is not the cause or reason for these decisions.
11.I will not cancel her credit card yet, or cut off access to the $300 in savings, that is hers.
12. Anything in the house she can have, except my family things.
13. I don't hate her. The last two years have killed our relationship, especially the last four months. My fear of aloneness kept me from being truthful with her. The first five years, the love was real.
14. Pack first, then tell her.

****

Gail was in a fury the day she came back to get her things. She stormed around the apartment screaming at me that I must be having an affair with someone, and she wanted to know who it was. She lost control when I said there was nobody, and started throwing my things around the room. First the little hand-painted porcelain statue— a Victorian woman in an overcoat, muff, and bonnet— was smashed to bits. It had been Granny Kirkwood's, a gift from her when I graduated from nursing school, because I had coveted it so much as a child. I was too frightened to stay there, so I told Gail I had errands to do and left for a few hours.

When I got back she was gone, her things, too. I started to inventory my own belongings in each room, looking to see what she might have claimed as hers. While almost everything seemed intact, I was disturbed to keep finding notes from her, in drawers and closets, in the medicine cabinet, and on my bed pillow. They were threatening notes, most of them saying I would regret and pay for what I had done. Some were painful diatribes of what a contemptible person I had become, of what heinous acts I had commit- ted. Each one cut me deeply, as if she were there in person, cutting little pieces out of me with a surgeon's scalpel.

As night fell, the silence and the emptiness of the apartment wrapped around me like a thick coating of tar and feathers. I found more notes inside the refrigerator and in food containers as I tried to prepare my supper, and at that point I broke down and cried. Later I found she had shoved a favorite photograph of the two of us into the sleeve of my night shirt. There were four-letter words scribbled in ink all over it. Another picture of us was shredded into bits between the sheets of our bed. It seemed there was no end to where she had put evidence of her and her craziness.

I didn't sleep all night. I began to wonder what she had done with the gun. Since I hadn't come across it in my search, I decided she must

98

have taken it with her, and I worried through the night that she might come back to kill me. Every sound I heard seemed ten times magnified, most certainly a threat. I felt like I was the only person left living on the planet, aside from Gail, and she was deter- mined to take revenge. At half past three the ringing telephone snapped me back to reality. It was Gail.

"Did I wake you up?" She sounded subdued. "No, I can't sleep," I said.

"Neither can I. I'm having a real hard time with us being apart like this. And yet I know it's the right thing. You need to get on with your life, Becka. I'm just making it worse for you. You deserve some peace and happiness. I'm really sorry for all I've put you through. Can you forgive me?"

She was doing it again— trying to manipulate my emotions, making nice talk. I couldn't trust it anymore. I didn't answer.

"Becka? Say something. Talk to me."

"I don't know what to say any more."

"I just want us to be friends, and maybe we can still see each other. I know it's been hard for you. I don't want to lose you. Do you believe me?"

I was feeling so hurt about the notes and the way she had behaved that afternoon, that I couldn't forget it just like that, like none of it happened. "How can you say that after leaving all those notes?" I asked.

"What notes? I didn't leave any notes. You must be crazy."

It was starting again. Her voice got louder as she spoke. "I'm trying to make up to you, and you're just being a witch." After a long silence in which neither of us spoke she shouted, "I'll bet you have your new lover there, don't you? You can't talk right now because someone is with you, isn't that right?"

Gail continued her harangue into the phone, so I made myself hang up. It rang again a few moments later, but I let it go. The answering machine picked up in the next room, and I could hear her shrieking into it. I ran to the kitchen and turned down the volume, but her accusations that I was crazy continued inside my head. I put my hands over my ears and screamed out loud, "I am not crazy!" I disconnected the phones from the outlets, and my own negative voices continued the tirade against me.

In the days that followed, Gail left messages on my phone machine, knowing I would check it when I got home from work. In one message she asked if I had found the gun yet. That sent me on another search through the entire apartment, including the holding tank for the toilet. Each day her cruel messages included the taunting question, had I found it yet? She was out of the house, but she wasn't finished making me miserable. Then she began to leave clues, one at a time, as if I were enjoying a playful scavenger hunt.

The clues were: It's not low. It's in plain view. It's hard to get to it. It's gonna require a special piece of equipment to get it. If you're looking inside, you're cold. After that last one, I finally found that she had gotten the gun up on the roof, and I had to get the ladder out of the storage shed to get it down. I knew she was taking some sick delight in knowing how difficult it would be for me to get all three hundred pounds of myself out on the roof to get it. I cussed her and everything else as I inched my way across the shingles on hands and knees, certain that I would lose my balance and roll right off the edge to the demise I deserved. Then she had black roses sent to my office at the hospital with a note that read: "We'll leave this hell together. Don't worry."

Chapter 16 - Therapist's Story

The events of the week in which Becka threatened to kill herself were no small matter in my own life. I had been out of town on business, returning on a Monday. My husband picked me up at the airport and said that my secretary had been through a frightening experience that day at my office involving a vagrant who appeared to be mentally ill. He had been camping out during the cold March nights in the sheltered vestibule outside my office door. When Patricia, my secretary, had come to work Monday morning, she had found him there with cigarette butts and empty food wrappers littered about the doorstep. At the bottom of the stairs was a pile of ashes from a small fire he had built on the cement sidewalk.

The man had been hostile toward Patricia. She had told him to clean up his mess and leave, but when she tried to go out during her lunch hour, he was still there. She was afraid to attempt to pass by him. There was a mental health clinic in the building on the first floor below my office, so she called them. They indeed had recognized him as someone they had discharged from their program for being uncooperative and told Patricia to call the police. She did so, but by the time she went home at five o'clock, the police had never come, and the vagrant had gone.

When my husband relayed this ominous news, we went directly to my office. The man was not there, but I saw evidence that he had been, because there was more trash on the upper landing.

Seeing the burn mark on the pavement from the previous night made me very uneasy. I called the police and asked for a special watch on the building that night. I tried to reach the owner of the building, without success. At five-thirty in the morning I was awakened by a call from the police, informing me that the building was on fire, and the fire crew was nearly finished putting out the blaze. They wanted a description from me about the man I had reported, but I had never seen him. The story they gave me was pathetic. They had caught the arsonist within an hour of discovery of the fire. Another call had come in for a stolen vehicle, which was quickly located, and the thief arrested. Police believed it was the same man who had started the fire, since they had detected the odor of gasoline on him. They had confronted him about being at the scene of the fire, and asked why he had stolen the car. His story was he was passing by and spotted the fire, so he had taken the vehicle to go find a fire extinguisher and call the fire department.

Most of my office was destroyed. I had very recently moved into it, and was struck by an added piece of irony. I had been shopping for office insurance for a few weeks, and just before going out of town, I found a company to give me coverage. I had an appointment with the agent for that same day, the day of the fire. In effect, I was not covered for any losses. The vagrant had set fire to the building. He was angry over his discharge from the mental health clinic so he had broken in with a can of gasoline. He had poured it throughout their offices, then went out to the parking area and smashed in all the windows of their van. Since my office was located just above the mental health clinic, the fire had burned through their ceiling and collapsed my office into the room below.

It was a bleak moment in my life, which felt at the time like a signal to end my career. That was the start of a week with a series of crises like nothing I had ever experienced. I was ready to say "I quit," and not find a new office, just to try to somehow bring my practice to a close. I didn't think I had the stamina to start all over— search for another space, purchase new furnishings and equipment, redevelop forms and files— yet, I couldn't escape the clients calling me that week in their own desperation. It was as if some mysterious force had a grip on me with a determination to make what was already a bad situation something far worse.

I had canceled all of my regular appointments for the week, and still there were four emergency calls in as many days. The first was someone who had injured his eye and was in excruciating pain. He wanted some assistance in coping with it through hypnosis. I went to his home to work with him. The next was a former client who had successfully used hypnosis with me on a previous occasion for test anxiety. She was about to take an exam to become, of all things, a fireperson, and begged to see me immediately. She came to my home for the session. The third person was a man I had been counselling through a series of major losses, including a son who had been killed in an automobile accident, another child who had been abducted and never found, and most recently a wife who was demanding a divorce. I was called because he had barricaded himself in his garage and was threatening suicide.

And the fourth was Becka doing the same thing: threatening to kill herself, although I didn't know it until late in the day. The crisis call about the male suicidal client came around ten in the morning. While I was away taking care of this problem, Becka had been calling my service, requesting that I call her as soon as I could. She somehow reached my husband who explained to her that I was handling a crisis and didn't know how long it would take. As it was, it took all day and into the evening, and by then, Becka had called several times. The suicidal man was in the midst of a full-blown nervous breakdown. I had never seen him in such a state of confusion and delusion. He was so paranoid that it took me a few hours to coax him into an ambulance, then more hours at a hospital to have him evaluated, and even more hours to transfer him to a psychiatric facility. It happened that this hospital was in Loveland, so once he was finally secure, I went to Becka's apartment at 11:30 at night.

Becka opened the door and let me in to a very pleasant living room. There was a fireplace with a sofa and coffee table in front of it, a leather easy chair, a rocker, and many bookshelves with a host of little things she had collected— statuettes, rocks, shells, feathers, boxes and framed photographs. The whole apartment felt warm and comfortable, and was well kept.

She first handed me a package she wanted me to give to Chris in a few days. She also gave me the .38 revolver Gail had used to threaten her, and asked me to store it safely. Then she asked me to follow her to the bedroom. We sat on the edge of her bed, facing an aquarium with one lonely tropical fish in it.

"That's Glenda," she said. "And the dog is Ernestine, and the cat is Tiger Lily. I've made arrangements for Ernestine and Tiger Lily, but I suppose Glenda will die. Gail wanted her and the dog, but she can't haul a fish tank around with her, with no permanent place to live right now. She's going from one friend's place to another."

Becka was calm and had little energy. She was wearing a worn old sweatshirt and faded red jogging pants. "I have everything ready here. These are the pills I'll take, the alcohol, and the plastic bag I'll put over my head."

She picked up one oblong cylinder from the bedside table

from amongst the huge pile of pills. "This is a suppository that I'll use to keep me from vomiting the pills and alcohol."

"So that's the plan," I said. "You'll use the suppository, ingest alcohol and pills, then tie a plastic bag over your head."

Becka nodded. "This is the Hemlock Society formula. The tricky part is going to be to know when to tie the bag on. I have to be careful not to do it too soon or too late."

"Becka, this is all too gruesome." I was exhausted physically and emotionally myself. I struggled to find the resources to respond appropriately to this nightmarish scene. I never could have imagined a week so fraught with events that I would question what I was doing with my life. One suicide threat in any therapist's lifetime is enough, but two in one day was somehow unreal, especially when it followed on the heels of a major fire loss. The fire itself had been a shock, since it was the third one in my life in as many years.

"I don't blame you for giving up," I said. "I feel like giving up too — not on living, but on being a therapist. I'm feeling low enough to crawl under a rock and stay there until I can face another problem. My husband told you I was handling another crisis today, a client who threatened to kill himself in his garage, and I had to hospitalize him. About all I can say to you right now is that I don't want to hospitalize you, too, Becka. I believe you can get through this difficult time and have a better quality of life.

"I will say that I don't know how much longer I'll last in this profession, though. Since the office burned, I've been thinking all this week that I'll just go sell shoes. You know— everybody needs shoes, you don't have to convince them of that— just help them find the right style and size, and they'll be happy. It's that easy. I think I'm just going to sell shoes."

I felt too down to say much more to Becka than that. The next thing I knew, she had her arm around my shoulders and began to rock me slowly. Tiger Lily spread himself across both of our laps and purred loudly.

"You've had a really rough time, haven't you?" she said. "But, Kathleen, you can't stop being a therapist. You're so good at it. You help so many people."

I sighed deeply. "I'm not so sure of that, Becka. People will do what they're going to do, and just caring about them and loving them isn't enough. I think that's the lesson I'm supposed to be learning out of all this. You can't cure people with love, and that's what I thought I could do, just like I tried to cure my mother with love. That's my unfinished business, and it's getting in the way of giving you proper care. I think you must go to someone else who can help you better than I can."

"I'm sorry I've made you feel this way. You think you're a failure because I want to die, but that's not it. You are a good therapist."

"And you are a good nurse. Think of all the people you have helped— many more than I have. You've spent all these years taking care of people, and caring about them. You're that kind of person; and little do they know of what you've been through in your own life to survive. Becka, I can't tell you to go on living for other people, just because you're such a good care-giver. I do know there are a lot of people who want you to go on living, not the least of which is me. I also know you have to get something back from life, too. You're a bright, charming, and talented person, with excellent experience and training. Surely you must get something back from your patients and from friends that helps to make your life worthwhile."

I knew that besides her job, Gail (until recently), and a few friends, Becka didn't have much invested in anything else. Becka stared at Glenda and didn't answer for a while. She still had her arm around my shoulders.

"You don't understand. Times like this, none of that makes a difference. It isn't enough to overcome the feelings I have of worthlessness and despair. If that challenge is all there is to life, then it just isn't enough.

I couldn't come up with any more reasons for her to go on living, and I didn't want to lose my foothold regarding her concern for me giving up. As she rocked me gently, sitting at my side, I now had some leverage that the roles were reversed: she was comforting me. I had clearly shown her my vulnerability at one of the lowest points in my life.

"Well, I'll make a deal with you, Becka. If you will make a contract with me to keep on trying for three more months, I will keep on trying, too. Clearly, the Prozac isn't right for you, but I'm sure there is a medication that will work. I know we can lick this depression with the right treatments. I deeply want to help you through this pain, and I want you to keep on trying to overcome it. Just give us three months; I know you'll see a brighter life."

Becka and I looked at each other through a glassy wetness for a few moments. "Okay. Three months."

"Let's make it clear what we mean. I won't give up on you, or on being a therapist, as long as you are willing to give me your stash of pills for safekeeping, to come to therapy at least weekly, and to get a change in your medication from your doctor."

Becka nodded. "Deal."

"Good. Now all I need is an office for you to come to."

Kathleen's Reflections

I began to think I would go crazy myself with the timing of events in my life and those of my clients. I felt overwhelmed that the possibility of quitting my practice grew more likely. I asked myself if I could have done things to set myself up for the profusion of problems I was facing; or whether the satisfaction of several people's needs was truly dependent on me, and if that was a mere coincidence. And if it were coincidence, I would have to say I was cursed with bad luck. It was very clear that I needed to simplify my life. I needed to spend more time with my family, yet the circumstances made it difficult to do so. I had two clients critically unstable, a fire mess to clean up, no office in which to practice, and a decision to make: whether to find a new office, or give up and sell shoes. I needed to continue employment somehow. Economically, I could make far better money by maintaining my practice, which was part-time, than at any other job I might find full-time.

Becka's story about Gail's crazy behavior reminded me of things my mother did when she got sick again, just a year after we moved to an apartment with her. One warm, late summer afternoon Mom came into my room with a glass of tomato juice in her hand. She was wearing a strapless, red sundress and all the remaining costume jewelry that hadn't been "stolen." She wore a lot of makeup, her cheeks and lips a bright red, as she had been prone to do lately. Her nails were red, too. There was a strange expression on her face, as if she were angry or upset about something.

"What's wrong, Mom?" I asked. "Are you okay?"

She didn't answer me; instead she went to the window and stared down at the driveway below. She tilted her head way back with a dramatic twist as she gulped down more of her tomato juice.

"I have a secret to tell you, and I want you to keep it. Can you do that?" she asked.

"Sure I can." I was surprised that she had a secret, and I

figured it was worth creating a pact, as a sign of bonding which any teenager in my position would love to have with her mother. She drew the tomato juice glass close to her chest and sat down beside me on the edge of my bed.

"I'm very serious about this, Kathleen," she started. "You must not speak of this to anyone at all. Especially not Grandma.

"I promise. Girl Scouts honor. So tell me."

Mom pressed the glass with both hands between her breasts and looked down into it for a long time. I was puzzled by her actions but shocked when she finally announced her secret.

"I am going to have a child. But . . . not just any child, Kathleen, and I swear this is true." She spoke in a whisper, "I am going to be the Mother of the next Christ Child."

I sat there, speechless. Thoughts raced through my mind about how she was losing it, how that meant all kinds of trouble ahead, about her going back to the hospital, and then about what I should say to her. But she went on talking.

"I've been preparing my womb for the pregnancy by drinking tomato and cranberry juices and eating strawberries and tomatoes. I must have many things that are red. It will produce the blood to line the womb. This is what I'm supposed to do to prepare for immaculate conception. When I am ready, God will plant the seed."

Almost a year before this she had given me the birds-and-bees talk, and shortly after that I had begun menstruation. Now I was confused.

"But Mom," I protested. "You told me you have to make love with Daddy to get pregnant, and Daddy hasn't been here."

"That's right. What I told you is true, but that's for a normal birth. This is different. You also know the story of Jesus' parents, Mary and Joseph, and that Mary was a virgin when God planted a seed in her to bear His Son. And he chose Joseph to be the mortal father. The Bible tells us that Christ is to come again to help us some more. God is going to send Him through me."

I listened with disbelief. Mom had never talked that way before, but she had the same look on her face as when she claimed that thieves had broken in and taken her costume jewelry. I knew she was having a delusion, even though I didn't know that's what it was called. To me, she was just crazy. It hurt a lot and made me very sad and frightened.

"How do you know all this is so?" I asked.

"An angel's voice told me. The angel told me to prepare myself."

"I think you might be mistaken, Mom," I ventured. "It doesn't seem like God would send His Son through somebody like you. I mean, you don't even go to church very much. Wouldn't He choose a nun or something? Why you?"

Mom smiled at me. With her bright red lipstick painted on crooked, she looked even more insane. Her eyes brightened as she said, "It isn't for us to know why, my darling. God works in mysterious ways. You'll see. God has chosen me, and in my prayers I've been asking His forgiveness to cleanse me of all sin. I am going to take communion this Sunday. But this miraculous birth will cleanse me completely."

Mom hugged me, then went to look at herself in the mirror over my bureau. She dabbed at the rouge on her cheeks with her finger and puckered her lips to spread the lipstick around. Then she looked down at her belly and pushed it out, rubbing it with her hands.

"I'll probably start to show soon. Remember your promise, Kathleen."

Mom continued to make a point of eating and drinking things that were red. I prayed that God would intervene and make her well. Almost every night I cried. In the couple of weeks that followed, she did and said enough crazy things that my grandmother knew she was quite sick again. Preparations were made to send her back to the hospital, and temporary homes for me and my brothers were sought. By the time she left, she looked about five months pregnant. The mind is so powerful! What you think about, you bring about. Not an immaculate conception, surely, but apparently one can fool the body into believing it is pregnant, enough to produce significant hormonal changes.

Chapter 17 – Becka's Story

Journal Entries: March 26-27, 1990

Deciding to work again— to move on in therapy— has set loose a host of demons. My body feels like a corpse I saw once in a field, out in the heat and humidity for three days. The skin was writhing from the maggots underneath. I haven't had a thought today but what the part of myself that is strongest, the negative, hasn't twisted and contorted in an effort to hurt me and keep me down. I hate mirrors, but today I have been transfixed by them. Each time I looked in one, there was "a talk" from that negative part about dying and doing the world a favor; about ugliness, pain, sorrow, aloneness, isolation, fat, guilt, unworthiness. You say I've "helped" so many people . . . what about the people I've hurt, anyone I ever loved or who loved me? Everyone. You . . . you doubt yourself because of me. Chris, a violated hermit in a state of feeling and involvement she never wanted. Gail, alone and abandoned, homeless, crazy. Leslie, cast aside, for what? Her faithfulness? My brother, raised by me, a psychotic child. My mom, burdened with children she never wanted, both needing from her and she unwilling to give to them. My dad, I must have driven him to do what he did. Before, he was a gentle man that read poetry. My Granpa, I killed him by what I did with his son. My Granma, I never was the child or adult she wanted me to be, a source of shame for her and her son. Balance that against the people I've "helped."

You, Kathleen, say I feel sorry for myself. You're close, but no banana. I am sorry, as in a pitiful excuse for a human being. I'm selfish and manipulative. I must be crazy— why else would I be the way I am? I need, need, need. My body hurts from lack of being touched, but when others reach out, I can't feel it. The fantasy you created in our hypnosis session, about hours of being held by my mother made my skin crawl with repulsion— how can that be?

What I am fixated on as THE want/need/desire actually repulses me. I can't let myself need again and be rejected — then stiff-armed, like it was with my mother. If I lapse into feeling the need even vaguely, I'm consumed by anger, frustration, pain, and an absolutely unbearable ache in my chest. It sucks the air and blood out of me

When I was five I felt it and I nearly died. My Granpa brought Mom back and I tried and tried to take from her. Then Roy was born and I began to give. Cast your bread on the water and it will return to you, but nothing came back or reached me. The need got so deep it was beyond feeling— larger than myself. Then I was eleven when I felt it again, the day Mom left, the night the incest be- gan again. I saw the truth in the mirror today— why no one can love me. There is no me— only what other people see in the space this body occupies, each image their own fantasy, and me trying to live up or down to it. Life has to be more than just plodding through each day— else why would anybody bother?

I don't know if I've ever had one honest or real feeling about anything since the day I realized that no matter how much or little I needed, the ache would never be filled. I can't live feeling that something must be inherently wrong with me causing such pain and evil to those that have had anything to do with me. Bad Seed. I never saw that movie or read the book for fear I would recognize myself. Now there is no me to recognize, because what fills that space is the thousands of fragments others have imagined they have seen there, no whole. I must be too hideous and evil to exist intact.

April 3, 1990 - 21:10

Chris has opened the door to her heart and her mind, at least a little crack. She is beginning to let me in, to know more about who she is. What a mystery! I want to creep inside her head and peek into her shadows. We made dinner together at her place, and she drank a lot. That's when she changed. I never heard her talk so much, nor reveal her feelings like she did. She told me about her two best friends getting killed in an auto accident the night of their high school graduation. She felt like it changed her whole attitude toward life. It didn't stop her from drinking, even though alcohol is what killed them. I guess she figured if it's going to get you, it will. She doesn't drive when she's had more than one or two slow beers.And she talked some about Dana, her lover. They seem to share very little, it's hard for me to understand how they came to be lovers. But that is partly what makes Chris so intriguing. After all, why would she bother to spend her time with me?

April 22, 1990 - 20:25

This new medication isn't doing anything . . . except messing up my hormones. Now the doctor has me on birth-control pills to try and balance out my moods, plus an anti-anxiety drug. I just keeping taking pills, and none of them make any difference, except to make me more uncomfortable with some other symptoms. About half of the three month contract time has passed, and I don't feel any closer to the light. The memories of him persist and haunt me. Will I ever be free of them?

April 26, 1990 - 20:45

I talk to Chris almost every day. I'm working the evening shift now, so it's hard to get time to see her. She keeps reminding me she likes her privacy anyway, and doesn't want to get too involved. Then she asks me to go hiking in the mountains, to a movie, or to just hang out at her place. She seems to like being with me. I have to believe it. I don't care what we do, as long as I can be with her. She likes to get drunk, and I like it because she loosens up so much and talks about herself. I learn more about her when she's had a few. I found out she grew up on a farm with three brothers in Indiana, and her folks thought she was the best hand of all four of them. Imagine… growing corn in Indiana! Somehow it's hard to picture that, now that she's a whiz bookkeeper in hospital administration. She's so lean you wouldn't expect her to have muscles, but I guess that's all she is— "a lean, mean, quiet machine."

April 30, 1990 - 10:15

Last night Chris finally broke loose and admitted strong feelings for me. She couldn't call it love, quite. We made love all night long, so that counts for a whole lot. It was the most delicious delight I've had in years. Then this morning, trying to recover from her hangover, she became distant and quiet again. She wouldn't talk or let me touch her any more, not even a hug, so I came home. What an enigma.

May 23, 1990 – 08:30

Where is this going to lead? Chris is there, close, so tender and loving. Then she is gone. She needs her space. She has to see Dana. What am I? What do I mean to her? Is she using me for some- thing? No, Chris is not the kind of person to use people. I don't understand what her behavior means. I'll just take it as it comes. If only I could stop wanting more from her. It is never enough, and I know she will not make any commitments. I keep hoping that she feels the way I do and will admit it to herself. If only I could stop thinking about her all the time. I am torn up by this obsession. Kathleen's self-hypnosis exercises help to diminish the thoughts some; it helps for a little while, but then I get all caught up in her again.

May 25, 1990

       i cannot believe it Chris is moving back to Denver she comes into my life like this captures my heart and all my thoughts and then she runs off and leaves it is too much to bear

June 13, 1990 – 06:00

       She did it. She is gone. My life is empty, worthless, and very lonely. I sleep all the time— when I am not at work— to escape the emptiness. The TV is always on, but only for the company of noise. I can't be bothered with preparing food. On a good day, I microwave a frozen dinner. The rest of the time, I eat pudding and tapioca and cakes—junk. I like things that are soft, that I can squeeze over my tongue without having to chew. It's like baby food. The apartment is a mess. I don't care. I'm a mess, too. Not bathing more than twice a week. What does it matter? The contract runs out in four days.

June 27, 1990 – 04:50

       I never should have agreed with Kathleen to extend the contract. I can't take any more of this aching, meaningless life. It is more pain than anyone should have to bear. Pills don't take away the depression. Chris can't take it away. Kathleen can't do it. It's my pain. It's my punishment. I must be paying penance for everyone I ever hurt. We had a long talk today about suicide, and you say I want to take the easy way out. What makes you think killing yourself is easy? Have you ever thought about going through with it? Do you know some easy way to leave? Yes, it is hard to stay here, plodding through this meaningless existence. You don't have any answers for me, so what is so great about being alive? My career? A sham. My love life? Doesn't exist. My family? Also doesn't exist. My friends?

       What can they do to take away the pain of knowing I am about the lowest worm on earth for what I have done— and not done? My lease on the apartment is up for renewal. I'm going to give notice and move back to Denver. If I don't, the isolation will kill me.

July 17, 1990 – 21:30

       Coming back to Denver was harder than I thought it would be. If I survive another move—just physically—it will be a miracle. Chris saved me by helping me with her truck. I couldn't have done it without her. I need to be near her, even if we can't be together much. Just to know that she is nearby is lifesaving. She keeps saying that we're not going to see each other any more, but she always backs down. Her ambivalence is my hope. It feels right to have moved back here, even though it was full of problems. I have my own place, but unfortunately it is on the other side of the entire city from Chris' place. It was all I could afford, so I have to be thankful that at least I'm closer than I was before. Thanks to Gail, I found Chris in Loveland, and thanks to Gail, I had to move myself back to Denver with- out any help from her, so I can still see Chris.

Chapter 18 - Therapist's Story

One hot August evening when I got home late, I found a message on my personal answering machine from Becka. Actually, two messages from her, back to back. I guessed she must have called around eight-thirty. She sounded intoxicated, and I knew she had taken up drinking quite heavily since she had been seeing Chris. Her messages were difficult to decipher, but she seemed to be saying goodbye to me. The last bit of the message sounded like, *Tell Chris I love her.* At that, I was sure she was in trouble.

I dialed her number quickly, and Becka answered, barely audible.

"Becka, this is Kathleen. I got your messages. What's going on?" She didn't answer. All I heard was the sound of heavy breathing and then a moan.

"Becka!" I shouted into the phone. "Talk to me."

"Kathleen." Her speech was slurred. "I just wanted to hear your voice again."

"You've been drinking, haven't you? How much have you had to drink?"

"I'm not sure. Quite a bit."

"Have you taken pills, too? Becka . . . "

"Damn it. I must have pulled the bag off. I didn't wait long enough. I panicked and pulled it off. Shit."

There was only heavy breathing again. There was no doubt in my mind that she had taken some kind of drugs. "Becka listen to me. I have to hang up and call for help. I want you to hang up the phone, but I'm going to call right back. I want you to answer it when you hear it, do you understand me? Answer the phone."

"Yeah, okay."

I wanted to keep her on the line, but there was no way I could get help to her unless I hung up. First, I had to find out where she lived so I would know where to send the police. It would take me forty-five minutes to reach her, even if I knew. I called a friend of Becka's who could tell me where she lived. Teresa said she would go there immediately to check on her. Then I called the police to dispatch an ambulance.

I redialed Becka's number and prayed she would answer it again. She picked up the phone, but she had deteriorated so much that all she could do was moan. It was impossible to understand what she was saying. I shouted into the phone to try to reach her better, but she seemed to have drifted off to sleep or into a state of unconsciousness. All I heard was her breathing. I followed the pattern of it, noticing whenever it changed pace, and tried again to awaken her by shouting. Sometimes she snored or snorted, which gave me hope that while she was heavily sedated, she was not yet dead. I waited to hear if someone entered her house, but nothing happened for what seemed an hour. Then I heard glass breaking, her dog barking, and soon Teresa was calling Becka's name to awaken her.

I shouted again, hoping Teresa would hear me and pick up the phone handpiece. It worked.

"Hello, is this Kathleen?" I recognized Teresa's voice. "Yes. I'm so glad you made it. How is she?"

"She's really out of it, but alive. I hear the ambulance. I'll go let them in, and then call you as soon as I can tell you more. I had to break the window to get in. Her dog is totally freaked out, but she didn't bite me, thank God."

I waited for an hour before Teresa called me. She reported that the emergency team had pumped Becka's stomach first, before trying to get her in the ambulance. They said there was little time left. She was then stabilized and being transported to the hospital as we spoke. It was likely she would be asleep or unconscious for hours.

They said there was no point in our going to the hospital since Chris was going and nothing we could do. One friend was enough. It would be better for us to phone in later to inquire about her.

"How did Chris get into this?" I asked.

"She showed up just as they were loading Becka into the ambulance. She wants to be at the hospital with Becka until she regains consciousness."

Knowing Chris was with Becka was a help. She would be

cared for, but I couldn't sleep. Every three or four hours I called the hospital, each time learning that Becka was still in a deep coma with no signs of it lightening up. I felt like I was becoming a pro at waiting for unconscious people to wake up. It was nearly thirty-four hours before she came around at all, and even then, she was incoherent. When I went to see her, she could barely speak, and I doubt she recognized me.

I talked at length with the attending physician just outside Becka's door. He said it was miraculous Becka had lived through ingesting the dosage and combination of medications she took, attributing this fact to her size. He said it would take her a couple of days to become more alert, and it could be weeks or months for her body to completely detoxify all of the poisons. There could even be some lasting effects, physical or mental; he didn't know. Brain damage: I knew about that, too.

Fortunately, Becka showed significant improvement in her mental functioning over the next few days. She was moved to the psychiatric unit once her physical condition was stable. That is where I visited her each day, even though she did not remember that I had come the day before, nor anything we had talked about. She did remember the day she decided to kill herself.

"Something in my head just clicked," Becka said. "I just knew it was time to take the pills. I was ready. I felt completely calm and rational, certain that suicide was the right thing to do. I knew it would be easy to slip over to the other side, painless— all my pain would end. I just left work like I did every other day, drove home, and started the plan. I wanted to die, and it was very simple."

Becka pounded her fist on the table and snarled through gritted teeth. "And I screwed it up! I'm so stupid I can't even die without making mistakes. Do you know what happened when I woke up in that damned hospital bed? I saw a clock on the wall. It was 4:45, and do you know what I said to myself? I said, "Damn! There are even clocks on the other side.""

I had never seen Becka angry in this way. She had become hostile and aggressive toward everyone and everything. She pushed chairs out of her way when she moved around. She dumped her ashes on the ground instead of using the ashtray. She complained that she had to beg for her cigarettes from the attendants, and that she wasn't allowed to smoke in her room, or anywhere except the courtyard. She complained that the food tasted bad and the coffee was always cold. The staff had had to put her in seclusion during the night. She had shouted and sworn at them for hours until reluctantly they broke down and injected a sedative to get her to quiet down.

Each day Becka asked me what had happened and why she had been rescued. I recounted the story each time, that she had left messages on my answering machine, and I had called for help. I said, surely, if she had truly wanted to die, she wouldn't have called me to tell me she was going to kill herself. But Becka denied that she had wanted to be stopped. She was very angry to be alive and to have failed what she thought was a certain means to death. She was angry with herself for calling me, for answering the phone, and felt stupid for not unplugging the phone.

I discovered during our conversation that she had also called Chris. That was how it had come about that Chris had appeared just as the ambulance was about to drive away. I believed Becka had kept the phone beside her because she hoped that Chris would call, more so than that I would. But I knew Becka wasn't ready for any further confrontation in her current state of mind.

The suicide attempt gave rise to an occasion to meet Faye O'Brien, Becka's mother. Chris had called her and told her what happened. She showed up from Dallas on the third day, when Becka was still incoherent. I talked with Faye at length about Becka and the events leading to the suicide attempt. She seemed to listen only barely to the answers I gave to her questions, as though she were very distracted. I suppose she must have been in shock, but I felt extremely uncomfortable with her. It wasn't that I didn't like her.

There was something more to my discomfort that I couldn't identify. Faye was a thin, nervous woman, bearing little resemblance to Becka at all, even though Becka had reported looking like her mother's mother. She had dark dyed hair, almost metallic in color, cut short and permed in the current curly style, amber eyes, and a deeply lined face. Her summer suit was short-sleeved, rather stylish, and she carried a linen handkerchief which she continually twisted through her fingers. Faye kept referring to me as Dr. Carr, even though I tried to explain to her that I was not a doctor, but a psychotherapist, and she could call me Kathleen or Mrs. Carr. After reminding her several times, I gave up and answered to Dr. Carr. She needed to believe that I was a doctor. It gave me some insight into Becka's feeling that her mother lived in constant denial and was very concerned about her image and her reputation. Faye might be having a hard time dealing with Becka's suicide for how reflected on her, having lost one daughter already to suicide.

After explaining what I knew about what had happened, I tried to learn more about Becka from Faye's side, but it wasn't going to happen. She kept herself closed by asking me questions, instead of answering mine. She did bring up her first daughter's suicide, and said she had never been able to understand why it had happened. Her daughter had had a lovely family and husband. Faye was in a very fragile state, facing a second daughter's near-suicide, while worried at the same time about leaving her bed-ridden, helpless husband at home. She knew that wouldn't reflect well on her character, either. She stayed only two days, then had to go home to care for him.

Meeting Chris was much as I expected; Becka's description of her was thorough. She held an expression on her face that was perpetually somber, her jaw set tightly, the corners of her mouth turned slightly down. I imagined I could read some deep, buried anger in her face. She never smiled, although it was hardly a pleasant time to be meeting. I was most surprised at how slim Chris was, even though Becka had described her as small-framed. Her shape was indeed boyishly straight, with her brown hair cut close, adding to the boyish look. One could certainly say that she and Becka were opposites, at least physically.

Our initial discussion was brief. We stood in the hallway outside the locked psychiatric unit. Chris described to me the events of Becka's return from unconsciousness, how she was in and out of awareness over many hours, and how long it was before she was able to hold down any food. Chris had stayed at her bedside for two days and nights, explaining that she wasn't working at the time, and was fortunate to have the freedom to stay.

"How did you know she was in trouble?" I asked.

"She called me a couple of times that evening. The first call, I could tell she was drinking. The second time she called, she was growing increasingly depressed. She never said she was going to kill herself, but I had an uneasy feeling about the way she was talking. Then I went out for a couple of hours, and when I got back there was a message on my answering machine. She sounded drunk, didn't make any sense at all. The way she said goodbye I could tell something was wrong. Something was really wrong. When I tried to call her, I kept getting a busy signal. Finally, I just decided to drive over there and see for myself. It takes me about forty minutes to get to her place. When I got there, the EMT's were putting her in the ambulance. They had already pumped her."

"I'm curious, Chris," I said. "Becka has been telling me for months that you don't want to develop a relationship with her, yet you've been at her side through this. Why?"

Chris looked away from me and down the hospital corridor to hide the tears in her eyes. "I can't abandon her like this. I know what she's been through. I know I'm giving her a message that I care — and I do, obviously. I don't know whether she did this because of me, but I sure feel guilty. Maybe that's what she wants me to feel. But I have told her many times that I do not want involvement; I'm not going to commit to anything. We can be friends, but not lovers. I've told her that till I'm blue in the face." Her face was strained with fatigue and the stress of that guilt.

"So I assume you plan to stick by her through this."

"Yes, but after she's doing better, we have to make some things really clear. I may need your help with that."

"What things?" I asked.

"For example, we have to set some limits— some boundaries, and I need her promise to abide by those boundaries. I need my space. She knows that."

"It seems her perceived need is quite the opposite of yours.

She has been seeking fusion in a relationship, and that's not very healthy for either of you. But Becka does need to find a healthier relationship than what you can offer, and I will continue to advise her accordingly. Are you sure you don't want to just walk away from her problems altogether? You could."

"I can't do that. I'd rather try to ease out of the situation gently. I don't want to hurt her any more than I have already."

"Okay. I'll do what I can to help the two of you establish some agreements. If you define exactly what it is you expect and want, we'll negotiate that with Becka when she is ready to discuss a new contract."

"She's got to take responsibility for her depression, take medication and counselling. I know she has some heavy stuff to deal with from her past. That's part of what I insist upon. And I can't have suicide as a threat hanging over me. I've had more than my share of that and loss of friends."

"You're absolutely right. Becka has to do those things

whether you require it or not. Be sure to think about what you need, Chris, and make it explicit, so Becka will have no doubt about where you draw the line. Let's not have any ambiguity. Then I can continue to reinforce that with her in therapy. As she grows stronger, I will also continue to encourage her toward independence and a break from you. You need to know my position."

Becka's hospital stay was tumultuous. Something about her experience had brought out the venom she had buried from all the years of abuse and neglect. At one time, she became so violent that six men were required to subdue her. She was straight-jacketed and restrained on a bed in the quiet room. Such restraint was necessary because she had been banging her head against the wall. She screamed to be freed, begging to be allowed to hold onto her head. She said she was afraid her head was going to come off. The staff interpreted her behavior and words as delusional, and she was given a tranquilizer.

Surprisingly, being locked in the quiet room became a positive experience for her, rather than frightening. She found she felt safe in there, especially when she learned she could look out the window in her door and see the staff, ask to be let out, or have the door left open. Erratic memory loss was very disturbing to Becka, more so as she improved and realized what was happening. Gradually, she calmed down and became more lucid with each day, until she was allowed to go home after nearly three weeks. While she was in the hospital we had established a contract to resume therapy, and continue the tranquilizer prescribed by the hospital physician.

Due to her wild, psychotic behavior as she withdrew from the overdose, her doctor felt she needed an anti-psychotic medication as well as an antidepressant. I felt it was excessive therapy, but since I am not a physician, my opinion held little weight with him. In time it became clear the psychotropic no longer helped and needed to be changed.

Kathleen's Reflections

Becka's coma plunged me into painful memories of my own past. I couldn't spend any time with her while she was unconscious, because it was too much like when Mom was dying. This was my third round with a comatose person and it hadn't become any easier for the experience. My nephew had been hit by a car just two years before, and was comatose for ninety-two days. I took turns with other family, sitting beside him, reading to him, talking about things I thought were familiar to him. With Mom, I knew there was little chance of her coming out of it. I only wished for her to know of my presence, that I stood beside her, telling her how much I loved her. I wanted her to know I was ready to let her go. I wished her to have peace, to be free of the suffering she had borne so long. At that time, I still believed in heaven, so I prayed she would go there to be with God.

Maybe people think therapists and psychiatrists have perfect lives, that they have all their problems figured out so everything goes smoothly for them. But we're people, just like everyone else. We don't know any more about life and the way it is or why humans do what they do than anyone else, really. Maybe we just think about it more than most.

A close friend of mine, also a therapist, was going through difficult growing pains with a teenage son who had become a drug addict. Nobody would think the family was struggling, from outward appearances, but I knew what they were going through. Both parents were in high profile positions in the community; on the surface they appeared to be a model family. The son's addiction and related behaviors were causing a multitude of problems that included marital stress and temporary separation, alcohol abuse, and potential bankruptcy. Actually, therapists understand more when they have undergone experiences similar to what their clients have suffered, not because they read about it a textbook.

Chapter 19 – Becka's Story

Journal Entries: Monday, August 27, 1990 – 10:20
       It has been extremely difficult to write my treatment contract.
Spelling words is a challenge. They look strange on the paper, just geo-
metric shapes instead of letters. Or they should be pictures of things. I know
they are words, but they don't look right. My brain is gone.

My contract, to be signed by me, and witnessed by Kathleen:
- Find out what life can be on my own, and what I want from it.
- Learn how to be with Chris in a new way, fulfilling to both
- Learn freer ways of relating to Chris that benefit us both, singly and together.
- Spend time with other people, whether I want to or not: 2-3 days per week, 2-3 different people, 2-3 hours at a time.
- Expand creative outlets: painting, writing, quilting, piano, reading, exercise, music.
- Identify and learn to rely on my own inner strengths, develop them.
- Join a co-dependency group and attend regularly.
- Therapy with Kathleen, twice a week. Therapy with Chris and Kathleen??
- See a doctor for follow-up of medication.
- Have a set routine to fall back on— intervention if depression or suicidal thoughts return.
- Have a list of support people to call for help. Ask for help when I need it. Get help when I need it. Start early— don't wait.
- Learn to control my impulse spending.

Sunday, September 9, 1990 – 08:30
Kathleen has given me an affirmation:

"I am a good person. I am learning to love myself."

I keep thinking and saying it, and it's working. I don't feel so stupid. But it isn't
quite the right message. There is something missing, something more is needed. Maybe she can help me find it in trance.

Tuesday, September 11, 1990 – 22:4

I have trouble hearing the affirmation that I am a good person. We explored "the parts" today, and what they each want, the little girl and Feisty Becka. It is because of that Feisty Becka that I have trouble accepting myself. Kathleen made this list of what I said while in the trance state.

What the Little Girl Wants

*retain freedom to leave *not be empty

*not become ugly *not be sloppy

*not be a pushover *continue to speak my mind

*stay selfish *get the attention I need

*stay loved *stay clean and intact

*not become afraid *keep one part that is mine

*not be used *not get fatter

*not cry *not have trouble breathing

*not stink *not be depressed

What Feisty Becka Wants

*not be abandoned *not be self-centered

*not be held down *not be angry

*not be a pollyanna *not be selfish

*not be empty *not be vain *not be a priss

We got some other parts to talk, too. The eleven-year old is a lot like the Little Girl, but she is more outspoken, and so is the teenager. It's like how Feisty Becka as a four-year-old would be as a teenager, and she is even more feisty. She's more demanding and vain, more of a priss than ever, and very self-centered. She wants what she wants, when she wants it. One thing is common for all of them: they're afraid of being alone and empty.

Monday, September 24, 1990 – 20:15

I'm back at work, but I don't know if I'm working. The staff are all very patient with me. I have to take everything slowly; I'm not sure I trust myself yet. They have more confidence in me than I think they should. It is such a miracle that I still have a job!

I still have trouble making sense of some written words. They just seem meaningless to me, and my mind goes blank. I have to make long lists and follow them carefully, because I forget everything. Then I forget the list. This morning I left the house without the files that I took home to work on, after I so carefully set them next to the door so that I wouldn't forget them. Then I nearly missed an appointment with the Director of Staff, but luckily for me, Chris reminded me. Otherwise, I wouldn't have gone, and who knows what they would have made of that?

The love and support at work is overwhelming. Sometimes I have to go into my office and lock the door. They have no idea what I'm going through— the memory problems, the insecurity, the anxiety that nearly swallows me alive. I feel like I'm going to be engulfed by some unseen, gigantic monster, and swept totally out of myself. That would be a blessing. I wish I wasn't here, trying to make this work. Why did I fail? Why can't I leave this place?

Monday, October 29, 1990 – 12:00

Chris is so close, yet so far away. She won't let me through that hardened shell she wears. I need to be touched, to be held. I won't ask for more, if she'll just be with me a little while, every few days. The loneliness is almost more than I can bear. I don't want to live this way. It is even more painful since my suicide. Chris is with me, but she is like a vapor. Sometimes she won't talk. I can't read what is in her eyes— something secretive, as if she doesn't want me to know what she feels or thinks. I want to believe she loves me, just as I love her, but she cannot let herself go. She is too committed to Dana to let herself do that. But when she has a few drinks, she be- comes lively, a spirited puppy ready to play and pounce, and that is how I love her best. That is when I know she loves me. I will wait.

December 27, 1990 – 23:50

What to write? What to do? I have to get my life together. I am alive. I didn't die. Despite all, I'm still living — but am I alive? Everything is forced — or just waiting — but for what? The New Year is coming, and it must not be the same.

April 17, 1991 – 15:10

Gail killed herself! She finally did it, just like she said she would. She blew her brains out. Poor Chaylene and Clive. I called them, and they are in total despair and shock. Gail never let on to her parents that she was suicidal, and they were completely unprepared for it. I begged Gail not to use such a violent method, for their sake. The sight of her body blown apart would be too much to bear. Her parents were so good to her, and to me, too. They seemed to care so much about Gail, yet she kept them in the dark about her manic-depressive illness. Now their lives are shattered with grief and guilt about what they must have done wrong, and wondering what they could have done to prevent it. They didn't deserve this to happen the way it did.

I will send my condolences, but I cannot go to the memorial service. There is no way I could bear the emotion of being there, and besides, I'm broke and can't afford the airfare. Chaylene and Clive said they understood. They also said they were sad when they learned that Gail and I had split up. Gail requested cremation in her suicide note. She always said that is what she wanted.

I know it is not my fault. I almost don't know whether to feel glad or sad. I knew better than anyone how she felt about the torment she was living with. And she understood mine. I can't help but wonder what would have happened if I had let her stay. It's strange to envy her, but I do. Maybe we would both be dead by now. What is the reason she was allowed to escape, and I was not?

Chapter 20 - Therapist's Story

Nearly a year and half of counselling sessions went by in what felt like torture for both of us. Becka insisted on calling it suicide and not an attempt, hence she behaved as if dead throughout that time. She felt tortured by her failure to escape. For me, sitting through her sessions of long silences was the torture. She simply would not talk. I often dreaded the time I had to spend with her.

When I felt as if I was going to fall asleep, I had to hide and stifle yawns, drink water, or get up and move around the room. Nearly everything I tried with her went nowhere. She had no motivation, no desires, no energy. When I tried to suspend the appointments until she was ready, she insisted she was paying me just to avoid being alone.

Each week Becka came into my office and moved across the room like a giant tortoise. Once she became ensconced in the recliner, she appeared to be finished with all the work she was able to do for that day, and sat silently. I asked the same questions and got the same answers: *I guess so*, or *I don't know*. She had little insight to draw upon about her suicide, other than that she wished she had unplugged the telephone, and that she had never called me.

Surprisingly, she did not express her grudge against me for saving her life. She had made up her mind to die, and she did her best to act as if she had. Even when Gail committed suicide, Becka had little to say about it, no matter how much I tried to draw out her feelings. Because Becka was unwilling, or unable, to explore any of her child- hood in trance, we focused primarily on matters that pertained to her daily existence, such as whether and how she was meeting the terms of her contract. When I made interpretations for her, she agreed flatly and dropped the subject. I felt useless and ineffective. I confessed to her I felt I wasn't earning my fee, simply because we seemed to be motionless, or at best running in place on a treadmill. She only offered an apology for not being a more ideal client.

Becka was long past having the psychotic delusions that had been present during her initial overdose withdrawal. She was deeply depressed and could benefit from the correct type of medicine. I tried many times to get her to ask her doctor to review her medication. At first she resisted by saying she had learned her lesson about challenging physicians' orders. I raised the fact that she was now a patient, not a nurse, and had a right and personal obligation to question her doctor. Eventually, she agreed to let me speak to her doctor. I told him I thought she only needed an antidepressant; he maintained she should continue his prescription because she had been so delusional in the hospital. He felt it would be risky to take her off it, and even prescribed an additional medication for anxiety. When that failed to bring any change, I urged Becka to find another doctor; that too, was to no avail.

I also proposed other forms of therapy. One thing I really tried to get her to do was go to a group for survivors of incest. She said she couldn't bear to listen to other people talk about their problems because it would make her more depressed. She had gone to a co-dependents group a few times, but she hadn't allowed herself to become a part of it. The group members were all straight, and she believed she wouldn't be accepted if they knew she was lesbian. Then I tried to get her to go to a massage therapist, believing that touch would be therapeutic. It might also open her up again to her feelings, perhaps even to her past. But Becka declined this too, saying she could not afford an additional expense in her budget.

On occasion, she came to the session with an agenda, for which I was grateful. She wanted was to stop obsessing over Chris all the time. It was distracting, and it depressed her, because every time she thought about being with Chris, the reality of its impossibility came back to her. Becka would play a fantasy in her mind of the two of them doing things together, taking walks, playing cards, or going to a movie. She loved Chris' beautiful hands, and her eyes, when they were soft. At first, the fantasy images would make her feel really good. Then she would feel the anguished longing for the fantasies to become real. The longing came to outweigh the good feeling she had had initially, so she wanted to stop fantasizing. While under hypnosis, I taught her how to change the pictures, or movies she ran through her mind to make them images that ultimately repelled her from making them. I had her imagine Chris' face with grotesque expressions, her skin aged and cracking or in florescent colors, her hair growing out of her head like snakes, and other such disturbing imagery. The repulsion served to condition her not to run the fantasy images anymore.

On another occasion Becka made a request that resulted in a small breakthrough. She asked for help with insomnia and with keeping focused on her work. She wanted to like what she was doing enough to look forward to going to work. She also wanted to be accurate and thorough in her paperwork. Her evaluations by her supervisor indicated she was not performing as well as she should.

She was still suffering from chemical toxicity, a year after her overdose. Becka seemed especially tired that day, drained of energy, and somewhat anxious. Her sleepless nights were spent worrying about how to keep up with her work, as well as the facade that everything was going well in her life. I felt that even if I couldn't cure her insomnia, she would at least get some rest during the trance work. I did a time distortion to suggest she would have had a full night of restful sleep by the end of the induction. At best, I hoped my suggestions would carry over to better sleep in the long run.

First my words guided her with some pleasant imagery of being in the mountains near a stream, which I knew she loved. I played a tape of background sounds from nature —birds, and the stream. After she began to relax, I started the suggestions: "Select a tree . . . you want to sit under it . . . so you stretch out on a blanket beneath its boughs. Looking up through the branches . . . you notice the deep blue sky . . . occasional white clouds drifting slowly across its expansive face . . . and you feel comforted to know that nature goes on, doing what it does . . . effortlessly . . . even as you relax, more and more. Birds are singing . . . and the stream is slipping by . . . making soft bubbling sounds . . . and it makes you want to drift deeply . . . into a comforting state of sleep . . . a very deep sleep. And while you sleep . . . you can dream of better days . . . of better health . . . of peace in your soul . . . and of a life of laughter and joy and satisfaction. You deserve that, Becka.

"Resting so peacefully under this tree, you sleep for a long time . . . like Rip van Winkle. And all the while you sleep, you are healing. Your soul is healing from all the hurt and pain you have suffered ... from all the terrible acts of crime against you . . . from all the injustice you have had to bear. The parts of you that are so very

128

tired . . . will go on sleeping and being healed . . .. all while there is
another part of you that is very focused . . . that can get things done .
. . a resourceful part of you that will take care of everything with
great satisfaction and enjoyment. That part of you will awaken later
today . . . fully refreshed from just enough rest . . . . and that part of
you will happily go to work . . . and will be fully alert and attentive to
completing what is assigned each day. That part of you will take care
of you . . . and your job . . . and all of your responsibilities . . . easily,
and thoroughly. That part of you will be able to sleep naturally and
healthfully each night . . . while the other parts of you go on
sleeping . . . like Rip van Winkle . . . becoming healed. It is no longer
necessary for those wounded parts to participate. They need time to
sleep. . . and to heal. They have suffered so long. Now they must
rest. . . And nobody knows . . . just how little time they might
need . . . how long it will take . . . how quickly for the healing to be
complete. So relax deeper now . . . and sleep deeply in your Rip van
Winkle sleep. The organizer in you taking care of everything . . . and
enjoying doing it . . . going to work each day . . . fully capable . . . all
your faculties restored . . . efficient and competent."

Becka responded profoundly to this session. She reported
the next week that she was able to sleep well through the night. Her
work performance took a leap in improvement. And she felt a deep
sense of peace that stayed with her for many weeks. She asked me
a few times to repeat the Rip van Winkle trance suggestions.

After several weeks went by, I tested Becka to see if she
was ready to awaken from that special sleep, by giving her some
suggestions that she would soon be healed enough to awaken.
When I tried to bring her back out of trance, she would not return.
After a bit of coaxing, Becka informed me that her parts were not
ready to awaken from the Rip van Winkle sleep, and I needed to
give her permission to sleep longer. Once I did that, she came back
readily. The Rip van Winkle sleep was permission. It was permission
to forget, and to relax without responsibility, as well as to recover in
her own time. She was not yet ready to do the work of delving into
her past, and the suggestions gave her permission not to do so,
without having to feel guilty about it. She had been wounded many
times by life— emotionally, psychically, and spiritually, but she had
never allowed herself to show signs of those injuries, nor to take
time to heal from them. She had had no mother, and no nurturing
part of herself that could do that for her.

The months wore on, as the wounded parts of Becka slept and recovered, yet always seemed to be in a low-grade depression. During this time she was gradually letting go of her dream to have a relationship with Chris, becoming somewhat more realistic about their friendship. The movie-making exercises had reduced most of the obsessive thoughts, and Chris was apparently happier, according to a brief conversation she and I had had, that Becka was giving her the space she needed.

Kathleen's Reflections

Becka was emphatic that she had wanted to die from her suicide attempt, and yet she lived through it, having overcome an enormous amount of toxic medication. Her will must have taken over in her state of unconsciousness and fought to stay alive. I have seen people live with tremendous handicaps and physical pain, over and over again. It happens every day, all over the planet. Quadriplegics go on living and functioning. Brilliant or slow, educated or not, people everywhere survive against unreal odds. And there are some who don't survive, who appear to give up. Why?

My nephew is a survivor. He had run into the street at the age of six and was struck by a car. He suffered severe brain damage and was comatose for ninety-one days. When he regained consciousness, we learned that his functioning had been reduced to the level of a newborn. All memory appeared to have been wiped out, as well as areas of speech and motor functioning. His parents took him home and gave him the best care they could possibly provide. It has taken years, but the boy has been gradually relearning much that he had lost the ability to do; feeding, dressing, and toilet training were re-accomplished within about four years. Rudimentary speech began about that time. You could say the boy's will took over and assumed the task of healing. Yet, another factor that seemed somehow relevant was the set of attitudes and beliefs of his parents. My brother-in-law, in particular, had such strong faith that his son would recover, he maintained a spirit of optimism at all times. He has given the boy an enormous amount of love, patience, and training, such that he must have strengthened the boy's will. They both keep trying, and progress continues, however slowly.

A story I had heard recently on the news gave me additional fuel for my speculations on will to survive. It told of a lumberjack who had a tree fall on him and trap his leg beneath it. He was alone in the woods and far from anyone within earshot of his cries for help. With whatever force of will was driving him, he took out his pocket knife and cut off his lower leg as his only chance for survival. He dragged himself to his truck and managed to drive it, clutch and all, to get the help he needed. There are similar stories of coyotes caught in traps that chewed off their own foot to get free. I became fascinated by this survival mechanism. What is that force? Does everyone have it? Is it chosen? Is it acquired or taught? What does it have to do with quality of life, life worth living for? What gives life the quality worth living for, enough to cut off one's own leg, just to have that chance?

And from where does the force of will come that people like Gail and Becka can sever the thread of life? When does quality of life get bad enough to drive people out of life? Historically, human suffering has taken many forms in great extremes, with countless examples. Just one of these was the Holocaust, the torture, the in-credible pain, and the prolonged misery of thousands of Jews. Cer-tainly there was little quality to life in concentration camps. Each day must have been lived at the level of survival. Do the survivors even know what kept them alive? From where came their hope? How do they differ from the ones who could not bear the injustices and killed themselves? I couldn't claim to have valid answers, but my own suspicion is that hope and faith are rooted in learned religious be-liefs. And maybe in our genetic makeup.

Chapter 21 – Becka's Story

Journal Entries: Friday, January 3, 1992 – 20:30
> I haven't written in my journal for over a year, except the one entry when Gail killed herself. I've had nothing to write, it seems. I fell like I've truly been in that Rip Van Winkle sleep, only nothing has really changed. Everyone is the same, acts the same. Gail is gone—that's different. Chris is unchanged. Life is about the same, and I can't take it like it is. I still want it to be different— for ME to be different. I want Momma to be a momma. I want to tell her how much I need her. She won't understand— or care, maybe. She can't face the truth about Daddy. I can't tell her what really happened. It would tear her up. She would be so hurt. I hate to be alone in this house. I long for closeness, touching, and love. My body aches with the need.

I am going to a new doctor this week. Kathleen has prodded me to try a new medication. I figure it's the new year, and I have to try something. I can't go on like this. It's not worth it.

January 19, 1992 – 22:00
I don't want to get my hopes up too high, but the new medication seems to be having some effect. I'm going to get Dr. Feinberg to increase it— it's not quite enough to lift the depression, but I believe it will.

February 14, 1992 – 19:15
> For Valentine's Day, I decided to look at my photo albums and my baby book. This is what I found in the baby book, written by my mother when I was three.

> *Before this year ends i have started this 'Memorie Book' for Rebecca Ann for her to look at in later years and remember — of how from a baby her daddy and I were completely raped about her in our love — for her. To My Beloved Daughter Lovely, Mother*

Raped for *wrapped?* I know my mother's spelling and grammar aren't too good, but how could this be? What kind of twisted irony is this?

February 17, 1992 – 19:00

Another terrifying hurdle: I have to go back to the gynecologist for a second visit. He wants to do a cystoscopy— maybe a cyst or a polyp. I don't know where— maybe on my uterus or an ovary. I had to escape from my body when he examined me. I don't remember anything he did or said. The whole time I was in the examining room is gone from my memory except I wished badly for a window in there so I could get out. After I got dressed and went to the receptionist, she handed me the form for the tests and an appointment card. That was the first I knew that the doctor had any concern.

Maybe I should have gone to a female doctor. How am I go- ing to get through this? It's bad enough with excess fluid, dizzy spells, leg cramps, and insomnia. The incontinence is the worst of it. I stink all the time, and I'm so embarrassed. Help me, Kathleen — I know you can.

February 18, 1992 – 02:30

The dreams are sheer terror. I don't sleep because I'm afraid of the dreams. I'm afraid of him. He can still get to me — he comes in through my dreams. He was in the room. I know — I saw him. I hate him! I burn candles to keep away the evil forces.

February 20, 1992 – 22:30

I did what you told me to do — I left my body and told it to stay relaxed and do whatever the doctor said. I asked the doctor to go slowly, but I couldn't tell him — like you said I should — that I was scared because I'd been raped. I opened my mouth, but no words came out. I had already left.

Friday, February 21, 1992 – 20:45

I don't understand why I have so much trouble with getting the right medication to work. I've been a nurse for twenty-three years, and I've seen people benefit much more than not. But I have to be one of those who's sensitive to everything. Just my luck. Nardil has been helping, and I refuse to give it up and try another one, just because of some fluid retention and a few other little symptoms.

Feinberg isn't going to win this one. If I let her reduce the dosage, I just know I'll get depressed again, and I couldn't take it. I will die first. I'm setting my suicide date for the end of March if these problems aren't cleared up by then.

I WILL NOT SUFFER THROUGH ANY MORE DEPRESSION!

I've started my plan: I'll get my will written and all my affairs in order while I've got the energy to do it. Chris will be my executor. Rhonda will notarize the will and living will. I'll be completely thorough so as to cause the least amount of grief possible for anybody I leave. Momma won't have to do a thing— since she never has anyway.

Tuesday, February 25, 1992 – 16:30

The results are negative— no cancer. Just a cyst. But there was still bad news. He said there was scar tissue on my urethra, and asked me if I had ever been raped! And my uterus is scarred, too. You see? HE's still getting me. His nasty poison is in my body. His ugly signature is carved indelibly on my guts. No matter what I do he is always there — the hideous evil. How can I ever get rid of him? I hate him!

Friday, February 28, 1992 – 08:00

I've gotten control over the dreams. I do what you said to do each night, I plan for the dreams to resolve things in a productive way. I got rid of him completely from the dreams, after we did the banishing session. But now I have another problem: I don't sleep long enough sometimes to have dreams— maybe fifteen minutes to an hour. I have to have the lights and TV on, and I sleep sitting up.

When I wake up, I'm SLAMMED awake. I stay confused and disoriented for a long time. By the time I figure out where and who I am, I can't go back to sleep. I get slammed at least twice a night. Then I get waves of chills that start at my feet and go off the top of my head.

Tuesday, March 10, 1992 – 22:20

I cannot believe my rotten luck! A man tried to break into the house while I was in the back bedroom. I saw his face through the window next to the front door. He was a young dark-skinned man—not black, but maybe Hispanic—with a mustache and a little fuzz on his chin. Terrified, I shriveled up into a little ball on the floor, and dialed 911 on a portable phone. The dispatcher stayed on the line with me while I waited for someone to come. She told me to keep quiet and stay in the back room, but I heard the intruder breaking a window, so I looked around the corner and saw his arm groping through the broken glass, trying to reach the lock. I lost my control and ran to the door, still with the phone in my hand, and screamed at him to go away. I told him I'd called the police. He reeked with alcohol so much that

I could smell it through the broken window. I pounded and pounded on his arm with the telephone. He cut his hand on the glass as he pulled it back, then ran. I saw that he was carrying a knife.

I sat down and shook uncontrollably for hours. It took the police eighteen minutes to get there. The 911 operator admonished me for making my presence known, but who knows what would have happened if I had waited until he got inside? And just when I was starting to get the dreams under control, now I'm having nightmares about shadowy male figures in my room, beating me up.

Chapter 22 - Therapist's Story

An antidepressant became the impetus for getting Becka moving again, motivated to use her therapy sessions actively. She had concluded that the Rip van Winkle healing sleep had been effective; it had allowed her time to grieve the loss of an unsuccessful suicide attempt and regroup for the next action to take. She seemed able to tolerate both a change of doctor and medication. I arranged for her to go to a female psychiatrist, Dr. Feinberg. She was someone who I thought would be sympathetic regarding Becka's background of sexual abuse, would take time to listen to what she had to say, and would work with her to find the proper medication.

When Becka came to her session several weeks after she had started taking the antidepressant, Nardil, she seemed to be transformed once again, just as she had been when she first took Prozac. It was like meeting a new person. She was exuberant with energy and a positive outlook, had taken on all kinds of new activities. She had started a water aerobics class, added more patients to her case load, finished her unpacking and organizing, and gotten caught up on her correspondence. She had begun dropping weight quickly, due to the increased activity and a reduced appetite. I felt very cautious about all these changes, yet I tried to hide my concern, just as I had the first time that a drug had lifted her so high. I knew Becka was overjoyed to be out of the depression, but such dramatic responses are like a double-edged sword. I worried about her going too high, only to crash later.

One benefit of Becka's elevated mood was that she agreed to go to a massage therapist. I sent her to Ruth Donovan, a specialist who did what she called body psychotherapy. While she massages the body, particularly the places that are stiff and tight, the client is encouraged to talk about her inner experience. Touch, of all kinds in this therapeutic context, will often elicit emotions, even memories, that appear to be physically stored in muscles and other tissues. Becka agreed to try this, knowing I would consult with Ruth about her progress, and that we would all work as a team, along with Dr. Feinberg. With the addition of this therapy, Becka began talking about her mother, in terms of both her childhood memories and her present feelings of abandonment. I was relieved that Becka had at last reached a stage of being able to handle the difficult work of uncovering past traumas.

Becka came to her session dressed in a new, over-sized jersey top and black stretch pants. I hadn't seen her look so radiant before, maybe because of the bright pink color of her shirt. She had generally been dressing much better since she began taking Nardil, but on this day she looked vibrant.

"I've been talking to my mother a lot more lately," said Becka, "and she seems to be more like a mother for a change. Now, I'm not going to get too excited about this yet, because I know she runs like hot and cold water. But actually what I think is going on is that she needs a confidante, not that she is so concerned about me."

"So she confides in you. Have you confided anything in her?" I asked.

"Oh yes. I've been telling her about how great I feel to be out of depression, and about all the things I've started doing. But she just wants to talk about her life. Get this: she's seeing her original husband again, from back before she married my father. Said he called her up and asked about how she was doing. They hadn't talked in over forty years. He had remarried and raised a family, and his wife passed away two years ago. So Mom told him she had just lost her husband, and they figured they ought to get together again. He flew out to see her from wherever he lives, and Mom said it was just like they had never parted. They're still in love with each other and are talking about marriage. Can you believe her? That'll make nine times she's been married."

"So how do you feel about all that?" I asked.

"I think it's great for her if she can be happy. It sounds like Lee is a pretty nice man, claims he's never been abusive to his wife and was sad about Mom's story about why she left most of her marriages. I think Lee and her last husband at least treated her pretty well. Maybe she never should have left Lee in the first place. But I don't think she's really changed any. She can't live without a man in her life. It's just one more way for her to keep her distance from me and avoid being a mother."

"It sounds like she's changed enough to have quit finding abusive relationships. But you feel like you're being shoved aside for a man again. That must hurt."

"Of course it hurts. You're right, though. He does appear to be a decent man, and maybe I should give her a little credit; maybe she has changed some. Lee has told her and me that he wants to meet me, and he wants us to be a family. Linda, my sister who committed suicide, was his daughter. He doesn't want to have another suicide between them. He sounded very kind on the phone."

"What do you think will happen?"

"I figure they'll get married; like they're already talking about making a big trip to California to see some of his family, and they want to stop by this way to see me. So great. I'd like to meet him.

But my mother, I could say to her, 'I'm going to kill myself at the end of the month,' and she would say, 'I'm going to move to Oklahoma to live with Lee on his farm.' It'll be a bit of a change, but I'll get used to it."

"Is that what you said to your mother?" I asked, uncertain. "No. I said I was having some side effects from the medication, and that it is the price I have to pay for not being depressed. Then she answered by saying she's thinking of going to live with Lee. I felt totally unheard. My problems don't mean anything to her."

I was concerned now, because this was the first I knew that Becka was having difficulty with the medicine. "Tell me more about the medication later— I need to hear about it, but let's stay with the subject of your mother for now. How much have you and she talked about your father's abuse?"

"When I was in therapy with Myra, I told her my father raped me; but it was Myra's pushing me that made me do it. She said I had to confront both of my parents somehow if I was going to heal and get over the memories. Well, it did nothing but push us further apart. Mom didn't want to hear about it. She dismissed it as one little incident where maybe Dad felt my tits or something. She disapproved of me going to therapy and said I should be able to handle things without telling some stranger about my personal life. She wanted to know if the therapist had told me to press charges. Mom thought I should be able to forget about it and get on with my life."

"Your mother just can't handle hearing about it. Do you think she knew that he was using you?"

"I'm sure she knew. She had to be able to figure it out. At least the physical abuse. All I ever thought about was her coming back to save me from him, and I never saw her. I began to believe my father's accusations of her as a whore, and I thought, why would I want to be with her if she's a tramp? I felt pretty worthless myself that she didn't want me."

"It would be an important step toward your healing, Becka, for you to confront her again. Can we make that a treatment goal, that sometime in the future you'll tell her again, and in more detail about what happened?"

Becka's face showed skepticism. "Are you sure it's something I need to do?"

"Well, is it?"

Becka sighed deeply. "Yes. You're right, I do. And I will—when I'm ready."

"And now tell me, please, what's going on with the medication and what Dr. Feinberg has to say about it," I requested.

"At first the Nardil didn't do anything, so Dr. Feinberg increased it a bit, then more. That's when I started to feel so good, when she raised it to the maximum allowable dosage. But I've been having some problems with water retention and lightheadedness.

She wants to cut the dose back, but I'd rather wait and see if I'll adjust to it. I don't want to get depressed again."

"Keep me informed. It's so difficult to get in touch with Dr. Feinberg that it would help if you tell me what is happening with the medication."

Two weeks later Becka came to her session depressed again. She was not smiling any more, and she sat in her sulking position, head down, hands wedged under her thighs.

"What's going on?" I asked. "Where is all that bubble and bounce, all that spit and vinegar you've had the past month?"

"Gone. Just like that. I told Dr. Feinberg it would happen, but she didn't believe it would make this much difference. The side effects continued, and she insisted I had to drop back on the Nardil, and as soon as I did — WHAM! back into the pit again. I can't take this. I don't want to live like this, Kathleen. Do you understand? I won't live like this."

I felt deeply sympathetic. "There seems no end to the cycle of problems and the position of victim that you find yourself in constantly. Your hopes were so high for the Nardil to change everything.

Does the doctor think you will improve some on the lower dose?"

"She doesn't know. She just won't allow me to take the higher dose any longer, and I told her if something doesn't give this
week, I'm going to set my suicide date for the end of the month. I've
already been outlining a plan, as far as getting my things in order
and writing a will." Becka looked at me with a flat expression that
showed only fatigue. "In the midst of this, there is only one saving
grace . . . . " she said.

"Which is what?" I asked when she paused.

"I am going to move into Chris' house and share it with her."

"What?" I couldn't conceal my astonishment, nor my dismay.

"She asked me if I wanted to share the cost with her
her. . .as. . . as roommates, and with a clear understanding that I
give her space and not expect anything from her. For her it's purely
for financial reasons, she said. I don't care the reasons; I'm just glad
for the chance to be near her, under any terms."

"But the terms always come up short for you, Becka," I ob-
jected.

"That's just how it has to be right now. I can't stand being
alone. It just adds to my depression, and maybe this will make things
a little easier. I know I have to leave Chris alone and let her live her
own hermitic life, but at least I can be closer to her and feel more
calm not being alone."

"You pay a price for everything nice." "That's the truth."

"I know you've heard me say this before, Becka: you deserve better. We know you can't get it from Chris, and as long as you
are so involved with her, you won't find anybody else. Chris is just as
unreachable and distant as your mother. Wasn't this what your
Granma meant by saying you are always taking up the rear?"

"Yeah," said Becka. "With one gigantic butt."

I decided to level with her. "As you can probably tell by my
reaction, I'm not at all happy with your decision. It looks like a step
backwards, after all the work you've done to adapt to living alone,
becoming more independent."

"Well I'm not adapting very well. It's part of the reason I'm
depressed. You don't know how much I hate being alone, even if it is
better for me. At least this way I can be near Chris and feel her
strength. I still have to accept that she does not want a relationship
with me."

"But that's the point," I said. "Why do you have to put your-

self in the position of a puppy dog in a window, wishing for someone
to take you home so you can become their obedient pet?"

"I just have to do it for now. When — or if—I get stronger,
then I can address living alone."

Two more weeks passed, and Becka reported to me that Dr.
Feinberg had reduced the antidepressant dosage even further because her symptoms had not subsided sufficiently. She was still retaining fluids and experiencing a dizziness that interfered with her
work and general functioning. I was most surprised to discover that
Becka had been keeping the severe extent of her symptoms a secret
from me. She came to her session with an elaborate chart she had
made, with columns for each day, listing all of her symptoms. These
she rated daily on a scale of 0 to 10, a requirement by Dr. Feinberg.
The symptom list covered a page and a half and included anxiety,
insomnia, leg cramps, headaches, dry mouth, frightening dreams
when she did sleep, sweats, heart palpitations, ringing in her ears,
joint pain, muscle cramps, chills, tongue ulcers, tremors, hallucinations, and incontinence. All she had told me about previously was
fluid retention and dizziness.

"Why haven't you told me about all that has been going on
with this drug, Becka?" I demanded. "I asked you to keep me informed."

"I couldn't tell you because of the pressure Dr. Feinberg was
putting on me to take less of it. I was afraid that the two of you would
gang up on me and make me stop taking it completely, and I just
can't bear the slightest chance of going any deeper into depression
than I already am."

"But this list of symptoms may *be* the reason you are depressed. I imagine anyone would feel that way if they were going
through all of this. This is a terrible state for you to tolerate. What is
Dr. Feinberg doing about it now?"

"I have to keep this chart and rate all the symptoms and call
in a report to her daily. Oh, and there's one other thing she mentioned. . .she said I should go to a group for survivors of incest."

"So where have you heard that before, right?" I said.

Becka blushed and smiled. "You're always right about this
stuff, Kathleen. But I am doing better. See? Look at the daily im-
provements on the chart. I dropped twenty pounds overnight when
she first prescribed Lasix. I was on the pot more than I wasn't. I also
have to take something for the anxiety, a sleeping pill, and an antibi-

otic for the bronchitis. It's a whole pile of pills."

"Does this mean you're willing to go to a group now?" I asked.

"I've told Dr. Feinberg I would, and I try very hard to keep my word to people. I'll go, but I'm going very reluctantly."

"Great. I'm just certain you will benefit from it. You really need to be with other people who know what it's like to suffer through sexual abuse, partly because you will feel less alone and better understood. It's so good to have you out of that zombie stage of deep depression. I know you're still not feeling well physically, but you seem to be able to handle the therapy on the emotional level, after a long, dry spell of going nowhere. Let's plan to keep you moving along with this as much as you can take it."

Becka asked, "Do you think I'll ever get to where I don't remember the horror and him? If I bring up more memories, will I ever be free of them, like when I had completely repressed them?"

"Yes and no. It's not that you'll forget again, just not be as affected by them. Your self-esteem will be strong enough to live with the memories. As time goes by, you will think of the past less and less. I know it's difficult to go through the memories again, but believe me, Becka, it will be worth it. I am so pleased with how you're doing now, that I know we can restore you to greater wholeness than you've ever felt. You have a lot more support now, too. You have Ruth, Dr. Feinberg, and me, and soon you'll have others, and you'll discover that you get strength from each one to rebuild your self-worth. And . . . you're worth it. Remember that."

Becka hunched up her shoulders and tucked her hands under her thighs. She had the worried expression that I recognized as hunkering down for a challenge. "According to your plan for me, Kathleen, what else do I have to do— besides get to the emotions and memories I've buried? Then what?" She seemed to know what I was going to say.

"Then comes a period of emotional integration. Usually that includes some powerful insights, which are followed by a form of forgiveness, *or*, a peaceful acceptance of the past, which can be released. Part of what would facilitate that is to confront both your mother and your father. I suspect it would help somewhat to have words with your brother, too. But mainly your parents. It would be something like the unfinished business work you did a couple of years ago. Do you remember that?"

"I remember it well. It helped a lot at the time. But I am not going to get in touch with my father. I told you I never want to see him again . . . ever."

"You don't have to see him to confront him," I said.

"Well I won't talk to him on the phone either." Becka was adamant.

"That isn't necessary either, although it might speed up the healing process. We can approach it some other ways when the time is right. For now, don't spend any energy worrying about it. That bridge is still a ways down the path."

I was dismayed that Becka had let her health deteriorate without my knowledge of it, and further realized how truly desperate she had be to have tolerated the symptoms for so long. She was taking so much medicine, just to be able to continue the antidepressant, and the poor success had caused her to be even more discouraged about recovery. Her suicide date was set for March 31, pending the effectiveness of getting medications and symptoms stabilized. She told me she had written and notarized her will, and was still working out arrangements for her pets. She said she was putting her life in order so that everything would be taken care of in time for her death. Each week when she came to her therapy session, she told me what percentage of her death-preparation plans was complete; she had informed Dr. Feinberg as well. She planned to rent a garage in which she would asphyxiate herself with exhaust from her car.

Getting the side effect symptoms under control was first priority, but I knew that I had to do something else to turn around her death wish. I decided to call Becka's mother and ask her to come to Denver. Faye admitted that she knew Becka was suicidal again, and sounded quite upset about it. I wanted her to join Becka and me for some family counselling, and told her I thought there were some positive benefits they could both derive from such a meeting. Faye asked if I thought her visit would stop Becka from making another suicide attempt. When I said definitely it could help save her, she agreed to come. In spite of the concern Faye exhibited for Becka, she seemed ambivalent about coming, and see-sawed back and forth over her decision. The ambivalence seemed to have to do with not wanting to leave her new lover.

Kathleen's Reflections

Becka's troubles never seemed to cease. I began to wonder if she could have made up the story of the intruder, as if even a day's lull in her life without some sort of problem was too much to bear. Or like my mother, may have staged her robbery. That seemed unfair to her, even as a passing thought, because I knew how true it was. The irony was amazing: that a strange man should find, or choose, to harass Becka, a woman who was in therapy at that very time in her life trying to cope with a serious lack of trust in men. It was as if she were a magnet for abusive men, as if she wore a sign that read, "Hurt me."

I also had a long-running pattern in my life of people with problems of the mind, beginning in my early childhood: my mother with a brain tumor, my nephew with brain injuries, and numerous psychotic and suicidal clients. In retrospect, I could see how I had al-lowed her to become too significant among my several clients. I had paid so much attention to the patterns of similarity between us that I had come to over-identify with her. My need to help could be getting in the way of true help. There had also been the fire in my office, tied in to severe mental illness, as well. When I had moved into my new of-fice a couple months before the fire, the rest of the building had been vacant. Within two months the day clinic for psychotic adults moved in below my office. That was precisely the kind of work I had done for years, before I started my private practice.

I no longer wanted to work with chronically and severely dis-turbed adults. I chose to do hypnosis so I could work with relatively normal people, in non-crisis situations, most of the time. My clients were mostly people who wanted to quit smoking, stop biting their fingernails, or get over a fear such as public speaking or flying. My caseload had a frequent turnover rate, which allowed me to concen-trate on a handful of long-term clients. When the day program for psychotics moved in I felt as if my past was stalking me.

And it didn't end there. Luck would have it that after I got a new office, the day program people also found their new location across the street from mine. Life is so strange.

Chapter 23 – Becka's Story

Journal Entries: March 13, 1992 – 19:00

I haven't cried so much in years. I mean HARD, deep, full-body
sobs. Ruth's hands can do that— bring me to the places where the sadness
is buried. She's such a little thing, and yet she can get those bitty fingers
and knuckles into places where it hurts, and the next thing I know I'm sobbing. Ruth says that's good, because the sadness is buried in the tissues.
When she works at the tightness and the emotions surface, I need to let
them go. She says there'll be anger that she'll dig up, too. All the years of
pain and sorrow and longing have been neatly stored under fat and muscle.
Sometimes I have a *déjà vu* experience when she touches certain spots, and
sometimes pure emotion comes spilling out without my knowing why, or
where it came from.

I always knew I needed to cry, but I couldn't. Daddy wouldn't let
me cry; Momma looked so upset when I cried that I kept my crying inside.
And now I need to let it out. After it's all over I feel so much at peace— and
lighter. Afterwards the world has more colors. At first I cried for Chris. I
wanted her to hold me, to stroke my head and rock me. I wanted it in every
fiber of my being, and I couldn't have it. Then I realized that's the way I
want my mother— the way I've always wanted her— so I was crying for
Momma. She was never there when he took what he wanted. She didn't
protect me. She was never able to fill the vast pit of need and longing— the
pit that has only grown more immense as time goes by. Maybe I AM the pit.
Perhaps that's all there is to me— just an enormous, fat void. Maybe there's
no end to the grief. What if it keeps coming and never stops? What if I keep
crying and never stop?

Friday, March 20, 1992 – 21:30

The things I hear in that group, Incest Survivors, make me wonder
about survival. Is any of this worth surviving for? And to have to listen to
more of it when my own memories are almost unbearable! I don't want to
listen to some of them in the group. What good can it possibly do to hear

about S_, whose stepfather took liberties with her when her mother was working, or out. Little Miss Prima Donna who sits in group with her make-up and "fixes" herself in her pocket mirror, smearing on more lipstick when she's worried that she's licked it off. He bought her with money, and clothes, and cars. That makes her a whore. She accepted the goodies and gave him what he wanted. Miss S_ has no problems remembering what happened to her. She's feeling a lot of guilt about it because she says that sometimes she liked it. Sounds like he was real nice to her. I don't know if that's the same kind of incest some of us have experienced, but S_ claims to be pretty upset about it now. Sometimes she tries to act like it wasn't that big a deal, but you know she feels guilty. Denial? There's just no way anybody who went through what I did could worry about having liked it. You'd have to be pret-ty sick yourself.

Then there's L_, who doesn't even know for sure if she's been had. She just thinks she has, she is so hung up over sex. She's married, and every time her husband approaches her for sex she starts getting panicky. He can't get her calmed down enough for her to enjoy it, so he goes ahead and takes it anyway. While he's doing it, she leaves her body, and she doesn't know why she does. I didn't know other people left their body like I did. I guess it's common with rape. L_ thinks she must be repressing memories, and she's terrified to let them come to the surface. That's what her therapist is telling her she has to let happen.

F_ is another story, and hers is somewhat more like mine, only she is straight and about five years older than me. It was her father, and she started having dreams about it. She wasn't sure if the dreams had a basis in fact, but then she was telling her older sister, and found out their father got both of them. They talked, and more started coming back to memory for F_. She now remembers he was abusive to their mother, too. He belittled her and slapped her around a lot. Sometimes he was mean to the kids. But when he was doing her sister, he let the sister get away with all kinds of privi-leges. He was mean to F_during that time, but when the older sister left home, he got real nice to her, and that's when he started taking his favors from her.

J_ was used by her uncle over a period of seven years when he lived with her family. He started with her when she was seven years old. There was a playroom in the basement of their house, and he would come down to play with her. It involved his touching her genitals, and then after a time he told her that she was very grownup for her age and she could play grownup games with him. He always told her she was beautiful and sweet, and that he loved her. In time he got her to touch his genitals and let him put his penis in her mouth. The games got more involved and more intimate. She said as she got older, she grew very uncomfortable and didn't want to play any more; but he threatened her. He said if she didn't keep playing he would tell her mother what she had been doing. She knew she shouldn't be doing it, and it would make a lot of trouble if her mother found out. As the years passed, he went all the way with her, and was always very pushy to get her to go to the basement with him. Then he told her that they could both go to jail if anyone found out. J_says now she has a hard time having a sexual relationship, and has tried with both men and women. She became very promiscuous in high school, and was raped by her girlfriend's brother when she was sixteen. She was also raped by a stranger about six months ago, and that's when she went to a therapist for help.

Two others haven't told much yet, nor have I. It's not easy to listen to it. I get so angry sometimes, and other times I can feel myself trying to escape out the window. I want to be there for them, be supportive, but sometimes I just can't. I watch the clock and wait for break time to get outside and have a cigarette. My turn to talk is coming up soon.

One thing that is coming out already for all of us in the group: that is that the incest eroded our self worth. Every one of us is having trouble with self-image, feeling like we're whores, like we're to blame for what happened. Even the ones who haven't got all the memories have felt worthless or bad during their entire lives, not realizing why. Each story is different, but none of us can like ourselves. We know we have to do something to change that, but it's not easy to do after so much time has gone by.

Monday, March 30, 1992 – 23:00

Feinberg is threatening to put me in the hospital. She's reduced the Nardil again. She also threatened me with electro-shock therapy. I can't live like this anymore. I re-negotiated with Feinberg and Kathleen to hold off for two more weeks on the suicide date. If the symptoms haven't been relieved by then, I am going through with it.

Thursday, April 16, 1992 – 18:00

Many of the symptoms are gone. Some are reduced enough that I can live with them. I still have a little flush and dry mouth, and my energy is low. The sleep problems are resolved, the depression is under control, and the tongue ulcers gone— as are the chills and palpitations. I still have trouble with dizziness, a little with hallucinations, excessive appetite, and incontinence. I'm also retaining water. My legs look like piers— not just logs, but piers. Feel like 'em, too, if I were to guess what it feels like to be a pier.

Chapter 24 - Therapist's Story

The bodywork massage Ruth did with Becka was like cracking ice cubes out of a tray. She broke up old patterns, chipped away at memories, and softened Becka's attitude about having to work through the past. Becka had formed a trusting relationship with Ruth, and the material that came out on the massage table was powerful. Ruth described how she had pushed into various tight muscles, and Becka's body had become even tighter. On occasions she would growl a deep guttural sound, and then she would breathe heavily, as if she were animal. When Ruth massaged her scalp, Becka curled into a fetal position and held onto her head, just as she had done in the seclusion room after her suicide attempt. Ruth reported that Becka was terrified something would happen to her head if she let go of it. And when Ruth tried gently to remove Becka's hands, she held on with an iron grip. Gradually, Ruth was able to gain enough trust to get Becka to ease up one finger at a time, until she could place her own hands where Becka's had been. She assured Becka that she was there to help protect her head, and she wouldn't let anything happen to it. It seemed as if there had been some head trauma about which Becka had no memory. But that memory would soon emerge. I began to apply more pressure on Becka during her therapy sessions to uncover the anger that had evidenced itself during the bodywork with Ruth.

"Taking a look at your treatment contract, I would say it's time to do some hypnosis to resolve buried trauma. You're doing so well with Ruth and your new group. Do you feel you can handle some forward movement with repressed anger?"

"I am scared to death of it, Kathleen." "I understand."

"What does it entail? What do I have to do?"

"My plan is to take you into trance and tap into all the resourcefulness within you, drawing upon your greatest strengths. And you have many, I must add. We'll start with the part of you that is most mature and adult, the part that is most capable of looking back into the past. This, in effect, would be a part of you that never actually experienced the trauma— the way we speak of parts. It would be the adult self giving support to the little girl, Feisty Becka, and to the eleven-year-old, depending on which part or parts show up in trance. We'll be looking for the situations that were most traumatic for the younger parts, trauma that cut off their healthy development. Our goal is to reintegrate the split parts of you, drawing them together into a complete, whole, and sound person — YOU. They will stay split as long as they have to handle the memories alone without a full awareness by the adult, resourceful you."

"You sound like you know what you're doing. You know I trust you, Kathleen. That's why I keep coming here, but I am scared. I know I have to keep moving, and I'm not ready to talk in group yet. This is where I want to do the hardest parts— in therapy with you.

So . . . with sweaty palms and shaking knees, I'm ready. Let's do it."

I took some time to develop the trance state and to ease Becka's anxiety by reviewing some imaginary places she had visited during trance, places that provided her the greatest sense of safety and most reduced her stress. I reminded her of the beautiful Southwest mesa, where she had resolved so much unfinished business in previous therapy sessions, and of the support she had had from her Granpa and Granma from "the other side." I reminded her of the deep, peaceful sleep she had had under the tree, where for months she found relief and security in knowing she could take all the time she needed to heal and grow stronger. I suggested she review other places in her memory where she had actually been during her life, places that gave her feelings of comfort and safety. When she was deeply relaxed, I had her reflect on the power of her inner strengths and resources: her skill in handling difficult and life-promoting situations as a nurse; her extremely valuable common sense; her abilities to organize, to evaluate and work things through, to accomplish a great deal, and to be fair and communicate clearly; and not least of all, her compassion, caring, and understanding. These were the traits she had named years before, when I had first begun therapy with her. I was building her sense of self before taking her back in time to painful memories.

"Now intensify and multiply the feeling of all these resources into what is the adult Becka; feel deeply every positive feeling you can imagine having. It is that adult Becka who is traveling with me now, and together we are going back in time, hand in hand, safely. We will watch what happens on a big screen, like a movie screen.

We can cope with what we see because we are strong adults. We go back in time to something that happened to a much younger Becka . . . something that was very upsetting to her. We are watching it happen on the big screen in front of us, Becka. . . What do we see?"

Becka squeezed my hand yet remained trancelike and motionless.

"It's Becka, the eleven-year-old." "Where are we?" I asked. "We're in Becka's room."

"Is anybody else is in Becka's room?" "Her daddy."

"What is happening between Becka and her daddy?" Becka was silent for a few moments. "He is talking to her.

She is afraid."

"Why is she afraid, Becka?"

"He's drunk. He is mean when he's drunk. He's trying to hold her close to him. Becka the eleven-year-old doesn't want him to. She pushes him away. He loses his balance and falls onto her bed."

"And now what is happening?" I asked.

"He gets up part way and grabs her arm and pulls her on top of him. His hands are strong. They hurt her arms."

Becka's face and body continued calm, even though her grip on my hand was intense. She used the present tense, yet she was observing the action from the third person. I wanted her to remain distanced from the experience the first time through. Becka's history of disassociation and "escaping out the window" was evidence of a valuable defense mechanism protecting her from trauma.

Becka went on. "He gets up, dragging Becka with him, and pushes her off the bed. He holds her on the floor by her throat. She can't breathe. He is squeezing . . . squeezing. Her face is red. Her mouth is open. He tells her to be quiet. She can't make a sound anyway. He says, 'Don't you want to make Daddy happy?'"

Becka suddenly held her breath and clenched my hand even harder. Her face froze in a pained wince.

"What is it, Becka? What is happening now?"

"He's . . . pounding . . . her head . . . on the floor.

Pounding . . . pounding. . . holding her by her throat. He is going to kill her. I'm scared!"

"Okay, Becka. You've done very well. That's enough. I am with you, right here. Become aware of my hand and feel the safety of it. You are safe, and somehow, because you are strong, you survived what happened. You are fine now. We come back to the present time when you are a brave and powerful woman; you have learned and survived so many things. . . .Your unconscious mind will make note of the useful learnings from this experience and add them to your repertoire of positive strengths, so that this unfortunate event can have some value to you now, as an adult.

"I want you to imagine now that you and I, the adults, are with Becka the eleven-year-old in this present time. We bring her out of the past to the present so that you can hold her and comfort her. In your imagination, hear yourself tell her that she is safe now; she has survived what happened to her. You as the adult will help her to grow up and become a healthy part of you, not left alone in that past experience, or any others. Reassure her, Becka, that she is not to blame for what happened. It is not her fault. Tell her that it was her daddy who did something wrong. He did a lot of bad things, and we might not know why. But it was not because of anything she did. The adult part of you knows that what I am saying is true. You must convince the younger Becka now. Tell her you will help her and the other parts of you— will all come together as one complete, whole person. Ask her to join you now."

Becka's squeeze on my hand had gradually eased off while I talked. Her face and body relaxed, too.

She said, "Becka the eleven-year-old came to me right away. She is so happy— so relieved. She feels a little bit of safety for the first time. But she worries about the younger ones, and the teenager. They need to be safe, too. We have to help them."

"That's right, we are going to help them, too," I said. "All the lost and lonely parts will come together."

"Can we go get them now?" Becka implored.

"Do you feel ready to go on? Can you do some more work today?"

Becka's hand tightened on mine. Her eyes were still closed; she was still in trance. She whispered, "Yes, I think I can."

"All right. We are going back in time again. . . . This time it is the eleven-year-old, the adult Becka, and I. Three of us are going back together, safely -- back to another event when Becka was terribly frightened or hurt. . . . And what do we find now, Becka?"

Becka stiffened. Still holding my hand in her sweating one, she began to tremble, and then she pulled in her arms and legs, drawing my hand with hers, as if she were trying to get into a fetal position. Her breathing became short and quick.

"What is it, Becka? Where are we?" I asked.

"He is in my room. I'm scared."

"Why? What is happening?" Even with my guidance to keep her in the third person, observing the event, Becka had slipped into the first person and was experiencing the memory live.

"OOooh, no-o-o-o! It's happening again. He's raping me. NO! Stop!"

"Does he stop, Becka?"

"No. I want to leave. . . . I have to go out the window." Becka suddenly opened her eyes and turned her head so she could see out the window in my office, just above her chair. Intuitively, I grabbed a small pillow from the floor next to my chair and held it just above her face so that it blocked her view. I sensed she was trying to leave the trance state and not continue, but I felt she could handle staying in it. Becka tried weakly to push my arm holding the pillow but had little strength. She whined and turned on her side in the chair, trying to cover her head with her arms. She trembled and whimpered, barely audible as she answered my questions.

"How old are you, Becka?"

"Teenager."

"What is happening? Why are you so frightened?"

"Daddy is watching. His friend is raping me. Daddy laughs. He says, '*Have a good time with her . . . she's a good time from behind. Get her from behind.*' Oh, please, I have to get out the window. . . I can't . . . "

I stood up next to the chair and leaned over Becka with the pillow. I wanted to mobilize her anger and not let her submit — as she always had.

"You have to fight back, Becka. Fight! The eleven-year-old and the adult Becka and I are all here to help you. We can fight him. He's doing a bad thing, Becka. Push him off!"

At that I pushed the little pillow down on her arms. She didn't respond, so I held it against the side of her head, hoping to incite her rage. Then she pushed back. I made her work against the pillow, coaching her to get angry and push him off. She became stronger, but with my adrenalin pumping, I did, too.

152

"He won't back off until you yell at him, Becka," I said. "You have to yell at him to get him off."

We pushed and struggled with the pillow between us for a few, eternal and agonizing minutes until she finally let loose:

"Get the FUCK OFF!"

I backed off and dropped the pillow behind the chair. Becka sobbed deeply, and I let her cry for a while. The catharsis could come only through reaching the height of the emotions involved.

Rage comes out of a deep well of hurt, shame, and the most poignant sadness there is. All of that was buried in her somewhere, and it needed to be released. In time, her crying tapered off. I held her hand and stroked her head and cheeks. Then I began to drone suggestions to calm her and give her time to integrate the experience.

"So now you can relax . . . you have earned the rest. You worked hard to release the poison from inside, and now it is out. And as you breathe deeply, you draw in healing oxygen with all the magical power it contains to sustain and promote life. With every breath you take, you relax even more . . . and more . . . finding the power you have inside to bring yourself back to a place of safety where you can gather the eleven-year-old and the teenage Becka with you, adult Becka . . . now.

"Take some time, as before, to talk to the teenage Becka. Let her know you understand how terrifying it has been for her to be lost, and separate, as if she was all alone. But she no longer needs to be alone. You are using your adult strength and knowledge to help her cope with the past. It is all over now. She has survived so many things . . . just like the younger parts. Now she is safe to grow up and keep on learning . . . becoming more at peace, more whole. Comfort her as the mother she never had."

At that, Becka began to sob again, releasing more of the deep sadness that she had kept buried most of her life beneath layers of fat and a strong demeanor of nurse-in-charge. When she had recovered, she opened her eyes, still wiping the tears and blowing her nose.

"My parts are so relieved to be reconnected," Becka said quietly. "I never realized the teenager was there until now. It's strange — to feel as though they actually have reconnected. Does this really work, Kathleen?"

"You will be the best judge of that, in time. It takes time. We can't expect you to become fully reintegrated in one day, but it's working. You had done a lot of work before this to prepare for what happened today."

"But what about the others? They're still alone . . . will we be able to get them soon?"

"As soon as you're ready, but not today. There is still more rage inside you, and it will continue to come out. What we want to do is control the way and the rate it comes out, so you don't have to worry about getting out of control. We control going out of control."

"I do worry about that. Especially when I'm with Ruth doing the bodywork. I feel the rage, but I'm scared I'll explode and hurt her. She's such a bitty thing, I'm afraid I'll mash her without wanting to."

"And Ruth is uncertain about it as well. She and I talked about it, and what we would like to propose is that we have a session of psychodrama, sometime soon. It would be the three of us. We would plan it carefully so that you would have an opportunity to release all the rage in a therapeutic way."

"What do you mean?" Becka asked.

"It would be similar to what happened today, when I was coaching you to let the anger out. We will set up a situation for you to confront your father symbolically, using props. I have some soft bats, called batacas, that can be used to pound on cushions or the furniture. Ruth and I will help you get into a state in which you can beat out the anger safely. I will do hypnosis with you in a session before the psychodrama to establish other safety controls."

"Such as what?"

"For example, you can have a code word and a physical gesture — by touch — installed, so to speak, in your subconscious. These would be signals that any one of us can use to call time out, as a way to pull back if it gets too scary. It usually isn't necessary, but you'll feel better knowing you have a way to stop if you want to . . so will Ruth and I."

Becka had been listening carefully to everything I said. I sensed that she was receptive to the proposal.

"It sounds pretty scary, but I'm more ready now than I was when Myra tried to get me to beat on pillows. Can I bring some props, too?"

"Of course. If you'd like, I'll provide a dummy to simulate a man. You also need to think about what you want to accomplish in this drama, and we'll talk about it before the actual session. I should think we'd be ready to do it in about three weeks."

Becka left that day in high spirits. She had pulled herself together quickly, considering how much she had emoted, and later she reported having slept deeply the next few nights, without recalling any dreams or other disturbances.

Kathleen's Reflections

The brain/mind is the greatest frontier yet to be explored, beyond space. I am certain we have little idea just what can be achieved, or will be, someday. The future awaits those discoveries. Becka's story is full of examples of the interconnection of the mind, body, and emotions. During the abuse and abandonment she suffered as a child, she was prone to severe illness, a form of self-punishment for being bad, as she believed she must be. She had to learn to dissociate from the pain and helplessness of her situation. She learned to deny that her primary sources of basic support would leave her (her mother), or would be the source of her suffering (her father), and thus blamed herself. This was important to her survival at the time. In order to protect herself from the pain of finding herself the bad one, her mind also depersonalized: it created a separate self that was the bad one, allowing her to believe in some inherent goodness in herself as well. She made the painful events happen to the bad self, while the good self escaped, denied, and watched. Later, her mind suppressed all the memories in order to let her live in peace, without continued suffering.

Once the memories resurfaced, she suffered from depression and anxiety that interfered with her beliefs and decisions, and thus, her health and relationships. Each time she felt the threat of abandonment by someone close to her, she became physically ill. Her emotions depressed her immune system to the extent that she got pneumonia, bronchitis, and kidney infections.

I recalled feigning illness, as do so many children, in order to avoid going to school. As the day wore on and I lay in bed thinking about my upset stomach and my headache in order to build my case, I actually began to experience those symptoms. I didn't have any of the fun I thought I would by being truant, just added misery to the guilt I felt about the lies I had told. We have little control over many of the events that occur in our lives, but we do have control over the conclusions we draw and the thoughts which we hold onto about those events. The differences among people in whatever conclusions are drawn come out of intrinsic nature and experience.

Take a thought such as, "Everything I do goes wrong," and dwell on it for a while. Repeat it to yourself during and after each thing you do. You soon find yourself believing it, and further, the phrase begins to affect your performance negatively. Then take a thought such as, "I can accomplish anything I attempt with great success." Dwell on it, repeat it over and over, and imagine yourself fulfilling this statement. The mind is full of such beliefs, many of them decided when we are just little children. Children are fed beliefs by the people around them, mainly family and teachers. These statements are accepted as truth because of their source, and those beliefs may become deeply embedded and difficult to change. For the most part, hopefully, the beliefs are positive and enhance the healthy development of the child. But a child who is told she is not living up to her potential may accept that notion and then live her life proving it to be true. Or a child who is labeled worthless may never have sufficient self-esteem and feel worthless for a lifetime.

Children develop beliefs on their own. Many of these beliefs are faulty, simply because the child has not had time to experience enough of life to have all the data collected about how things work and don't work in the world. Becka believed her father's threats, that he would harm her brother or her, if she revealed to anyone what he was doing. She already had the belief she was to blame for what happened, then would have another reason to feel guilty if her brother were also abused, or killed. And still at the same time, she believed her father loved her, fully in the face of all the cruelty he inflicted upon her. He was all she had to rely on.

Becka had a host of negative beliefs about herself and her potential which needed to be changed. The psychodramatic "exorcism" could help her begin to change her beliefs about her early relationship with her father, give her a sense of control and restore the self-esteem she lost during that time.

I had dealt with my unfinished business about abandonment in therapy while I was in graduate school, attempting to change my belief about what I deserved. It was difficult at first to feel anger toward my mother for getting sick and dying, because logically, it seemed out of her control. To disgorge the anger and sadness is far from rational. In a psychodrama training group, I spilled my guts of the rage I had buried, including anger about my father leaving me. I *realized that I had been sustaining a pattern of abandonment in my life, whether I did the leaving or someone else did. The issue of loss had been repeating and reinforcing my unconscious belief that I didn't deserve a stable love life. It took many years and more poor choices before I had the "Aha!" experience which led to the actual changes I made to improve the quality of my life.*

Chapter 25 – Becka's Story

Ruth usually starts out by giving me an overall massage to get me to relax. I'm always so tight, especially in my lower back,that it doesn't take her long to find spots that needed help to loosen up. This time she dug hard into the muscles, burying her knuckles in my flesh. The pain hurt and felt good at the same time. Suddenly everything went black; I couldn't see anything. I started to tremble, and then the trembling turned to hard shaking. I turned on my side and curled up into a ball. I am in the closet. I don't dare make a sound. I don't want him to find me. He'll make me do sex things with him, and I hate it. He is coming into my room, yelling my name. I hold my breath. He is beating me with his belt. I escape out the window. From outside, I can see him beating Becka. She is lying on the floor near her bed, but she doesn't cry or make a sound. He hits her thighs and buttocks three or four times with the belt. Then he drops it and opens his pants.

"Why did you do that Becka?" he sneers at her. "Why did you hide? You know I don't like to have to hurt you, but when you're so devious, you know I have to punish you. You know the rules, and you have to play by the rules, now don't you? You know we play games when I come home from work, don't we?" He turns Becka over on her back, pulls off her jeans and panties, and then stands over her, naked from the waist down. He is masturbating.

"You won't get hurt or punished if you just play the way we always do. You know Daddy just likes to play, isn't that right, sweet Rebecca Ann? You're Daddy's girl, and Daddy makes the rules of the games. We play our own secret games, don't we? Just me and you." He gets on her and takes what he wants. He makes a lot of noises, grunting and groaning, and then he is finished.

"Now you get in the bathroom and clean yourself up. I can't have you stinking all the time. And come right back in here."

I do what he says. I come back, and he grabs my arm and pushes me into the closet. He throws my jeans and panties at me, shuts the door, and locks it. I hear the lock click with a final, metallic sound, and then I hear his footsteps as he leaves my room. Now it is dark and quiet. I still don't cry. For a long time I don't even move. I am back from out the window, but I don't feel anything. It is hours before I feel anything, and then when I do, it is hunger. I find my clothes and put them on. I hear him coming again. The door opens.

"Here you are, sweet Rebecca Ann— some crackers and water. You'll be getting good and hungry by now. It's going to take you some time to sit in this closet and think it over what it means to hide from me. I'm sorry that you were so stupid to do that, but you'll learn. I wish you didn't make me have to do this."

He locks the door, and it is quiet again. I think about Roy and wonder if he knows I am in here. He must know. But he can't do anything about it. Or maybe Daddy left him off at Granma's. I bunch up some clothes and move things around in the darkness until I can curl into a sleeping position. For a long time I don't sleep. I just listen to hear if he is going to come back. I know I will stay in the closet all night, at least. At first it isn't too bad being in the closet. As time drags by, I sort, count, and organize every object in there. Sometimes I worry that he might keep me in the closet always.

My hunger pangs have subsided after the first day, and it won't hurt me to lose some weight. I make up a good fantasy and play it a hundred times, but then I start to feel a little like I did when I went out the window. I want to escape out the window again, but I need to see it to do that. I put my cheek flat on the floor with one eye peering under the space beneath the door; I try to see my bedroom window, but the bed is in the way. At least I can see the beautiful light from it, reflecting on the floor.

Ruth had to shake me pretty hard to bring me back, and then I started to sob. All I could do for a long time was cry, taking in big gulps of air and slobbering my way through dozens of tissues. My body shook with every sob. Ruth held me for a long time. She is just a little bit of a thing, but her arms and hands were full of comfort, and her heart was full of patience.

When I finally finished all the crying I needed to do, she asked me what was going on. She said I laid trembling in the fetal position for several minutes, not making a sound. She couldn't reach me at all. I told her about the closet. It wasn't the only time he locked me in it. That was the first time, and it was the longest. It was three days and nights. I was around twelve or thirteen years old, maybe a year after Momma left. He only let me out to use the toilet and to take sex. All I got was crackers and water twice a day. After that first time, he would lock me in it if I wanted to go out somewhere, and he said I couldn't go. He put me in there to make sure I didn't sneak out. I wanted to sneak out, and I would have, but I knew the price I would have to pay. I quit trying to go anywhere except to school.

Chapter 26 - Therapist's Story

Faye O'Brien came with Becka to two family sessions during her two-day visit. I arranged the chairs in a triangular formation so that everyone could see each other well, and so that we would each be an arm's length away from one another. I wanted to seat myself close enough to Becka to keep my alliance with her. I also wanted to create an alliance with Faye by showing I could be equally close to her, and perhaps give her a connecting touch if I sensed it was appropriate. My goal was to assist these two women in reconnecting with each other enough to become intimate, and to talk to each other about things they had avoided for so long.

Faye, as was typical of her, was dressed tastefully in a tan rayon skirt and a colorful paisley blouse. She carried a crocheted sweater over her arm. "How nice to see you again, Dr. Carr," Faye said, extending her hand.

"Nice to see you, under somewhat better circumstances, Mrs. O'Brien. But please call me Kathleen, as Becka does."

"Fine. You call me Faye, then." She smiled and squeezed my hand harder.

Becka looked happy, a healthy flush on her cheeks. She was looking much better physically than she had in months. As I guided them into my office from the waiting room, I waited to let Becka select the chair she wanted. Faye asked me where she should sit, and I gestured to one of the remaining chairs."Faye, I felt it was important to have you come to Denver at this time because Becka is going through so much stress. As you may know, she has been clinically depressed for some time, and her medications are causing severe enough side effects that her doctor wants to hospitalize her again."

Faye seemed surprised and looked at Becka. "I didn't know she wants to put her in the hospital."

"That has been a fairly recent development," I continued. "Dr. Feinberg feels that if all the side effects are not controlled very soon, like this week, that it would be necessary to hospitalize Becka in order to have her withdraw from the medications safely. Her plan is to introduce an alternative medicine after clearing out the current drugs. Hospitalization would be to ensure she is in a safe place, in the event she drops back into the very deep depression she was in before."

Faye continued to watch Becka while I talked, and Becka just looked down at the floor.

"Rebecca told me the symptoms are going away," Faye said. "They are," said Becka. "Over the past three days, most of them have been subsiding. I phone in my reports daily to Dr. Feinberg, and she is pleased. And I haven't been any more depressed, so far."

"Good. While the physical problems are the most critical right now, I have been concerned for some time that there are some emotional things Becka needs to address. She needs your help to do that, since these are matters that relate to her relationship with you."

"I know," said Faye. "I haven't been the best mother, but I always done the best I could. You know that, don't you, Rebecca?"

"Yes, Momma," Becka answered softly.

I went on, "I've told Becka that I believe it would help the two of you to go over some of the things that happened in the past, partly to make sure you both understand it the same way. So, I'm going to let Becka start."

Becka looked at her mother. "We've already started some of that since Mom got here. She said she left me and Roy because Daddy was beating her up all the time."

Faye said, "I told Rebecca about her father and the way he was. I never told her before, and I probably should have. I didn't want her to be afraid of him like I was— but I found out she was anyway. I didn't think he would hurt the kids. I thought it was just me he wanted to hurt."

Faye had a tissue in her hands and was twisting it around her finger nervously. "We just aren't the type of family that talks about what another one does, you see. The only one I had ever told — about him beating me— was my mother. She always said I shouldn't have married him to begin with, 'cause she never did like Bobby, you see. But she never liked none of my husbands, really, but she never gave them a chance. She never even knew them that well. I suppose Rebecca told you I've been married several times—

twice to her father.

"Well, I had other husbands beat me, too. That's why I left them. Now my latest husband, God rest his soul, never laid a hand on me. Nor did my first husband, Lee. Maybe Rebecca told you I'm about to marry him a second time, too. But Bobby was the strangest one. I was fascinated by him when we first met. He was kind of quiet and serious, and I thought he was real smart. And he was . . . well, always reading books and all. After a time I learned he was quite a Momma's Boy, you know what I mean? His mother was over-protective; I guess that's what they call it. She seemed like a cold, unloving woman, but she did everything for him, and so of course, he expected the same from me. He was very demanding. The funny thing was, he didn't learn that from his daddy, 'cause he wasn't that way. His daddy was as gentle and kind as could be. But Bobby was her only child, and there wasn't anything she didn't do for him. I even sensed sometimes when we were around his folks that his daddy was jealous of the way his momma hopped to his every whim.

"Well, we got married, and I soon found out Bobby was the jealous type. Fiercely jealous. He was certain I was having affairs, and he would just accuse me of it— that, and of flirting with every man I met. Well, I wasn't, but I might as well have, since I got beat on no matter what. He forced sex on me, too. It didn't matter what I said, if I was tired, or sick. He just seemed to enjoy forcing me."

Through the telling of her story Faye continued to twist the tissue she held, pausing to touch her nose with it from time to time."I left the first time when Rebecca was three, but I took her with me.

Bobby came after me and threatened to kill us both. He had a knife, and I thought he was going to cut me. I went back, but after a couple of weeks I left again by myself, thinking I could hide from him better without worrying about her, too. I knew her grandparents would help look after her. They loved her so much.

"I went back to him again, because he swore he wouldn't hurt me no more. He said he'd changed, and I believed him. I got pregnant with Roy John, and he just started up the beating again after Roy was born. It didn't take him long to forget his promises. I tried to keep the family together. I tried to put up with his meanness, but I couldn't take it. Bobby threatened to kill me many times, and I believed he was going to do it. When I told him I was going to take the kids and leave, he just said he'd come find us and kill all three of us. I was too scared to take them with me, and I figured we would all have a better chance if I left him the kids."

I was watching Becka as her mother told this story. She had a look of compassion on her face, apparently accepting of it as told. Faye was looking at me most of the time as she told it, but now and then glanced at Becka.

Faye continued, "He kept trying to find me. I can't tell you how many apartments I moved out of, and how many jobs I got, trying to get where he couldn't find me. After a few years, he finally let up on it. Now this business of Bobby touching her— I never thought he would do that. I guess I kind of suspected it once, but I just couldn't believe he'd do that. I thought more that he might beat the kids, like he did me. But sex with her— no. I know, now that Rebecca has told me— he did. And I am so sorry that it happened." She teared up now and used her tissue to blow her nose. Then she reached into her handbag for another one.

"And we're not talking about one time, Momma," Becka said. "It happened all the time."

I wondered if she would tell her that he got her pregnant. "Yes, I understand that now. And it just horrifies me to think of what you went through, Rebecca. It simply horrifies me. To think he would have sex with you. I am just so sorry. But you see, dear, I thought what I was doing was the best thing. I thought you'd have a better life to stay in one place, go to one school, and not have to be on the run with me. I truly thought it was best for you and Roy."

Becka had tears in her eyes now. Faye reached across and took Becka's hand. "Oh, Sweetness, don't go crying on your momma now. It's okay. There's nothing to cry over. It's all in the past. I love you, Rebecca, and I always have. I just did the best I could. I love you, Sweetness."

"Becka, is this the first time you knew why your mother left?" I asked.

Becka nodded as she wiped her tears. "I didn't know he was beating her like that, threatening to kill her. I have no memories of that at all."

"He didn't do it in front of you kids. He did it in the bedroom, usually. And he got real mad if I cried out or made any noise, so I tried to keep as quiet as I could. You kids were usually gone to bed."

"I didn't know he was rough on you sexually, either," said Becka. "So it wasn't just me he did that way."

"Oh, he was brutal. He wanted to do strange things— sexual

things. It embarrasses me just to think about it. I never told nobody before." Faye looked at me instead of Becka, obviously embarrassed. "But you see, I have had to put things like that behind me and forget about them. It don't do no good to dwell on what you can't change. That's why I don't understand why Rebecca can't just put it all behind her, the way I do, and go on with her life. She has so much talent and intelligence. My word, she's a nurse, and she can always get a job with good pay. Nurses are so well respected."

Becka replied, "If I had a clue about how to forget it all again, I would. I don't understand how you do it."

"Faye . . . you're having a hard time understanding why Becka is so depressed over her past?" I clarified.

"Yes. It don't make no sense to me to go talking to someone over it, as if that would change anything."

"I understand your confusion, Faye," I said. "Human beings are more complicated about some things than we'd like to think. One thing that's important is to remember that people are different, and they handle their problems in a lot of different ways. Becka is different from you, and she has also had different life experiences from you. Perhaps you can accept that, in part, Becka's personality style and her personal beliefs are what led her to handle things the way she has. But mainly keep in mind that Becka was very young when the traumatizing events began by father. She was at an age when she couldn't possibly understand why the things happened that did. She had no choice but to trust the parent who cared for her day by day, and probably loved her, I should add.

"When Becka began to have a sense that something was wrong about what was happening with her father, her conclusion was that she was the one being naughty. This is a pattern observed in thousands of cases of incest and sexual abuse. Because the perpetrator is an adult, the child can't reason that the adult is doing wrong, so it has to be the child who is doing wrong. It is not logical, because small children have not yet developed a capacity to think logically. Becka is just beginning to discover, as a forty-three-year old woman, that she is innocent, that her father is guilty of wrongdoing. She is going to a special group for survivors of abuse and learning that many other women felt they were the bad ones, and caused what happened to them. She is beginning to feel less alone and bottled up inside herself by sharing the truth with people who know what it was like for her. That is partly why you are here— to hear her story, too. She has been hearing yours. What else do you want your mother to know, Becka— about your experience when you were left with your father?"

Becka had been listening carefully, looking from me to her mother. Now she grew uncomfortable again, and stared at the floor. She sighed deeply, and then said, "It's pretty ugly, Momma. Think you can take it?"

"I'll sure try, Sweetness. That's what I've come all these miles to do."

"You probably ought to know that he got me pregnant." Becka paused for her reaction. Faye bit her lower lip.

"And he locked me in the closet sometimes, to keep me from leaving. I didn't get anything except crackers and water. He did a lot of unpleasant sexual things to me, and sometimes he hit me, smothered me, and choked me. He even brought a friend of his to the house and let him rape me, too. I learned how to not feel it, by leaving my body. I just wasn't there till it was over. You probably also should know it started after the first time you left, when I was four."

"When you were four? I don't understand how you left your body." Faye appeared stunned; her eyes became glassy and hard, a mean, angry expression filling her face. She went on, "I could kill him! I thought about doing it when he was beating on me, and now I wish I had. Sweet Jesus!"

"Faye," I interjected, "have you ever heard of post-traumatic stress syndrome, in relation perhaps to soldiers who were in Viet Nam?"

She said she had, so I continued. "Becka went through so much stress during her childhood that she now suffers from that syndrome. There is some research that indicates that the brain may actually undergo neuro-chemical changes as a result of the prolonged stress, and thus cause depression that is much more severe than the kinds of blahs and dumps that most of us feel once in a while.

"Also, the mind often uses a number of mechanisms to cope with horror and pain. These are generally variations of denial— a way to not have to think about the events or believe they happened— or are happening. Becka said she left her body, and that is one means for the mind to deny the reality of horror and its pain. A second way is for the person to kind of split into more than one person, letting a part of herself be the bad one that deserves the abu-
166

sive treatment, while some other part remains the good person. A third way is to forget— amnesia. Becka's mind conveniently provided her with all these ways to cope. Forgetting it all for many years worked for a while, but sometimes the memories come back. Perhaps they don't return until the psyche is better prepared to cope with them. Does your mother know when the memories came back for you, Becka?"

"It was right after Granma died, after the funeral, when I last saw Daddy," Becka said. "It was because he tried it again with me behind Granma's house."

"Just a few years ago? At his own mother's wake?" Faye was stunned again, as Becka nodded. This time she reached out further for Becka and put her arms around her neck. "Oh sweet Jesus, Rebecca. How could he! Why, he's come near ruining your life."

Becka seemed to welcome the embrace and the attention of her mother. They both cried, hugged, and patted each other for some time.

"Now, Dr. Carr, are you saying she's going to be able to get free of these awful memories by talking about them?" Faye asked.

"That's our plan. Part of it is releasing the memories, part of it is going through all the emotions that go with them, and then eventually it involves coming to a place of either forgiveness, or some degree of acceptance, so that the memories can be, as you say, put behind her. With the severity of trauma Becka went through, however, just putting it behind her will not help, now that she has the memories. Her group and her sessions with me are to help her come to terms with the past, and then get free of it in a healthy way. I think your coming has been an important step toward that outcome."

Becka and Faye returned the next day, and I was curious to learn how they had used the previous twenty-four hours to digest the meeting from the day before. They had gone to a shopping mall and a movie together, saying they had talked so much their jaws hurt.

Becka brought along some photographs of herself as a child, and reviewed stories for her mother's benefit of events she had missed out on in Becka's formative years. It seemed to be an excellent way for Becka to heal a little bit and fill in some of the holes.

I also used the second session to review the key issues of just how much Becka was affected by her childhood experiences. I wanted Faye to grasp the impact and current struggle for Becka in coping with her memories. I also wanted Becka to get into her mother's shoes enough to begin having some understanding of Faye's need to deny and avoid. Nothing could make it right for Faye to have abandoned her children, but certainly Faye had done the best she thought she could do at the time, given what she had to work with. That was the point from which Becka could begin to find acceptance.

I pointed out to both of them that their entire family operated with a mechanism of denial, and denial of many things more than the incest by Robert. Denial can serve a useful purpose of protection, up to a point, and in certain cases. But it is damaging when it creates distance between people who presume to care for one another, blocking intimacy and connectedness. Feelings and thoughts were not shared in their family; problems and worries were not shared— such as Faye never telling her children about Robert's abusiveness. I emphasized that it would hardly be useful to take my statements as a point of blame of anyone, but rather use them to begin making the changes necessary to increase closeness and support between them and among current family members.

Becka nodded in agreement and smiled at her mother. "It really means a lot to me that you came, Momma, and that we've had all these talks."

"It's important, Sweetness. I want to help in any way I can.

None of this would ever have happened if that no-good Robert hadn't been so crazy. I could just kill him. I know money can't buy everything, and I've tried to help you with that when I could. I know you still have those big hospital bills, just like I do with Joe's medical expenses— that whole mess still isn't cleared up, a year still after he's been gone."

I thought it significant somehow that Faye would shift to talking about money and medical expenses in response to Becka's gratitude that she had come. Perhaps money for her trip was a concern, and also a way to be somewhat less intimate. As time drew near to end our meeting, I asked, "What sort of agreements could you make with each other, to sustain and build on the relationship you've been fostering these two days?"

Becka spoke first. "I would like more contact with you and to be reminded that you care."

"Well how about if I just call you every Sunday, then?" Faye offered. "And I'll write more often, too. I'll have plenty to tell you about, what with all the plans Lee has for us."

"That would help a lot."

"Is there anything else?" I asked.

Faye went on. "Lee is planning a trip to California in May, to visit some of his relatives there. We're going to stop here on our way to see Becka. He's dying to see her again after all these years. He saw her only once when she was a baby, and he's heard me tell all about the kids. So we'll come see you real soon, Baby."

"Does that feel like it will cover what you need, Becka, with respect to your mother?"

Becka affirmed that it would, so I asked Faye what she needed from Becka. "I would like her to tear up her suicide plan and get rid of all those silly living will papers she has . . . that's what I want."

Becka looked solemnly at Faye for some time before she spoke.

Then she said softly, "I can't do that. I'm sorry."

Faye looked disappointed. "Well can you promise me then that you'll do your very best to follow the doctors' orders— Dr. Carr and that other one— and try to be happy? I don't want to lose you, Sweetness. I couldn't bear to lose another one."

"All I can do is promise to do my best, Momma. And I will."

"That's all I can do either, Baby. I'll do my best, too."

The session ended with both women seeming more at ease than when we started the first session. They talked and teased with what were obviously family jokes. They had plans to go out to lunch before Faye's return to Dallas that afternoon, and the two appeared to be a mother and daughter pair that had been close all their lives. No one would have guessed there had just been an unburdening of the sad stories they had told each other.Faye was good at making it seem everything was wonderful, while Becka was equally adept at going along with her, each one sweeping things back under the rug in their own patterned ways. But I would not let Becka leave them there.

Kathleen's Reflections

Denial is a powerful mechanism of the mind. One doesn't know one is using it, so it is difficult to do anything about it. It takes a lot of honest self-reflection to face what is hidden. Becka knew her mother was not likely to embrace the realities she had brought forth, at least not in a way that would change Faye's approach to life or her relationship with Becka. It had taken Becka years to reach a stage In her growth where she could step back and ask herself if she was lying to herself. Sometimes she came up with an admission that she was lying, but she was not always ready to do anything to change it, such as with her attachment to Chris.

My explanation of denial and the need for it was aimed at Faye's subconscious mind, with respect to herself as much as to have her understand Becka. It is typical in cases of incest for family members who are not directly involved to deny that the behavior could have occurred. Faye may have known or sensed it, but it would have required major changes in her own life to have acknowledged and acted on it. Such changes might have put her in additional jeopardy and created intense shame and embarrassment.

*Denial served the positive purpose of protection for the people in this family, including the extreme degree required by Robert, Becka's father. Her grandfather had apparently been well aware and took steps to stop it. Becka recognized this long after he had died, that he was trying to protect her. Other members as well, appeared to have known something was going on. Becka suspected that her grandmother knew, and her brother had found out, at the very least, when he interrupted the encounter behind the shed at their grandmother's wake. The denial of the perpetrator requires a powerful rationalization, especially for incest and child abuse. Some common themes are: Our relationship is special, unique; only we have this kind of love and can share it this way. She can learn what it takes to be in a sexual relationship being with me; it'll make it easier for her when she grows up. She's too young to know what it's all about. I'm her father (step-father, uncle, grandfather), and I know what is good for her. I can't get sex from her mother like this, so she'll have to be the one who gives it to me. No one will find out— I can make her keep it secret. Usually at a very deep and unconscious level is a theme of such anger and rage toward women that the resulting belief is: **Women are sluts, no-good whores.** It may arise from feelings of emptiness, powerlessness and lack of control, evolving from the person's early relationship with his mother.*

I knew little background of Becka's father. I did know, according to Becka and Faye, his mother was over-protective, cold and withholding of affection; Robert may have been abused or rejected by her.

His possessiveness toward his wife showed he wanted to dominate her. His sexual and abusive activity with Becka may have been his way of seeking power, and at the same time, fulfillment of the nurturance he had lacked from his mother and his wife.

I had no idea whether Robert had suffered any remorse for his behavior, or whether he had any conscience about it. I thought not when I learned he had approached Becka again many years later, as an adult. Sociopaths, as Robert might be diagnosed, do not have guilt or uncomfortable feelings about criminal or anti-social behavior. I speculated there was a chance that Robert was not sociopathically disturbed, but rather evil, in the way described by M. Scott Peck, regarding his idea of "people of the lie." I couldn't make such a judgement without meeting Robert, but I suspected the same thing of Faye O'Brien. I felt uncomfortable about some things she had said, and for some reason, I didn't trust her. It was an intuitive feeling more than a certainty, but I felt she had been less than truthful about her running from Robert and her explanations for having abandoned her children. Faye had managed to whitewash her past and had gone on to live a tidy life with her various husbands and her retail jobs, always dressed so prim and proper. Yet, her ex-husband, Robert, and her daughter referred to her as a "whore." Peck's dissertation on evil makes the point that it originates not in the absence of guilt but in the effort to escape it. Faye had made sounds of apologies that Becka had suffered, but her emphatic need to put the past behind her made me uneasy. She was quick to blame Becka's father for Becka's state of mind, and rectify her own position as faultless for what Becka had suffered.

Becka had complained to me many times of her mother's inaccessibility and denial. Now I wondered if Faye might actually be a "person of the lie." If so, Becka was probably right that there was little chance her mother would ever change, and that Becka could ever feel she had a real mother. People of the lie are not able to put themselves on trial, push themselves through denial, and judge themselves as sinners. The denial is their true evil, not the lies or ill-considered behaviors.

Chapter 27 – Becka's Story

There are seven women in the Incest Survivor's Group. Four of us have clear memories; two of them never did forget what happened. One has just started having nightmares and flashbacks, and two more aren't sure what happened. Some of them with memories aren't sure if their memories are real, or are fantasies they have in their minds. All I know is, nobody in their right mind would make fantasies about what I've experienced, I don't care how masochistic they might be. I can't tell them what happened to me — at least, not yet. The others seem to want to be there— in that group. I guess there's something wrong with me that I don't like to go there. I don't want to re-play those horrifying experiences. But you say that I have to get it out— my story. Must be the adult part of me that believes you, because all the kids in me are screaming and begging me not to go.

One of the women in the group tonight broke up and bawled. I had to leave the room. I was going to escape out the window in my mind, but it was so bad, I just took my whole physical self— and all my parts— outside. One of the group leaders came after me, and we talked for a few minutes out in front while I smoked a cigarette. I wouldn't go back until the crying had stopped, and then they made me say why I left. All I could say was, I understood it too well, and I just couldn't bear to go through it again.

Wednesday, April 22, 1992 – 21:15

Ruth's magic hands— they're like witching rods. She goes straight to the tight place, and the next thing I know, memories are spilling out. She triggered Granma's funeral this time. But this time I didn't cry. I felt the anger, and I still feel it. I am pissed off at every- body. I'm even pissed off at the dog, so you know I'm mad.

****

"

Granma died in May. It was the kind of spring day for her funeral that she loved best—when the temperature stays perfect all day long, and you can smell everything new that's blooming. I hadn't seen my brother, Roy, for several years, but my father—it had been more like ten years. There were lots of relatives and friends I hadn't seen since I left for college. The whole thing was like a big reunion more than a wake. Or maybe more like a circus than a reunion. We had gone to the funeral parlor for the service, and then the long procession to the cemetery. Momma and Grams were there, and I pretty much stayed with them. I saw my father looking at me during the service, but we never spoke until later at Granma's house where the buffet was held. Momma and Grams Kirkwood wouldn't stay there long. They just spoke to a few people and left. I found my brother, Roy, and we went out in the back yard. We were catching up on each other's lives when Daddy came out the back door. He let it slam, just the way he always had. I felt a sinking feeling then, from some vague memories that were stirred up by the door slamming.

"Rebecca Ann! I finally get a chance to see you again," Dad- dy said loudly. He reached out and embraced me. I tried to appear happy to see him.

"Hello, Daddy." I moved away from him quickly, feeling awkward since I hadn't seen him for so long.

"Let's sit down out here and visit a while. I want to hear how you've been doing."

Just then someone came to the screen door and asked Roy to come in and help find something. I was disappointed to be left alone with Daddy. I hadn't had any of the memories yet, but we had remained distant for so long that I didn't know him any more. We sat on the lawn furniture under the magnolia tree that had housed my childhood fairy lightning bugs. I told him about my job, that I had recently left Leslie, and I was with somebody new.

He had never accepted that I am a lesbian, and that was why we saw so little of each other after I left home. He talked for a long time about himself, and I soon realized I wasn't even listening. I don't have any idea what he said. Eventually I did hear him say, "I want to talk to you about your brother. Let's take a walk."

There was a large lot behind Granma's house, which she owned. She knew it was valuable and had held onto it through several offers to buy it from her. We walked back that way, and when we were behind the old tool shed where Granpa had had his shop, Daddy stopped. He had been talking about how he was worried about Roy joining the Ku Klux Klan, and how Roy was so hard-headed and ornery all the time. I still wasn't listening very well.

"I worry about you, too, Rebecca Ann. You living with a woman and all. Something's not right about that. And you being so fat like this. I worry you need to lose weight. You were always such a pretty little girl, even though you were a little chubby. You were always so sweet."

He came closer to me, and his voice got lower. "Maybe I could help get you set straight, the way you ought to be. Make it like old times when we had our games . . ." His face was up against mine now. I smelled the whiskey, and I smelled him, just the way he had always smelled. Everything went black for a few seconds. When I could see the light again, his hands were on my breasts, and he was pushing me up against the shed.

I opened my mouth to scream, but his hand slapped over it quickly. Just at that moment, Roy turned the corner of the building and found us standing there, Daddy's hands covering my mouth and one breast. I'm sure he saw the terror in my eyes. He did a classic double-take.

"Hey!" Roy said. "What's going on back here? Is everything okay?" Daddy had stepped back and released me the instant Roy appeared.

"Everything's fine," Daddy said. He looked at me the way I'd seen him look before, when he said something and meant for me not to forget it. Then he looked at Roy the same way and said. "You didn't see nothin', did you?" He turned and walked back to the house.

I slumped down against the side of the shed. My heart was racing, and I had broken into a sweat. Roy came closer and sat down beside me.

"You gonna be all right, Rebecca?"

"Sure, Roy. He didn't do any harm. I'll just sit here by myself for a few minutes, if that's okay with you. I'll come back soon."

"I was looking for you— to say goodbye. I'm ready to leave. Maybe you ought to leave, too. Can I give you a ride somewhere?"

"Thank you. I don't need a ride, and I will leave soon. You go on, and take good care of yourself, you hear? You're still my little brother, and I can tell you that."

I stood up and gave him a hug, but as soon as he left, I slumped down again and just sat for a while. I don't know how long I stayed there. I could barely feel anything. I just watched movies in my mind of my father, fucking, on top of me, his face breathing whiskey into mine; and from behind me, like a dog. I had managed to forget it all for seventeen years, and now it was coming back as fresh as yesterday. Suddenly I heaved, and all the buffet lunch was spewed across the wall of the shed where he had pinned me. I heard myself sobbing, "I'm sorry, Granpa. I'm sorry, Granma. I'm so sorry."

After the funeral I had started having frequent nightmares. I would wake up soaked through my night shirt, sweating, choking, and shaking.

Some of the dreams were of him choking or slapping me. He would cover my mouth with his hand and tell me to keep quiet. He told me to never tell anyone what we did. He told me I would be taken by the devil and stuffed in a black hole forever if I told.

I had dreams of him laughing at me— laughing and enjoying seeing me in pain. His mouth opened wide when he laughed, his head tilted back so I could see his gold crowned molars. He would call me a fat little pig, and pinch my butt hard, or a stupid, lazy whore. He told me that it was my fault he did the things to me that he did. He said if I had just behaved myself, he wouldn't have to do those things. Then he would laugh some more. I would awaken from the nightmares, and sob. The memories of what he really did to me came back through the dreams. The worst ones were when I would awaken, unable to breathe, choking, as if something was stuck in my throat. It was his penis. He would stick it in my mouth and I would gag. His come was disgusting. He got angry when it made me vomit, and he called me apriss.

In those days, I couldn't tell Gail any of the details of the dreams, but she knew they were about my father raping me. She had insisted that I go to a therapist, and that was when I started to see Myra. Myra got me to tell her a little bit of what had happened with him, but it was too painful to tell it all. I didn't want to have to dream it, then remember it ,awaken, and cry, and then tell it all over again to a stranger. Myra told me that I had to tell it— to get it on the outside of me, instead of keeping it inside. I really tried, but it was so frightening. I was afraid of some unknown retribution. He said I would be punished, and I guess the child parts in me believed him, and they were the strongest. They were the parts that had made me forget it all. They didn't want to remember— the four-year old, the eleven-year old, and the teenager.

Chapter 28 - Therapist's Story

Becka arrived early for her psychodrama session, carrying with her a list— she was so good at making them— and an assortment of props. Her list enumerated the things she planned to do to her father, as well as the signals we had established for helping regain control if she felt like she was losing it. Ruth and I were ready, too. We had fashioned a dummy out of pillows, a shirt, and trousers to represent Becka's father. I had a supply of batacas and assorted throw pillows, and we had pushed the furniture in my office to the walls to give us plenty of space to move around. Becka picked up the dummy. "It needs features," she said. "Can I draw on this pillowcase?"

"Certainly," I said. "The pillow case and old clothes came from the rag bag, so you can do whatever you need to do to make this work for you."

Becka took the colored markers I offered her and drew eyes, ears, a nose, and a mouth on the stuffed pillowcase that made the head. "I'm making the mouth open, because he's going to be doing a lot of screaming," she said with a tone of confidence. "I guess he needs a little hair, too. It might get pulled. And I may as well add some eyebrows to make him look more human and less like a cartoon. What a joke." She laughed at her handiwork. "I'm not much good at portraits, but this will do as him."

Then she reached into her little sack of props and brought out a small cloth bag. It was a square bean bag which she had stitched together in the middle so that it had two compartments of beans. "These are his balls. And for his penis … I brought this ratty rawhide dog chew. I let the dog chew on it for a while, of course."

Becka emptied out the remaining props and set them up with a look of impish glee. "Here's a knife. I was going to bring a real one, but I got scared and decided this plastic one would be safest. I think I'll be able to cut with that serrated edge on it. And this jar has dish soap in it. That'll be his come, which I'll put in this syringe to get it down his throat." Ruth picked up a tiny baby doll in a red and white dress. It was a cloth doll with a painted face, something like a kewpie. "What is this for?" she asked.

Becka's impish glee vanished. "That represents the baby I miscarried."

Ruth and I both took time to read Becka's list and tried to memorize the order in which she wanted to proceed. Then we discussed where in the room Becka wanted to put the dummy. She selected the sofa, since she rarely sat there.

"How is this going to work?" Becka asked. "How do I get started?"

"I've already explained it to Ruth," I said. "We are both going to be your *double*, which is something used in psychodrama. A double is a special player who is there to help the main player do and say what they're having a hard time with. It will be as if we are the parts of you. I will represent the youngest parts, and Ruth will represent the teenager. We may say things to prompt you to get started and also encourage you to keep going— like speaking for you— but only as it seems to be needed. If we say something that fits for you, you can repeat it; but if it doesn't fit, let us know or don't repeat it. You don't have to accept any of our words as yours if they don't accurately express how you feel. Does that make sense to you?" Becky nodded.

"I may also play the role of your father's voice, to say something he might say, just so it seems more real that he's actually here. I'll change my voice so that you can tell I'm speaking for your father. You can correct me on him, too."

I led Becka to stand in front of the dummy draped on the couch, and Ruth followed. We flanked Becka and stood just a bit behind her. I explained, "Here's how we're going to start: I want you to read this list of what you're going to do to him, but read it to him. Imagine he is hearing how he is going to be tortured. I'll help you with wording sometimes."

Becka stood looking down at the dummy, breathing heavily. She was still carrying extra fluid in her legs, and it was somewhat painful for her to stand. She read out loud: "First, I'm going to put a pillow over his face so he can't breathe."

I repeated what she said, changing the pronoun to *you*.

"First, I'm going to put a pillow over your face so you can't breathe." I also changed the tone of my voice to sound more threatening than Becka had.

Becka looked at me, then at the dummy and said it the way I had. "That's right," I said. "Tell it to him with feeling. Make him feel scared about what's about to happen."

Becka continued. "Second, I'm going to cut off your balls and jam them into your throat till you choke on them. Then, while you can still see, I'll make you take a good look at the little fetus-baby you made me pregnant with. Fourth, I'll make you swallow your own cum. Next, while you can still watch, I'll cut off your penis and ram it into your throat, too. Sixth, I'm going to blind your eyes, and then, finally, just beat you to a pulp."

While Becka was reading the list, she was building up stronger sentiment, which is what I wanted to happen. She needed to really feel her anger in order to get into an abreaction and cathar-sis of the anger.

"Here's the pillow I'm going to smother you with," I said, handing a throw pillow to Becka.

Becka took the pillow and stared down at the dummy. She began to tremble slightly. I picked up another pillow for myself as her double and said with emotion, "I'm going to smother you with this, you no-good . . ."

"Bastard!" Becka snarled through her teeth. She leaned for-ward over the dummy, but couldn't go any further. I leaned over him too, nearly putting my pillow on his face. I snarled like her, "You no-good bastard!"

Ruth added, speaking as Becka, "I'm afraid to do this. What if I lose control and go completely mad?"

"Yeah," said Becka. "That's what I'm afraid of."

Ruth as Becka continued. "But I can do this. I have my safe-ty valves all set. Ruth and Kathleen will help me stay safe. I know I can do this. I HAVE to do it."

As Becka I said snidely, "Sorry, Daddy, but I have to do this, just like you had to do it to me." Then I changed my voice to a deep, male-sounding voice and said, "Rebecca Ann, you don't have the guts to do any of those things to me. You wouldn't hurt your Daddy, would you?"

At that point Becka jammed the pillow down on the dummy's face. I kept up his role: "Oh! Stop! I can't breathe. You're smothering me." Becka smiled and kept on pushing the pillow down on his face. I continued making muffled screaming sounds for her to stop.

Becka began pounding the pillow on his face. She pounded harder and harder. Ruth and I urged her on by saying, "I'm going to make you suffer, like you did to me. See what it's like? You feel like you're going to die."

Becka pounded with the pillow until she was breathing very heavily. Then she held it again on the dummy face while she caught her breath."I don't want to kill him by smothering. I have too many plans for him to do him in yet. What's next on my list?"

"Next you make him see the little fetus-baby," said Ruth. She handed the doll to Becka who dropped it into a waste basket and placed it beside the sofa. Then Becka lifted the dummy and leaned it over the arm of the sofa, as if it could look down into the waste basket at the doll.

"LOOK!" Becka demanded. "Look at what you did. You never got to see it that day— the baby you made. The sad little bastard-child of incest. Look at it in the toilet. That's the life you made and then wanted to murder." Becka was looking at the doll, too, through the tears flowing down her cheeks. "Take a good look at the product of your sin, you filthy bastard."

With that, Becka pounded on the dummy a few more minutes, taking in big gulps of air between each blow. The gulps soon turned to sobs, and Becka dropped to her knees. She clutched her head with both hands and whispered in a raspy voice, "My head!" This was her signal that she felt like she was losing control and needed help. Ruth quickly knelt beside her and pulled Becka's head to her chest with both arms.

"You're okay, now, Becka," Ruth said. "You're safe. We're here with you, Kathleen and I. We're doing a psychodrama, remember?" Ruth and I both held onto Becka's head as Ruth talked, trying to bring her back to the reality of the room and the enactment.

"Don't let go of my head," Becka begged.

I spoke to her then. "It's understandable that the kids would get scared about this. Reassure them from that adult part of yourself that you can handle all this emotion, and no one is going to get hurt. You, Becka the adult, as well as Ruth and I, are here to make this work safely. This is a perfect opportunity to show those young parts of yourself that you can handle scary feelings, and that they can trust you. We're going to slowly remove our hands now, while you come back, calm and ready to continue what the adult part of you came to do here."

When Becka was calm again, and we had released our hold on her head, she said, "I'm okay. I want to go on. Where's my list?

The balls are next, right?" Becka asked.

Ruth turned to the dummy and growled, "Now I'm going to cut off your balls." She said it with as much emotion as Becka had.

"And I'm going to jam them down your throat," said Becka. With the plastic knife, she sawed at the bean bag cloth which she had placed in the crotch of the dummy. I suggested that she cut at the trousers, putting the bean bag inside. Becka hacked at it with her serrated plastic knife until she made a hole through the trousers. Reaching through the hole, she pulled out the bean bag and tried jamming it into the dummy's mouth. She had to cut a hole through the pillow case so that she could push the bean bag through.

"Now choke on your balls," she growled. "Get 'em in your throat and choke." Next she took the syringe and filled it with the dish soap. "Now swallow it all down with your own come." She was taking an intense pleasure in forcing the sticky substance into the hole that was his mouth.

"See how you like this disgusting, vile stuff in your mouth."

I made sounds of choking, coughing, and trying to plead in his voice. She seemed pleased to hear him suffering and struggling. "Too bad you don't like it," she sneered. "I thought you would enjoy your own medicine. I hadn't thought of this till now," Becka said, "but I might as well add one more thing to the list." She turned the dummy over and ripped a hole at the back of the trousers. "I'll just go ahead and ram this syringe up your filthy butt."

Then she continued. "And now for the penis. For sure you're going to enjoy this, Daddy dear."

I cried out in the male voice, muffled by the things he was choking on, "No! Not my penis. You wouldn't!"

"Oh wouldn't I? Well, just watch and suffer." Becka sawed at the cloth trousers again in the crotch area where I had placed the half-chewed rawhide bone. She then decided to cut on the rawhide itself, so I held it for her. It took quite a bit of effort to cut all the way through it, but Becka persisted until she had cut the rawhide in half. Then she pushed both pieces into the mouth-opening in the dummy face. She was sweating heavily, fully absorbed in the actions. While symbolic, the props served to stimulate the needed abreaction of her anger.

"While you choke on your gross penis for a while, I'm going to poke your eyes out," Becka said. "Now you can't see. You can never look at me again. You'll never see anything or anyone. You'll never have any pleasure or satisfaction." She was stabbing the plastic knife into the pillow-eyes. She punctured the cloth many times, until there was no longer any resistance of the fabric because it was so full of holes.

Becka knelt down in front of the couch to rest. Her respiration was very labored, her body hot and sweaty. When she had regained a more even breathing rhythm she said, "I'm ready to beat him to a pulp now."

I handed her the bat. "Do you want to use this, or the little pillow?" Becka chose the bat and started pounding on the dummy. She didn't say anything any more— just pounded— using both hands on the handle of the bat. She seemed to have gained extra strength from having rested and was able to keep up the beating for several minutes more.

"I have to get him on the floor," she said. Using the bat she beat the dummy off the sofa and onto the floor, and continued pounding.

Ruth and I had been watching silently for some time, as Becka seemed fully occupied and didn't need any further prompting from us. But now I started speaking again: "Take that from us little ones, Daddy. You made us afraid, and all alone. You wouldn't let us tell anyone how bad you were."

Becka repeated my words through clenched teeth. Then Ruth spoke. "And take that from me, the teenager. You deserve to be punished, to suffer and be tortured. You need to find out what it was like. Suffer, Daddy, suffer."

Becka kept up the pounding in a rhythm as she repeated Ruth's lines. By now she was sitting on the floor, beating relentlessly on the dummy. It was falling apart, and the rag stuffing was coming out. Each time a piece came loose, Becka whapped it hard with the bat and sent it flying across the room. She pounded on and on, until I began to think she wouldn't reach a point of satiation, and I wondered if I was going to have to stop her.

I said, "It seems like I'm so full of anger I'll just never get it all out."

Becka heard this, and without missing a beat said, "It just

keeps coming . . . and coming."

I said in her pounding rhythm, "I . . . HATE . . . you! I . . . HATE . . . you!"

Becka picked up the phrase herself, saying one word with each whack of the bat. "I . . .HATE . . . you!"

I knew she had pumped up enough endorphins to make her energized and dizzy, so I gradually helped her slow down her rhythm, suggesting she back off easily, pacing her down with my own voice. Finally she was able to come to a stop. The pieces of the dummy were strewn around the room.

Ruth said, as Becka, "I guess I pretty well beat him to a pulp."

Becka looked around and laughed. "I guess I did!" She suddenly seemed to be aware of Ruth and me. "Are you guys all right? I didn't hurt you, did I?"

We both assured her we were fine.

"We're going to take some time to unwind from all this and settle down," I said. "First what I want to do is a fairly simple art therapy exercise." I took some paper, crayons, and markers from my desk and spread them on the floor. The three of us sat in a circle, giving Becka enough room to spread out with the materials.

"I'd like you to pick out a color that represents how you're feeling right now. I want you to close your eyes and think about the color and about how you feel. Then you can draw something— anything— just make marks if you want. It doesn't have to be a recognizable object, but it can be. Just let something come out on the page." My purpose was to begin some closure to the session. Becka followed my directions, then waited for the next instruction.

"Now select a color that represents your father, and do the same thing," I said.

Becka did so, choosing to use a separate piece of paper for each drawing. She chose red-violet for the way she was feeling, drawing large spiraling circles all over the paper. She said she felt open, full, and expansive. She chose dark brown for her father and scribbled hard on the paper. She made a large square box and filled it in completely. That was how he was to her, crammed into a dark, dirty world, with hard, defined edges— a box where there was no light. Then she took the drawing that represented him and tore it into hundreds of little pieces.

"That feels pretty good," Becka remarked as she dropped

the bits of paper into the waste basket. Ruth had already removed the doll and put it back in Becka's sack, along with her other props.

"What do you think we should do with what's left of your father?" I asked, gesturing to the rags and torn clothing around the room.

Becka answered, "Maybe you should burn it. I don't want to touch it again."

"Fine. I'll take care of it," I said. "The last thing we are going to do is what is called 'sharing' in psychodrama. This is the final phase, and is just as important as the drama part that you just went through. Ruth and I will share some things with you that your experience stirred up for us. The purpose is for us to release some of what we're feeling, and also to let you know how we personally relate to your drama experience here, so that you know we were just bystanders."

I asked Ruth if she wanted to say something first, or follow me. She elected to wait, so I started.

"Becka, I'd like you to know that I felt as if I was just as angry as you were at your father, all through the drama. But my anger was over more than your father. I felt anger toward all the men I've ever heard about who have abused my clients— all the rapists. This was an opportunity to get some of my own rage out of my system.

"The other thing it stirred up in me was a host of memories of growing up with two brothers. There were never any serious incest problems, but the things that happened to me may often occur among young siblings. One brother wanted me to stroke his penis through his trousers when we were riding in the back seat of the family car, when I was about seven. The other brother later showed a lot of curiosity about my breasts developing when I was eleven, and wanted me to let him have a look. I recall being very embarrassed by these requests, so tonight I was feeling the anger about it. In retrospect, it makes me aware of how opportunistic my brothers were, to take advantage of their little sister. Both of them behaved very sweetly toward me, as they did only when they were asking a favor of me. I believe that if they had tried to force anything on me, my anger tonight would have been many times greater."

Ruth spoke about her experience next. "What you did here tonight has been extremely moving for me. It has brought up some things that I thought were over and buried, but I guess I still had more emotions to let out. There were times when I felt like crying, and other times when you were talking to your father that I felt just as angry and vengeful as you."

Ruth wiped her eyes and blew her nose, because she had started to cry as she talked. "You see, I was incested by my father, too. I have gone through a lot of therapy myself in order to come to terms with it. I feel such a relief tonight, that I have to thank you for a most incredible gift. It is a gift to have been part of this event with you, and to be able to let go of more of my own rage. You have helped me to go a step further toward coping with the horror and the injustice of what I was subjected to by my father."

Ruth continued, "I also relate to the denial by your mother. My mother is unable to deal with the knowledge of my father raping me. She continues to act like she doesn't know anything about it. I think that has intensified my rage— her denial, added to my father believing that the matter was never a big deal. I have confronted both of my parents, which helped in some ways, and made it worse in others. It helped to get the secrets out in the open, but left me with that additional anger about their denial. I'm starting to accept that they cannot change, that denial is their way of protecting themselves from their own helplessness and Angst."

Ruth moved closer to Becka and hugged her. "So thank you, Becka, for helping me while you were helping yourself."

"I hope this helps someone," Becka laughed. "I'd hate to think I sweated this hard for nothing. It's a heck of a way to get rid of excess fluid, that's for sure."

We continued to talk for some time, sharing more of our experiences and expressing our desires to see change in the consciousness of society, so that children are not abused by the very people whose job is to protect them. The evening had grown into late night by the time we had cleaned the office and walked with each other to our cars.

Kathleen's Reflections

I referred to Becka's psychodrama as an exorcism, not in the quite the same sense it is used in reference to calling out the devil from a person possessed, but what she had to do was just that powerful for her— and for me and Ruth. What had unfolded during the session had come from some primal place within Becka's subconscious mind. She must have had many fantasies of her own har-

bored within, and because of the twisted child-mind beliefs that evolved from the incest. During the drama, she had hypnotically regressed to an earlier stage of development, so her thoughts and actions came from highly irrational places in her consciousness. That she could use the props she had brought along and so realistically (seemingly) to tear and gouge and rip into the dummy-father was possible because of the state of regression she had achieved. It was in that state that she needed to release all the horrors of the trauma she had ever suffered from him.

The abreaction— the surfacing of pent up rage and deep, deep sadness— had come through exorcising of the evil father. It had allowed Becka to get the badness out of herself and put it back on him, where it belonged. She was finally relieved of the guilt she had carried for his behavior which was beyond her control, but would still take more time to integrate the full impact. The symbolic gesture of beating her father to a million bits and tearing up the drawing she had made, were her ways to release repressed feelings leading to emotional catharsis. I would watch and listen carefully in the weeks to follow for signs Becka was integrating this release. Integration would mean she was coming closer to a healthy form of acceptance about what had happened with her father, and becoming strong enough to love herself in spite of the incest. I couldn't really expect her to ever forgive her father, although, in many instances a full catharsis will lead to such action. The best I could hope for would be that Becka would absolve herself of her sins and find herself whole.

Chapter 29 – Becka's Story

Journal Entry: May 21, 1992 – 08:20

      Slept like a baby last night. Lost 23 pounds of water in three days after taking Lasix. Feel total relief from the side effects; blood pressure normal; pain in legs down to 3 on a scale of 0 to 10; dizziness, hallucinations, sweats, tremors, rash, flush, and muscle cramps all gone; appetite fair; energy up a little; suicidal desires down to 2 on the scale from 8 and 9, where it has been. Tapes have been helping me sleep. Nightmares have quit.

Goals:
- Integrate child/adult in feelings, not in head
- accept, love, integrate child
- accept,love, integrate adult
- accept,love,integrate child Becka
- listen to the child
- play: ladies softball, swim, joke, art, entertainment
- don't take everything personally
- learn to accept Mother and Becka, as is
- accept/work out anger/pain/guilt over old relationships
- no sexual relationship till goals are met
- resolve co-dependency patterns
- continue body work and therapy
- no lying/hiding in therapy
- no holding back feelings in therapy
- resolve mothering issues with Kathleen
- Cure agoraphobia
- do something other than work and therapy
- swim 2-3 times a week — start Saturday
- learn to have fun alone
- get wood
- movie/concert/play once a month
- night class this summer
- make one or more friends this year
- see old friends once a month or more

- Stop obsession with Chris
- accept Chris' need to be alone not as rejection
- give myself space and time
- love Chris as a friend, not a lover
- recognize importance of my life
- focus on other people
- accept Chris doesn't love or desire me
- recognize my own separateness and independence
- give up false hopes
- make expectations only for myself
- learn to masturbate to orgasm, enjoy it, feel satisfied
- Increase self-esteem
- stop negative head talk
- deal with feelings instead of getting sick
- dress better — clean, ironed clothes
- express real feelings to others
- bathe four times a week
- learn to see myself as a separate being
- learn to see myself as a sexual being
- skin and nail care, eyebrows
- lose 25# this year: exercise,
- desserts down 5x,3x,2x,1x per week
- Increase self-confidence
- call my own bullshit
- accept praise and integrate it
- accept criticism as constructive, not personal
- learn new RN skills and improve present skills
- accept/know that I am a good RN
- do things I want to do — music, garden, read, woods
- stop being paranoid.

Chapter 30 - Therapist's Story

The date Becka had set for her suicide had come and gone, averted largely by the success of adjusting her medication and reduction of fluids to a more normal level. The resulting physical relief from the side effects greatly improved her mental and emotional condition. I felt that her mother's visit, as well as the emotional release she had gotten from the exorcism, were also critical factors.

She sat in my office now, ready to make a new contract for the next phase of treatment. She chose to sit on the sofa this time, instead of her usual place in the recliner. She had always stayed away from the sofa, because it wasn't close enough to the window for her to see out, or escape if she needed to. There was something different about the way Becka looked now, less tension around her eyes and a healthy color to her skin. She wore a multi-colored plaid blouse and jeans, not her usual drab cotton jerseys or jogging suits. The strong warm colors made her look younger and happier.

I had something important of my own to cover in our session, and I wasn't looking forward to it. I read her long list of proposed goals while she waited, groping for a way to tell her my news, even as I read silently.

"Becka, this is excellent— right on target. It's wonderful that you're feeling better and have avoided another suicide date. Your timing is right in your renewed contract proposal, because I was going to bring it up myself. And I have to tell you something that makes it particularly important for us to plan our time ahead carefully."

Becka looked at me with an expression of curiosity. I took a breath and continued, "I know you are not going to like this, and I've debated with myself about when to do it. I have decided that a delay of this news is not in your best interest, even though I can give no definite time-frame; but it looks quite certain that I will be moving away from this area with my family, sometime in the next several months. It could be two months; it could be even ten months to a year. The most likely time-frame is six months."

I was watching her face carefully to read her true response, knowing her every expression, every gesture. She could hide little. Becka closed her eyes and let her head fall back against the sofa cushion. Her hands tightened into the round balls I had seen her make so many times when she fought tears of hurt. She brought her head back up and opened her eyes rather quickly, as if she didn't want to miss anything.

"Go on," she said softly. She needed time to absorb what I was saying. I felt as if I could read a hundred lines of thought in her mind.

"My husband has been offered a job doing something that has been his dream for many years. He is quite fortunate to have been selected for the work, which will require that we move to St. Louis. The timing for him to start working is up in the air; his employers cannot give him a specific date. He hasn't had a final interview, either. When that happens we will have about six weeks left. If he were to be called as soon as tomorrow for an interview date, that would give us at least two months."

Becka was nodding. "So you've known for a while that you would leave."

I knew Becka was devastated, yet she held back her feelings, trying to be accepting.

"Yes, I've known it's possible for a couple of months, but just recently he was told he will have a final interview. I have had it in mind as we've worked through the incest events, knowing we must do this work together and get you strong enough to handle my leaving."

"Do you really think we can do that now?"

"I'm sure we can. You just got through the hardest part last week, Becka. The worst of it is behind you now."

"But all the parts— the kids— are still not together with the adult."

"Becka . . . I'm still here, and we're still working. We have quite a bit of time."

Becka looked down at the arm of the sofa but didn't pick at it. She kept her hands in tight balls against her thighs.

"I'd like to tell you about something called *time-limited therapy*," I said. "It is a technique in which the client agrees to a contract from the first session for a specific amount of time to be in therapy, and that time cannot be changed. It would typically be something like nine to twelve sessions, not long. At every session the therapist begins by reminding the client how many sessions they have left, at which point they will have reached— or not— the goals. They will no longer work together or see each other again. The relationship is limited by the original agreement.

"As therapy progresses, the theory goes, the issues become resolved more quickly by working through the rejection and abandonment the client feels, and then saying goodbye. When it is handled properly, the client is brought to a healthier state by having a thorough termination with the therapist. The time pressure forces the client to address what she came to therapy to do."

"So you're saying we're on time-limited therapy, and I have to hurry up and do what I want to do."

"It is too late for us do start the method the way it was designed, but by approaching the remaining time as limited does put the pressure on. I'm not saying this is ideal, Becka. But maybe it's good . . . let's look at the up side. I believe that the time factor, and my leaving factor, can be a benefit for you. If you want to become truly whole, if you want to achieve these goals you have so thoroughly outlined, then you *must* separate completely from me. Sooner would be better than later. We have already prolonged that outcome. I think you're ready to handle it soon with a deadline. You obviously cannot do this with me the rest of your life, even if I were to stay here."

"When you say I have to separate from you completely, does that mean I can never see you again? What about after we finish therapy— can't we meet on a friendly basis for coffee or something?"

"Well, it looks like that's a moot point now, since I probably won't be here— but no, it doesn't mean we could never see each other. The answer to that really has a lot to do with just how whole you become. But suppose we terminated therapy, and then became friends, you wouldn't really have achieved your goal of separation and self-sufficiency. Or suppose you wanted to do some more therapy at some later point in your life. You wouldn't be able to do it with me, because our relationship would have changed. I could no longer be in the role of therapist that is necessary to do the work."

Becka nodded as if understanding, but she continued to pout. It was difficult to require the separation, was necessary therapeutically, but the hard part of getting the words out was over. It was like peddling a bicycle as fast as I could.

"Let's take a good look at your goals." I took out the pages she had brought, copied from her journal. "You see— you yourself have specified, even before you knew I'd be leaving, that you want to '*resolve mothering issues with Kathleen.*' And another goal is "*learn to see myself as a separate being,*" as part of increasing your self- esteem. You also want to "*stop the obsession with Chris and accept that she doesn't love or desire* you," again separating to become whole. These are all related— all of your goals are— and they can be accomplished. You have already seen it so clearly that you were able to write it down like this. I am impressed."

"You really think I can achieve all of that in two months?"

"I do. I think you're on the edge right now, and with a little encouragement, we can boost you into action on these goals very soon. I'll tape the hypnosis part of our sessions for you, so that you can continue to reinforce the positive changes, even after we've terminated our work."

Becka didn't look entirely convinced. "I still feel like all the kids are not back together with the adult part of me. We've gone back in time with hypnosis and retrieved them, but I feel like all I've gathered up is a bundle of twigs— they slip from my grasp, and they feel so fragile. The younger parts of me still feel scared."

"We still have work to do to strengthen them, that's true. And we still have the time to do it. You're so very close now— just bolstering their fragile little egos with various kinds of success and accomplishment, of which you are fully capable."

"Do you think I'll need to find another therapist? I hate the thought of starting all over with somebody new."

"No; plan on not doing it. Rather, I would like you to continue with your incest survivors' group and having body psychotherapy with Ruth. She works with you quite well, and that would be the perfect follow-up. Of course, Dr. Feinberg will continue to monitor your needs for medication."

Kathleen's Reflections

It was difficult to believe that just as Becka was feeling good again, ready to get on with her life, I had to sink her with another of life's blows. The timing of it was uncanny. I really had to wonder if there was some grand design to our lives that was unfolding, or if events happen merely by chance. I chose to believe that my leaving would be the boon for her that I suggested it could be: an opportunity to break cleanly from me and grow stronger for it, changing the pattern of abandonment in her life to a healthy outcome.

Each person in my family had had some degree difficulty with the decision to leave Denver so that my husband could pursue his dream, including him. It wasn't too difficult for my children, as they were making their own choices and going on to colleges. I would be giving up a practice I had worked hard to establish. We would all leave friends and community interests. We would all leave the home we had come to love as a new, second-chance family. My husband was going to a new career. I didn't know what I was going to. I would have a tabla rasa, a blank slate upon which I could write anything I chose. Just a short while ago, I was ready to sell shoes— but not really. It had seemed like a simple escape from the pressure I was under. Now I could truly choose whether to continue my counselling career, or start something new.

I saw how Becka had kept herself from moving forward by not making choices. She knew she needed to choose her freedom, but freedom meant no structure and having to make more decisions. She knew she needed to choose to leave Chris, as she had chosen to leave Gail, but that resulted in choosing loneliness. The price of freedom is a terrible anxiety.

During the early period of separation from my first husband I had a powerful experience, as if in a dream, but I was awake and in deep contemplation. I was sitting one evening in my bedroom— the one I shared for several years with my now estranged husband. The children were asleep in the rooms across the hall. We lived in a remote country setting, the closest neighbors at a quarter mile. Everything was quiet, peacefully still.

I was thinking about how alone I was, yet not afraid, when a memory popped into my mind of a recurring dream from my childhood. I had often dreamt that I would be walking alone in different settings, but usually in the woods, when I would unexpectedly step off a cliff and find myself falling. Before I would hit bottom and die— but just as I thought I would die— I would awaken abruptly, my heart racing and feeling breathless. I never would die or be injured, but I always expected it. Now, with my husband no longer living in the house, I felt as if I were dreaming again, this time of falling and falling in slow motion— so slowly that I could see all the detail in the wall of the sheer cliff as I fell. I could see small roots and trees growing out of the wall and thought about grabbing them to stop my fall. All of this was happening in a microsecond. I realized just as quickly as I saw the little roots and handholds that falling was not so bad, that I wasn't hitting bottom, not ending up crippled or dead; I was ok. I was falling, and that's all. I relaxed and accepted the falling, and soon it was all over. I had survived.

The adult version of that dream has become a symbol for so much of my life that it is shocking to think it had its beginnings in my four-or five-year-old child-mind. I have needed to remind myself of its significance over and over: relax, let go, and when I'm falling, that's all it is— just falling. There have been and will be other hard times when I will fall again and be okay.

No angels came to save me from my fall. Angels would come from a source of power other than myself. I did not need to invoke the angels or any of God's powers: I invoked the strength that is within me to let go of fear and accept what is. Perhaps it is God-given strength, but I cannot say with certainty where it comes from.

Chapter 31 – Becka's Story

Journal Entries: Thursday, June 4, 1992 – 22:40

I will not believe it. You will not leave. If I believe it enough, never doubt then it will be true. You caught me off guard with your news of leaving, or I never would have heard what you didn't say. What you didn't say sent all the children in me into a panic. They're all asking me what to do— like I know. You are my anchor, crutch, mentor, advisor, mirror, friend, therapist, magic mind alterer, the voice the real me responds to, my life saver, my advocate, my reality-sounder, island in the middle of the sea, voice that brings me out of terror, holder, peace, hands of courage (beautiful, saving hands), steadfast support.Do you know how many times in the past six years your voice or hands pulled me out of the craziness?

You won't leave me in the madness— not now— remember, we're sisters. Oh, Sweet Jesus. I know why you're leaving now. When my sister called for my help before she committed suicide, I wasn't there for her. I told her I had my own problems and didn't need any more. Whatever the Divine Presence or scientific laws are, they despise me.

Friday, June 5, 1992 – 23:50

You are officially dead to me. I had the earring driven through my ear to join the others. You're on the side with Myra. Granma and Granpa are on the other side— the four people I loved and trusted who left me. Mom is not there, because I never trusted her. Chris is not there, because she's a hole in my heart pouring pus. I've been cursing God for weeks, because for months I prayed for mental/physical health and believed it would happen. Hail Mary Mother of God—novenas never known to fail—till now. Hours of the Rosary. Months of believing again there was someone who would not fail me.

The last weeks I've been asking "What else?" You mother-fucking-bastard of a whore for a mother. Now I know— I've lost you. I've finally got the answer to why. I looked at my kid pictures, and I was a prissy, pretty little bitch. I drove— probably enticed— my father into fucking me and fucked myself in the process. I lost my Granpa because he saw the truth about me. My Granma died for the love of him. I've lost you because I threw Gail out when she needed me most. I lost Chris because I don't deserve pleasure or an end to the loneliness, because of what I did to Leslie and Gail. After years, I finally figured out: don't get up, stay down.

You've got your own life— go live it and leave me to mine. It can't last much longer. I'm all out of cope, and I've learned— I won't get up. "Don't shut you out?" you say. If you loved me, would you really expect me to hang around and feel this pain?

Saturday, June 6, 1992 – 20:15

I ache for the touch of your hands. I have your voice— it's what puts me to sleep every night. The voice is yours, but the tape is cold — no interacting, no hugs, no hands. I keep trying to make you dead, but you are alive in me— your voice buried deep in my brain. The things you've taught me— we've fought through together— won't let me shut you out and end the pain.

I'm beginning to think I'm a masochist— one pain bumps into the next pain, and on and on. Is there no end to the pain? If there is, I could have found it with your help. Now— Oh for all the time I wasted holding back. I'll have your voice, your image, your teaching, your memory, but I won't have the safety when you hold me, the anchor when we hold hands, or the assurance that some- one— you— will go into the terror to find me and bring me back.

Sunday, June 7, 1992 – 13:35

At this point, I never want to see you again. I want to forget that you ever existed. I want to take the easy way out. To live through this with my heart open is going to be excruciating. But since I love you, is there any other way? Can I honor what you've taught me and gone through with me, and not stay present and open— go through the pain of losing you? No.

Monday, June 8, 1992 – 06:30

Well, I re-read the previous days' entries. I guess I can get all balled up in this leaving— notice I did not say abandonment— and waste what time we have left, or I can grow up and get on with it.

There are still so many things I want to work through with you. Even if we cleared a problem per session, there's not enough time. What am I worth to you? Are you going to write me, drop a card, call, visit if you're in town, let me know when you move back here? Are you my friend as well as therapist? I had so many plans for when I completed ther-apy— lunches, movies, coffee talks. I will never learn not to make plans for other people it seems. It's something I've done over and over, only to have them fly in my face— usually painfully.

Tuesday, June 9, 1992 – 18:40

These are the things I want to finish before you leave, under hyp-nosis, since it works faster for me. If you leave by July 1, we'll have seven more sessions. If you leave by August 1, we'll have eleven more.

Priority 1. Incest— worked through— obliterate the memories
Change attitude about one pain/loss/trauma after another.
Integrate child/adult/Becka
Stop negative head talk — become a worthy person
Accept Chris doesn't love or desire me— be peaceful about this
Termination – peace

Wednesday, June 10, 1992 – 19:00

It was like being torn apart leaving you after the session today. I hug after hug, but part of me knew there would be a last one. I can't imag-ine not feeling your arms around me, or not having you to turn to when I'm out of control, or the world's too much, or the past overtakes me. I've asked an awful lot from you, yet time after time you were there for me, providing freely your con- cern and expertise, calming the storms, providing perspec-tive, snatching me back from the dark. The last hug, I could feel you slip away; yet your voice is in my head, my love for you in my heart.

Thursday, June 11, 1992 – 21:15

I wrote some things that hurt you, I know, but it was the rage of a child having its security blanket snatched away; fear of a child expressed as rage to be left in the dark and so near the light; the bewilderment of an eleven year old left alone again with known and unknown fears; and the angry rage of not knowing if she's ready to face them down alone. The adult me, as well as the children, the eleven year old, and the teenager, love you. The adult me knows that this must be, and gives you all my love and best wishes— wanting only happiness for you. The children and the teenagers forgot that you are the one who gave them life and the strength to express their misguided anger. That doesn't mean they don't love, but as all chil-dren, they are self-centered. They're very new at this.

Friday, June 12, 1992 – 21:00

The thought kept going through my head today that you have those writings I did— the hateful ones— they're not real -- oh, the children's anger was real enough, but what they said was to hurt you back, like they imagine your leaving will hurt them. Children can be very unkind while at the same time they love you. Please don't take their meanness to heart. You are very dear to them, and they are afraid and confused.

As for my cutting you off— that's me— the Becka inside each one of the kids who didn't feel when something caused pain, denied the existence of the person, because they weren't there when she needed them to stop the pain in her heart. But when I shut my heart to you, I found you inside my heart behind the door loving me, caring for me with no intention to hurt or abandon me, even though we will be apart in distance. You're here with me, in my heart.

Saturday, June 13, 1992 – 23:00

I wanted to call you tonight— hear you say you still care, despite what I wrote. I love you— believe me I do! If you didn't give up on me when I committed suicide— surely you won't give up on me over this. You are the one that wanted me to let out anger— you opened the Pandora's box again. Now I'm afraid, and feel like crap over what I've done.

Sunday, June 13, 1992 – 11:00

I miss you already. It will be like a piece of my life is gone when you're not here. I just re-read what I wrote. You're in my head, my heart, and since I'm listening to your weight-loss tapes every night, I guess you're in my guts now, too.

Monday, June 15, 1992 – 19:00

Two more days and I'll see you. Will you turn away, or will you have recognized what I wrote as blind anger from children, and that the real me loves you? What are your plans for us? I want to work till the last minute, because you're the best, and the two of us are a productive team, even if I do have relapses. Anger is very new to me, and I'm afraid I've done the wrong thing with it, hurting the one I never meant to. I wish I could erase the words from your mind and heart. Forgive me— I am truly sorry. I'd give or do anything to take the words back. See why I'm afraid of the anger? It strikes out at the innocent and the vulnerable, and not its source. Are you sorry you saved my life now? Kathleen, please forgive me.

Tuesday, June 16, 1992 – 23:30

Three in the Incest Survivor's Group cracked like rotten eggs tonight. Their pain was unbearable. Their crying distraught. Their screams all-encompassing. Each scream, each sob, each throb of pain set off an echo in everyone in the room. While others nurtured, I left.

Chapter 32 - Therapist's Story

It was now two weeks since I had given Becka the news, and I was still feeling uncomfortable about leaving her— a portentous feeling. Dr. Feinberg called me to say that Becka was retaining water again, and suffering from the severe side effects of her medication, this time blackouts as well. She had passed out, fallen, and twisted her knee while on a visit to a patient's home. The doctor wanted to take her off the medication before something worse could happen, but Becka begged to be given more time to straighten out the problem.

Becka had promised Dr. Feinberg that she would cut back some on the Nardil and take the diuretics that had worked previously. She had promised to chart her weight and blood pressure, and report her status daily to the doctor's secretary. Dr. Feinberg wanted me to persuade Becka to admit herself to the hospital in order to withdraw totally from the Nardil. It was a session I knew would be difficult, since I had a lot of difficult things to cover with her.

Becka waited for me while I read her second week of journal entries, starting with June 10. I had already read the entries for the week of June 3, which she had left at the end of our last session. I wasn't at all surprised by the angry words; in fact, I both expected and hoped for her to be angry in some direct way. Writing her anger is as direct as Becka can be, just because of the kind of person she is, and what she had learned about anger in childhood. Here she was begging my forgiveness, when now I needed to praise her for her anger. It was the poignancy in her suffering for which I wasn't prepared. She had never expressed her pain before in a way that struck me quite as it did when I read these letters. It was not simply because I would be leaving, which was the focus of most of the entries. I suddenly felt Becka's weariness, as if it were my own. She was at the point that having a check bounce or a bill paid overdue could tip her over the edge of that fine line she was walking between life and the other side. I watched her, week by week, looking more beleaguered, having her energy sucked out by everyday life. Now she sat in the chair opposite me, looking somehow very small for all the nearly three hundred pounds of her, bloated and water laden. Her fists were doubled up tightly and wedged as usual between her thighs and the arms of the chair.

"You said a lot in these pages, Becka." I looked into her sea-green eyes and saw the hurt that still burned. She also had a look of fearfulness, and expectancy. "I know you're waiting to hear if I forgive you for the mean words— and I do. Yet, the request for forgiveness, strangely enough, isn't even necessary."

"What do you mean?"

"For two reasons. First, it is normal, natural and even healthy, for you to be angry. It's what you should be doing at this stage of dealing with letting go. I'm relieved that you allowed yourself to feel it as quickly as you did, and then to express it in such an appropriate way, by writing it out. It would even have been okay for you to say those mean words directly to my face, and I still would continue to love and accept you. It isn't your style to say it directly to someone like me, and that's acceptable, too. I can accept your anger. You have very good reason for it. And I'm very proud of you for writing it out."

"Well I really didn't mean all those nasty things I wrote," Becka said. "They just came out from the anger."

"That's what we do when we get angry … fight back. Can you let it be okay to have normal anger and to show it in the best way you know how— without hurting someone?"

"Didn't I hurt you though?" Becka asked.

"I am a person who understands where it is coming from, and I trust your true feelings. You see how powerful it is to have trust? It means you can express anger and know that you'll still be loved. I have to model that for you. The children in you didn't know that, but they're beginning to get it, aren't they?"

"Yes, I believe so. And I trust your love, too. I just don't want to hurt you because I care for you so much."

"I want to let you in on something, Becka, (the adult): be prepared for the kids to get angry some more. It's normal, and I can handle it."

"That brings me to the second reason you didn't need to ask for forgiveness. You see, it is I who should be asking you to forgive me for leaving you. I need to show you my true feelings as well, if I am going to be a model. I remember a long time ago, early on when we began to work together, you brought up the concern that you were reluctant to get attached to another therapist for fear of being left again. At that moment, I thought to myself that it was very unlikely I would ever move somewhere else, simply because I love living here so much. There was no way I could have foreseen my leaving.

"It might surprise you," I went on, "that I have struggled with the leaving myself. It is truly difficult for me to leave you. A big part of the reason I am apologizing to you is because I have *allowed* you to become dependent on me; it's perhaps not the best thing I could have done; we've already discussed that. But I really mean it when I say I will miss the chance to be your friend. I don't know most of my friends as well as I know you. The intimacy we have shared is a powerful bond. We've been through a lot together."

Becka was staring at our hands as I talked, tracing her fingertip over the back of my hand. She looked at me, then reached around my neck and hugged me. "I know you've been having a hard time in your own life, let alone all my troubles," she said.

"I have also tried to not burden you with my life problems. I believe I have shown you I can handle them without needing anything from you, even though you have been very compassionate. More than anything, I have hoped you have gotten some positive role modeling from the way you see me handle my own troubles."

"There's no doubt about that, Kathleen. I've gotten a great deal of my strength from watching you. Rest assured."

"Well, your journal entries show you made some excellent progress in that. You sat on your pity-pot, worked through some of the anger, and went on with recovery. But there is something else I want to tell you. Perhaps my anticipated leave is bringing about opportunities to say things we might not have said."

I paused to gather my thoughts, because what I was about to say was important, and I wanted it to come out right. "I have realized in the past weeks just how much I do care for you, and how it hurts to see you suffer. It's painful to see you go on having to cope with blow after blow, feeling defeated every way you turn. And it hurts me a whole lot to add to that suffering."

Becka was able to keep eye contact with me as I talked, an unusual circumstance. I went on, "What I have to tell you is a promise: that I will not physically step in if you attempt suicide, as I did before. I know you are still planning it. If it is your choice— if it reaches that point— I will not intervene, only because I love you. You need to understand that I do not want it to come to that, ever. You know I believe you can— and will— have a good quality of life. All I ask is that you do one of two things. Either don't let me know you're going to do it, or be prepared to convince me that you truly do not want me to stop you. I came to this because of the way you insisted you wanted to die the last time and you were very angry that I stepped in.

"I cannot tell you anything more than what I've already said about why you should go on living. I can help you put the past behind you, but I cannot make it disappear. I can encourage you to go on trying, one little step after another. I have run out of new things to try, outside of a better medication for you and continued attempts in our sessions, to make you whole. I want to take all your pain away, but I can only do what I have been doing, and let you know your life is worthwhile to me. I have a personal opinion about suicide for you, which I will also share with you now. I tell you this, and everything I have said so far, because I love you and want to be honest with you. I have thought for a long time that suicide, in your case, is the easy way out. You sought it the last time as the easiest way to get control over your existence— to not exist at all. I can make that judgement from a position of someone who is NOT deeply depressed and only imagines what it must be like. But somehow I have been able to glimpse it even for only a moment, enough to truly feel your exhaustion and despair. But I selfishly want you to keep fighting.

"At the same time, I do not want you to live that way. I care for you too much to want you to keep suffering. I want to help you improve the quality of your life, but if I cannot, perhaps someone else can. Something else can. I will not give up on you. I will do my best to keep you trying, too.

"We still have at least a couple of months, and we'll work to get all of your parts integrated before I leave. But that is the best I can do. I care for you too much to say I know what is best for you, or to stand in judgement of the quality of life you should go on living. You alone must decide that."

Looking into my eyes through her tears, Becka said very

quietly, "Thank you, Kathleen," and my eyes flooded up as well. "I know you can't make the past disappear, but if you could just make me not remember it, Like it was before. If I've worked it through, why do I have to go on remembering it? It's just too painful."

"Working it through, Becka, means that you won't feel the pain the way you have been. It will feel resolved, and then you can forget it normally. You will be able to put it behind you."

After another moment I said, "I have some other things to cover with you today— another confession, actually."

"Well you're just full of them today, aren't you," Becka smiled. Her energy was up from when we started.

"Yes, as I said, termination brings about all kinds of things— some hard, some rather nice. Remember you had mentioned to me once that you thought you might write an autobiography someday?"

"Yes . . . ."

"Well, I've been thinking that it could be really interesting and helpful to read your story from my perspective as your therapist as well, and that perhaps we could write a book about you togeth- er— after I move. It's just an idea, a possibility. We would have to consult a lot, over the phone, and even in person. And, we would have to make sure to carefully terminate the therapeutic relationship before I leave, so that we could start fresh."

Becka's eyes widened as I talked. She looked uncertain whether to believe what she was hearing, and then got a joyful grin on her face.

"You knew I would love the idea. Of course we'll do it." She looked up, as if envisioning what it would be like. "You'll write your part and I'll write mine, and we'll have to coordinate how to make it all hold together. I want to write my story and stuff every page of it down my father's throat."

"I'll hand you the pages," I laughed. "It does mean we have some work to do on those goals, however. We'll have you whole enough by the time I leave that you won't need another therapist, as long as you still have your group and Ruth. What I said about termi- nation still holds," I went on. "We have to treat this as a situation in which we may never see one another, and will have to work through the anger and the disappointment, the fears, and the frustration— both of us. We have to be ready to say goodbye and not leave loose ends. Remember the work you did on finishing business with Myra, and with Gail? You've got to do the same with me. And with Chris, too."

"Why Chris?" Becka asked.

"You need to mourn the loss of Chris to become healthier and stronger. Accepting that she is not available to you is like a death of someone you love. Even more important, breaking with her will show you are ready to handle responsibility for your own life—being separate."

"You're right, but I hate to admit it. Letting go of her is the hardest thing I have to do. I know I'm going to have to move out of her house eventually, but I just can't bear the thought of being away from her right now. Even if it isn't much, it's still something."

"I have just one more thing before we finish: I am asking you again to please, please, admit yourself to the hospital to come off the Nardil and get on a safer medication. Dr. Feinberg wants you to do it, and I do too. I can't stand seeing you suffer with the edema and dizziness and all the other problems it's causing."

"I'll think about it some more. I can't say right now."

Kathleen's Reflections

I worried about giving Becka the wrong impression with the promise I had made to her, yet it felt right to do it. I needed her to know that my only desire was to see her free of her suffering. Becka was worn out emotionally and physically. I could not know or predict an outcome for her, nor could I make the judgements about what made life quality for her. I also have a strong belief in being a real, sincere person with clients who have trusted me so deeply, even though I had fought in peer supervision over this and many other things I did, seen as unconventional.

I had had glimpses of what I thought was similar to Becka's experience. There had been times when the weight of my own problems had grown to such proportions that didn't think I could go on, either. Yet, I always had something to live for. I could always think of reasons why I needed to keep trying, my family not the least of them. I have felt the potential is always there for a better quality of life, and I can make it happen. The outcome for my efforts seems very worthwhile. But I know that my blues cannot be compared to chemical depression. For Becka, it must have been what I have felt when at my lowest, then multiplied tenfold, or much more.

Becka had lost sight of any goals worth achieving. One source of much satisfaction over the years had been her career. In her depressed state, she had convinced herself her career no longer mattered. The only thing left was a loving relationship with another woman, and this too she had talked herself into believing would never happen. She had thoroughly formed the conviction that life is not worth living if she has to live it alone, while also holding a belief that she didn't deserve a relationship. Even if she could escape her debilitating depression, she believed the pain of her history would never leave her. There was no way she could trust, in advance, in the benefits of a true resolution with her past.

Becka's life was now causing me to think about suicide in a new light. She was not dying of a terminal illness; nor was she endlessly burdened with physical and mental constraints, like my nephew; nor was she crazily out of control, like my mother with terminal brain cancer. She was in the grip of a mysterious mental and emotional condition we call depression; for her it was a combination of chemical imbalance and a barrage of life's problems keeping her down. She might appear to many to be wallowing in the pain of existence itself.

The medical community has the job of trying to minimize the physical and mental pain of people who suffer. Religious and social service groups have the task of helping disadvantaged people find a better quality of life. When they have done the best they can, and the person continues to suffer, who is to decide how much pain any person should bear? Are such medical and social service groups the ones to make decisions about what sort of quality is adequate for any given person to go on living? Can individuals be allowed to choose for themselves?

AIDS and other terminal illnesses have brought to the light even more poignantly the difficult question of euthanasia. Will medically assisted suicide only be granted to those who are terminally ill or severely restricted in a physically painful or vegetative existence? If so, what about those in deep mental and emotional despair? Shall they ever have a choice whether to continue living or elect medically assisted suicide as well? Is all depression curable? Should someone who has intermittent, ongoing bouts of severe depression be required to live through them when medication doesn't help, simply because "it will pass" — until the next time?

Have we evolved in medical technology so far beyond the

ethical issues that we are now too frightened to make the moral decisions that accompany that technological progress? Where will it all
lead, when we can clone humans for organ transplant replace-
ments? Shall we also clone new brains or genetically alter them,
seeking a new emotional chemistry?

I was developing some opinions about these issues in relation to Becka's circumstances. She was making me see them, almost from inside her skin. I had been trying to guide her toward a life
of greater satisfaction and independence in which she would have
more control. Her interpretation of control went on to include a
choice about her destiny, something most people don't consider is
theirs to make. Rather than embrace her control over her life, she
was choosing to control her not living. That it was a cowardly choice,
and still understandable, was the only honest opinion I could give
her.

I believed that Dr. Feinberg, Ruth, and I could help her, but I
could not force her to go on trying, nor do it for her. I could only encourage her toward the wholeness I believed could become a reality.
I let her know I respected her right to choose whether she wanted to
continue running against the odds or hope for better ones. It was
her right to choose, but that didn't make choosing suicide the right
choice.

Chapter 33 – Becka's Story

Journal Entries: Tuesday, June 23, 1992 – 22:30

Another black hole. More memories came up on the table today with Ruth. I keep thinking I've remembered them all, and then another one comes. They surface like bubbles. NO MORE. MAKE ME FORGET. YOU CAN. I KNOW YOU CAN.

Wednesday, June 24, 1992 – 19:00

The pain from the edema continues— my body bound by pain. I just cannot risk the depression by going off the Nardil. Too much at stake.

Thursday, June 25, 1992 – 21:00

Went to sleep at 7:30 pm Wed. night, awoke today at 5:30 pm. The pain and stiffness are gone. Still bone tired and sleepy. The edema is gone. Lost 11 pounds yesterday.

Friday, June 26, 1992 – 22:10

Up all night except half-hour naps with your tapes. Hallucinating my father in the room. Can't face work. The swelling is coming back. There's an ache in my heart for you. I wish I could cry— the tears would be better.

Saturday, June 27, 1992 – 19:30

I have one small shred of hope to cling to — that you really mean it about us writing my story together. It is a ray of hope from out of the darkness — that this will keep us in contact with each other. I think you do mean it. I dare not let myself start making plans for you.

Here it is, nearly the end of June, and you haven't heard when you're going, so it will at least be a couple more months. You're still here.

Sunday, June 28, 1992 – 14:00

I'm afraid to write anything, for fear of convincing myself this is really true— you are leaving— now or later. The tight pain in my chest goes with me everyday, but whenever I start to feel it— when I'm not actively pushing it down— it takes my breath away, and the fear is immense. In the back of my mind— no matter how great the terror— I knew you were there, even as I was dying. What a blessing for me and a burden for you. What were you thinking when I was in a coma? Were you there too? Am I strong enough to stand on my own without you at my side? Obviously, time will tell. Ready or not— there you go.

Kathleen, I love you for your support and constancy— gifts unknown in my life after Granpa, till you. Don't they say that when an infant can't see its loved object, it doesn't exist? Guess who's an infant?

Monday, June 29, 1992 – 22:40

Fell asleep while driving— hit the curb. I can't stand the pain in my back and legs. I am so tired.

Chapter 34 - Therapist's Story

Before Becka was to arrive for the next session, I got a call from Dr. Feinberg telling me she had hospitalized her that morning. She said that Becka had called in to give her progress report, and she admitted that she had fallen asleep at the wheel and driven off the road. Dr. Feinberg stated, "I believe she actually blacked out, as she did before. And I know she has had erratic sleep patterns, so it's possible she fell asleep. Either way, she has clearly reached a point where she can no longer survive her symptoms. I have insisted that she withdraw from the medications she has been taking. After we get a baseline she can be prescribed another form of antidepressant."

"Could you tell whether the accident may have been another suicidal gesture?" I asked.

"Of course that is a possibility. Either way, I managed to get her to agree to hospitalization, under the threat that she is now a danger to herself and others, and I would have to have her committed. I told her we would prefer that she spare us all that effort and agree to go, and she did. She has found a ride out to St. Mary's Hospital by someone on the staff where she works. I had to admit her out there, since there are no beds available in the small unit we have here, and she needs to be in a locked unit."

Dr. Feinberg went on, "Becka was concerned about her appointment with you, so I assured her that I would inform you of these events, and how to reach her. She ought to be admitted by two o'clock . I said you could call her, or she can call you. I thought it might suit your schedule better if you call at your convenience."

"Yes, thank you. I'm greatly relieved that she's in the hospital, and very hopeful that this will go well. What do you expect from the detoxification, as far as the chance of dropping back into depression?"

"It's very hard to know. Everybody is different. I just know that she could accidentally injure or kill herself, or possibly someone else, and I feel much better about getting her off the Nardil. She'll have some ups and downs, most likely. She could also breeze through it. Let's stay in touch."

During the time that Becka would have been in session with me, I called her at the hospital. I heard the voice of the frightened eleven-year-old on the verge of crying.

"Kathleen, oh, Kathleen. Please get me out of here. I can't stand to be locked up. The doors are locked. Can you come and get me?"

"Becka, listen to me. I want you to rely on that strong adult part of you, the one that knows how to handle a crisis. Get together with her where you belong. Can you do that?"

There was a long pause, and then she spoke in the adult voice, "Yes. We're all together, and safe here. I have to admit I don't like being locked up, but I know it's something I have to do. I could have killed someone in my car yesterday when I fell asleep. I guess I was lucky. There can be something good even amidst the bad things that happen. I wasn't hurt, and no one else was, either. Just an ugly dent in my bumper to remind me of my stupidity."

I was relieved to hear that Becka could keep herself intact enough to be rational, given the stress she was under.

"Now listen carefully, Becka. You're going to have a job while you're there, of keeping all the parts of you as one strong whole, so you can recover as a whole. You have to be lovingly firm with yourself, and do whatever they tell you is necessary to detoxify— and ask for something when you need it. The people there want to help you. You know that as a nurse yourself— that they will help if you ask for what you need."

"I know. I have to ask to smoke every blessed cigarette. It's like a prison in here. How long is this going to go on? Will you come to see me? I need you so much now."

"I'm sure this is hard, and you're scared about how it will go. I want you to keep a positive attitude that it will go swiftly and easily. There is no reason for depression, because you are making such an excellent recovery. Remind yourself that you are strong, and you are going to make it— all the way to the top. Remember: what you think about, you bring about. So keep your thoughts positive. That's your job as the adult— to take care to keep all the parts from freaking out. They don't need me— they need you to be strong for yourself."

By Friday, Becka was into her third day of being off all medications. I found her smoking in a courtyard outside as part of the locked hospital unit. It was open to the sky, but surrounded with two-story brick walls. There was a small area of grass with trees and shrubs planted tastefully along the wall to detract from the austere, prison-like feeling to the court. She was sitting at a picnic table with other patients and a staff member, also smoking.

She got up and limped over to me, wrapping her big soft arms around my neck. Then she pulled me over to the table to introduce me to everyone. I was amazed at the level of her energy and enthusiasm, as she chattered to the others. It was as if the old Becka had been resurrected again, much like each time she had started on antidepressants.

"Walk with me around the courtyard," Becka said. "I'll finish this cigarette, and then we can go inside where we can have some privacy. Can you stay for a while? I am so glad you came. It's kept me going knowing that you would come. I hate being so far away from home. I want to get out of here. I just hate being locked up and having to ask to even smoke a cigarette. I can't eat the food— it tastes metallic to me. I've lost eleven pounds since Tuesday when I weighed in."

She went on at such a pace that it was clear she was heading uphill, rather than down into depression. I knew that change could also signal a swing to the other side at any time. The laws of physics seem to apply to moods for people like Becka: what goes up, comes down; and the higher it goes, the further it has to fall.

"You certainly seem in a good mood, in spite of not liking it here," I said.

"I feel much better than I did the first two days. At least today the food doesn't taste as metallic, and without so much water, it isn't as painful to walk or stand. I want to get out of here as soon as possible. Dr. Feinberg said I might have to stay two weeks, and that's what I told them at work, but I don't see why I have to stay that long."

"It's because detoxifying can take an unknown amount of time, and you can't start on another medication until you're free of this one."

"Dr. Feinberg isn't even treating me here. She doesn't have privileges, so these doctors don't know anything about me. They just give you a room, read you your rights, and tell you to keep quiet.

What a joke! This isn't treatment."

"It's medical, not psychological. You're in a safe place where people are keeping an eye on you. You can rest and be free from the stress of daily life, while your body adjusts to the chemical changes it has to go through. That's all Dr. Feinberg wanted, and she couldn't do any more than that if you were in the hospital nearer home."

"Yes, but this place is too far for friends to come and visit me," Becka protested.

"Have you heard from friends?"

"Yes. Two women from the group called, as well as the group leader. She said she would come to see me tomorrow, isn't that sweet of her? Terry called, too. My boss, Georgina, left work on Tuesday to drive me over here. And you won't believe who came yesterday. It's someone else you saw for incest history a long time ago. I didn't even know that you knew her. She asked me to tell you hello, and that she's doing really well. She gave me a lot of encouragement to keep working on this."

"You're doing well, then, in spite of the extra distance. And you find out that you have a lot of love and support when people will go the extra mile for you. You see, Becka? Many people love you and want you to keep up your faith that you will get your health and your life together, and be happy. I feel very confident that you'll be glad you came here to detoxify, and you'll be more comfortable on some other form of medication. Let's expect the most positive results that are realistically possible. This time period may be the most important transition you have been through yet."

A woman who appeared to be in her mid-fifties approached us along the sidewalk and said to Becka, "Is that your girlfriend or your sister?" She was wearing a bright pink bathrobe over a white tshirt and denim jeans, and large, fluffy pink bedroom slippers. Her dyed blond hair was matted to her head, the dark roots of her natural color exposed.

"This is my therapist, Pauline," Becka said, "and I'm having a private conversation with her right now."

"I don't mind," said Pauline as she raised her nose in the air and sauntered away. "I was just gonna ask if she'd like a cigarette. You probably didn't give her one, you bitch."

Becka looked at me and rolled her eyes back. "I just don't want to stay any longer than I have to. It's creepy around here at night. There's one woman in here who won't sleep at all, just screams. They put her in the quiet room at night so she won't disturb the rest of us. I don't sleep much myself."

"Let's go to my room where we can have privacy. I'm having a little trouble with being locked up. It's the walls. This place is a lot bigger than the closet was, but the panicky feelings come back when I think about not being able to get out of here. It's especially bad at night, staring at the walls when I hear that patient screaming in seclusion. Maybe hypnosis will help me handle it better."

Becka eased herself into a comfortable position on the edge of her bed, grimacing as she supported one leg on a chair. She offered the remaining chair to me. She opened her bedside table drawer and took out a worn spiral-bound tablet of lined paper. It looked like it had once been very thick, with ragged little strips of paper sticking out through the metal spiral. I recognized the paper as the same on which she kept her journal notes and periodically gave to me to read. There were numerous sheets with dogeared corners tucked into the back of the tablet.

"This is my journal and my accounting system," she said. "If I lost this, I'd be in trouble. It's got my whole life in it. Before you do the hypnosis, I want to ask you if you will help me with something else, too. I need your advice. I've been working on my budget, trying to figure out how I'm going to pay for everything. I have some checks coming from work, which I've asked Georgina to deposit. But I can't quite make ends meet right now."

She opened the tablet to a specific page and held it out to me. It was a list of her expenses and her resources. I glanced at it briefly. "So what is your question?"

"I'm thinking about writing to Lee, my mother's husband, and asking to borrow money from him. Mom says she will not take any money from him, because it's just not right. She has sent me some of her savings to help out, but she won't ask Lee for money, even if it is to help me. But I know he has it, and I believe he would lend it to me gladly. I don't want him to give it to me. I'll pay it back. I was thinking about writing to him and proposing a loan of about $1000, with interest. What do you think? Should I go around my mother like that?"

"You told me when you met Lee that he offered to help you in any way he could, didn't he?"

"Yes, even with money. And this may sound strange, but I think it made my mother jealous that he showed so much concern for me. He seemed very sincere in caring about me, and offered to

have me come for a visit at his place, just as soon as I can. He said
he would buy me a ticket whenever I'm ready. I think it's hard for him
to think of me going— like his daughter— you know, my step-sister
killing herself. Maybe it's his way to make up for her."

"I think you could write a businesslike letter to him, with a
sound proposal for how and when you'll pay him back, yes. I see
nothing wrong with it. You could also tell your mother in a separate
letter that you have taken the initiative to ask him for help as a business transaction. That way you won't be splitting them. By the way,
have you talked to your mother since you were in here?"

Becka changed her position again, and grimaced some
more. "No. I don't want her to know. I will write to her though, and
maybe I can figure a way to tell her. By the time she gets it, I'll be
home. Can you also give me some suggestions under hypnosis for
fast healing? And some help with the pain in this knee? I sure need
it. They offered me a painkiller and sleep medicine, but it seems like
that could interfere with the detox, so I turned them down. " Becka
stretched out on the bed, and I covered her with the blanket. "I might
fall asleep," she said. "In case I do, I'll just say goodbye to you now."

Kathleen's Reflections

*I left the hospital feeling relieved that Becka's withdrawal
was progressing well, and so far she had not become depressed. At
the same time, I knew she had a long way to go and could sag back
into depression, or plunge into it at any time. It was so good to find
her feeling better that I wanted to cling to all the optimism I could
muster. I had to consciously fight the tendency to expect her to be
knocked down again as soon as she was up, since that was the pattern to which we had both grown accustomed.*

*During the previous weeks, even as she had been trying to
accept my planning to leave, she had been making strides in dealing
with the incest issues. The surfacing of memories about the abuse
was critical to helping her get resolution with the past and gain acceptance that it was behind her, and most definitely not her fault. In
time she would build her self-esteem and master the painful memories naturally.*

*Becka had made some important connections to people in
her therapy group and the group leader. There were a few women
who would remain supportive of her, as well as being friends with*

whom she could do things socially. She had successfully handled the loss of one of the group's leaders after the first cycle of eight weeks, which had given her some practice before the time came for me to leave. She was certainly more deeply attached to me than the group therapist, but in one way, we couldn't have planned it better that she would have to deal with a loss at that time.

The realization of how similar her incest experiences were to those of other people in her group had come as both a surprise and a relief to Becka. It was helping her chance at a full recovery to be with other women at different stages of the process. Since she was much further along than some others who were just beginning to remember or talk about what happened, she could play the role of guide and compassionate supporter. That in itself would help to bolster her self-worth. The terror of the flashbacks and the nightmares was largely behind her, and certainly not new. She had been through a powerful catharsis in her psychodramatic exorcism. Once she returned to her group, she would be able to continue to release her anger. She was very close to the next stage— the stage of forgiveness and acceptance, and I would work with her intensively to achieve that in the time remaining. I noticed that she wasn't talking through her gritted teeth any more when she made reference to her father. Once she reached that point, I believed she would find inner peace with her past.

Quality of life being so dependent on beliefs as it is, a major task remained to strengthen the new, positive beliefs Becka had been creating. I was counting on her relationships with new friends in her group to help with that, as well as the plan to get her to write her story for publication. I knew the process of writing it would be additionally healing and help her attain further closure. All of these plans still hinged on the success of achieving a balance in her body chemistry, whether through another antidepressant or some other means.

Chapter 35 – Becka's Story

Journal Entries: Saturday, July, 1992 – 18:30

What an incredible relief to be getting rid of the pain and swelling — the fluid. And you, my breath of life, always there with such wisdom and good judgement. I believe the hypnosis is working again. These walls don't feel so dreadful now— must have been something you said, but I don't remember anything except "relax." You must say that word as the key to make me go under. Oh, I do remember seeing this beautiful, deep green light. I didn't hear you leave. I slept better last night than I have in months.

I'm beginning to feel almost normal again, after having you and Ruth visit me. The food doesn't have that metallic taste so much now — at least some things don't. I think I'll be ready to go home soon. Dr. Feinberg doesn't want me to work for a few more weeks, but I've got to have something to do. I need to make money.

Food Intake, July 4, 1992
cals./grams
toast 75/1 soda
90/0 fish 360/15
roll 60/1
potatoes 160/5
soda 90/1
Total: 835/23

Saturday, July 4, 1992, letter

Dear Mom,

By the time you receive this, I will be home from the hospital. I decided to be admitted, and get off the antidepressant that was causing me so many problems. It got to the point where I wasn't able to function safely any more, and I figured I should do it for my patients if I couldn't do it for myself. It is still scaring me that I could get really depressed again any time, but so far I am not.

I have been trying to get my life in order while passing the long hours here in the hospital. I am trying to find a way to cover my expenses. My insurance will not pay for all of this visit, and I am still paying monthly for the hospital stay from two years ago.

I know you do not have your own income, but I also know that Lee has plenty of money. I have taken the liberty of asking him for a loan, which I can pay back a little each month. I have offered to pay him interest at a rate that he can decide. You may not approve of this, but it is the only resort I have left. And Lee was very kind to offer his help when he was here. I wouldn't do this if I wasn't cornered.

I don't think we will be seeing much of each other for a while, so I will tell you some things in writing. I have been working in therapy on a mountain of anger that has been inside me for most of my life. A lot of that anger is still toward you. You came here to go to counselling with me, and that seemed to help some. But you made promises to me then that you have not kept, just like it always was. I cannot trust you—my own mother. I am too disappointed in you to bother to try any more. You're not going to change, even if you want to.

I'm finding out how hard it is to change, even when I know what it is I'm trying to change. But you don't even have a clue what you would need to change in order to be a real mother to me. You want me to forgive you for the past—for leaving me, for taking the beatings and the sexual abuse from Robert in your place, and for not having the guts to rescue me and Roy from him, and for not being the kind of mother I have needed. Just because you had it rough, I'm supposed to forgive you.

You wanted me to give you a chance to start over—to be there for me now. Well, I gave you a chance. We hugged and kissed and cried when you left. You made your promises, and you kept them for a couple of weeks. And when you got tired of phoning like you said you would, your calls got erratic—not every Sunday, nor even every week. You asked fewer questions, showed less interest in me, and spent your time talking about how wonderful life is with your new husband.

Meanwhile, life for me has only gotten harder. But you don't want to hear about that. You don't want to know about the many times my father raped me, beat me, and locked me in the closet. You don't want to face how pathetic you really are. I know you can't change, because you won't look at yourself honestly and see what you are. I see the truth now. I give up on you. I have too much to do to take care of my daily survival, and I can't count on you for help with it.

If Lee is willing to lend me money, I will make my business arrangements with him only. Please stay out of it.
Becka

Saturday, July 4, 1992, letter

Robert,

You have ruined my life. You have deprived me of the sanity and peace of mind that I deserved to have. Because of you I have not been able to have healthy, trusting relationships, or normal, satisfying sex— and now, any kind of life at all. I live with constant nightmares and horrid memories of the disgusting, perverted things you did to me. I live with the results of your sickness, while you go on enjoying life, as if you never did any of it. All you had to do was go to confession and you're free. What good is it for me to confess? Should I confess that I was innocent— a little child, minding my own business?

You had no right to do what you did to me. You have no right to call yourself a father of any kind. You are a monster— a perverted and sick beast. You are not worthy of the air you breathe every day, or the ground you step on. I cannot forgive you for the misery and destruction you have caused in my life.

Every day for me is filled with the flashes of memory of you, and that is painful. My life has become meaningless— hopeless— because of the things you did to me, and the twisted ideas you put into my head. You are dead to me. I never want to see you or hear from you again. Maybe God does forgive you, but I can't. It is too hard to believe any worthy human would do what you did.

Becka (I am NOT Rebecca Ann)

Chapter 36 - Therapist's Story

I got a call from Becka on Monday afternoon, saying she was going to be released the next morning and needed a ride home. She wondered if I could come for her. I was surprised to hear they were letting her go.

"Who is releasing you, Becka?" I asked.

"The staff doctor here at the hospital. He thinks I might as well go home. I'm feeling fine— the symptoms are all gone, and he thinks the Nardil is pretty well out of my system."

"What about Dr. Feinberg— does she agree with that decision?"

"She said she's going to call you. I suppose she agrees, but I don't care, as long as I get to go home. Can you help me -- come and pick me up tomorrow? I hate to ask you, but I don't want to bother Georgina again. She's got a lot of people to manage, and she shouldn't be running after me. I know you're busy, too, but I thought I'd at least ask."

I was actually glad she asked me, rather than Chris. I didn't doubt that Chris would go if Becka asked, but I knew the burden on her was far more than she had bargained for. I also didn't want Becka to have reason to feel encouraged by anything Chris might do for her.

"I can come in the morning, Becka. I just think it's too soon for you to leave the hospital, and I don't understand what is going on. You've only been there a week. Let's plan that I will be there around 10 a.m., but I am going to check on a few things."

"Are you going to try to make me stay longer?" Becka asked.

"I don't have any authority to do that, Becka, but I am going to try to find out what the doctor there thinks of your present status; that's all."

"Well, Dr. Feinberg said I would have to agree to be in touch with her and you or Ruth every day. She wants me to call in a status report every day, and to agree to take another antidepressant if I need it. She is making me promise, and I said I would."

As soon as we hung up I called to page Dr. Feinberg. She confirmed the plan Becka had described, but also said that she had not been consulted about the decision by the attending physician. She said that was not uncommon. I asked her if she thought Becka ought to be leaving this quickly, and she said she would have preferred that she stay another week. She suspected Becka had been pushing to leave because of the financial strain of a longer stay.

Becka had a good case; she was free of the symptoms from the Nardil and was not showing any signs of depression. The unit staff had said she could take over and start running the unit for them, she was doing so well.

I was ambivalent. Becka's signs of recovery were excellent, but I knew she wasn't out of the woods when it came to depression. I knew her better than the staff at the hospital, even better than Dr. Feinberg. I felt very uneasy about her being on her own. Becka's doctor at the hospital was not eager to talk to me about her release, nor anything else that pertained to her. He said she was doing very well and couldn't see that she was a danger to herself or anyone else. She wanted to go home, said she would continue several more days off work, and would stay in touch with her regular doctor. That was good enough for him.

The next day I went for Becka as planned. Through the hour-long ride home, she talked cheerfully and almost constantly, skipping from one subject to another with exuberance. I wanted to be positive along with her, since that was what I always told her to do, yet I didn't trust that her state could last. She was too high, too energized, almost manic.

"You know, Kathleen," Becka said, "I had time in the hospital to think about a lot of things, and I realized something very important. It finally clicked with me, even though it's something you have told me. It was like a lightening bolt struck me on the head, and I got it. And it was such a powerful moment that thinking about it since— or telling you— isn't nearly as potent as it was when it happened. Do you know what I mean?"

"I believe I do— rather like a mini-satori, as they call it in Zen practice. It's like a little piece of enlightenment, on a small scale."

"Yeah, I felt enlightened. You're going to think it was silly, because it's so simple— and so obvious. I really got it that my father is
a very sick man. That all my suffering has been because there is
something really wrong with him, and not me. I didn't make those
things happen. My kids all believed whatever he said to me. I didn't
have any way of knowing anything else. You see -- now, you've told
me that many times, but this time it was like all the kids finally heard
it too. You know? Does that sound crazy or am I just losing it for sure
now?"

"No, I think it's quite normal. It's part of the process of recovery. I'm delighted to hear it. It means you've moved through yet another phase toward becoming whole."

"Well, I realized some other things, too. Like that I don't
need a mother like my mother. I'm better off to get it together without
her. I feel like I've started letting go of her, or at least of needing her. I
have to stop planning how other people are going to be, or what
they'll do. I feel much stronger somehow. I know much more clearly
now that I have to do the nurturing for myself. I can't get what I need
from somebody else alone."

"It sounds like this hospital visit has been good for you in
many ways. I am impressed. Do you see it that way?"

"I have to admit it's true. As much as I didn't want to go and
didn't like it there, it was the right thing. But still, Kathleen, I just don't
understand why life is so hard. And why it doesn't seem to be that
way for everybody— just some of us."

Before taking Becka home, we stopped at Dr. Feinberg's
office for a brief, three-way consultation. Becka made her commitment to both of us that she would handle her time as if still in the
hospital. She would stay away from work for at least another week;
report her blood pressure, weight, and mental status to Dr. Feinberg's office daily; and call or see me and/or Ruth every day. She
had to make daily reports to us about her level of moods, and agree
to take the new medication at the first sign of her mood dropping.
She also agreed to report her plan of activities for staying occupied
every day.

Kathleen's Reflections

I stayed up late that night wondering to myself and out loud with my husband, about the mysterious nature of life— a favorite topic of mine. Such thinking involves asking a lot of questions and trying to answer myself, knowing there are no answers to be found. Why is life so strange? Are the things that happen part of a grand design, do they happen randomly, or do we unconsciously, even pre-consciously, choose them? Does God have a plan, or do we just grow this way and that, like crystals? Are humans being tested with suffering, and if so, why are some people tested more severely (seemingly) than others?

Was it coincidence that the events of my own life repeatedly tested my relationship with Becka, whether or not I would stand by her, through whatever she had to face? I was coached in my own super-vision to back off, for being co-dependent or having countertransfer-ence. Most therapists have several clients in desperate need much of the time, yet they don't do the hand-holding I had done.

Was I going too far in my concern for her? There were two therapists in my peer-supervision group who believed that Becka had a personality disorder, that I was overly involved with her problems, and that I was being used and wasting my time. I felt differently. Per-sonality disorder may have been the right diagnosis, but I did not see reason to give up on someone because of a diagnosis. I cared about Becka as another human being, not as if a mechanical therapist who followed rules from a textbook. I believed that I had to deal with her honestly, and each of my responses was honest, however faulty at times from over-identification. Further, I have always believed that if I could do anything during my entire lifetime to help even one person improve their quality of life, then my time and efforts would have been worthwhile.

I had invested a great deal of love and energy in Becka; I wanted to succeed in helping her improve the quality of her life. I knew I had wanted to cure my mother with love and it didn't work; and I still believed love made a difference. I believed I could use my own history positively, albeit not flawlessly, to help Becka.

Becka's plans for her death gave her a sense of control over her life. I couldn't blame her for wanting the control. I tried to guide her to the life matters which she might control.

When clients ask, "What am I to do?" I have some answers.

I can say, "You must grieve; you must deny; you must get angry; you must forgive; you must learn; you must accept; you must become stronger to live with your existential anxiety." And if they have enough internal fortitude, they do these things; and we call it recovery. Some recover well; others cannot.

My conclusions for Becka were not profound. I could not offer any concrete, reliable answers, other than what faith could provide. I believe people turn to religion because rationale and science do not provide enough answers. Religion offers at least something to believe in, something to give hope and to assuage the generalized anxiety of not knowing any answers. I concluded that the answers I sought are not to be known just now, that we humans are not technologically or evolutionally ready to know. Someday, perhaps, we will evolve to know more answers.

Life is NOT fair. Life is just the way it is, and that is all. I would have to live with unanswered questions. I chose the option to live my life by moral and ethical codes in which I do my best to do no harm, and attempt to improve quality of life for myself and those around me, to the best of my ability. It's a morality evolved out of Christianity, as I was taught, but that's about all I could say for it with respect to religion.

Chapter 37 – Becka's Story

Journal Entries: Wednesday, July 8, 1992 – 21:00

I found this poem by Galway Kinnell a long time ago. I keep reading it, finding some strength from its words:

Wait, for now.
Distrust everything if you have to.
But trust the hours.
Haven't they carried you everywhere, up to now?
Personal events will become interesting again.
Hair will become interesting.
Pain will become interesting.
Buds that open out of season
will become interesting.
Second-hand gloves will become lovely again;
their memories are what give them
the need for other hands.
And the desolation of lovers is the same:
that enormous emptiness carved
out of such tiny beings as we are asks to be filled;
the need for the new love is faithfulness to the old.
Wait.
Don't go too early.
You're tired. But everyone's tired.
But no one is tired enough.
Only wait a little and listen:
music of hair,
music of pain,

music of looms
weaving all our loves again.
Be there to hear it, it will be the only time,
most of all to hear the flute of your
whole existence, rehearsed by the sorrows,
play itself into total exhaustion.

Friday, July 10, 1990 – 02:30
I cannot wait any longer. I am tired. That's all I've been doing the past six years is waiting. There is no more wait left in me. You cannot know if you have never been to this hopeless place of depression. To wait any more would be waiting for another miraculous drug, waiting for another side effect, waiting for Chris to throw me one more tidbit of her time— or one more wonderful smile, wait- ing for memories to die, waiting for Momma to come back, waiting for the kids in me to grow up, waiting for the pain to stop, waiting to find a purpose when there is no purpose.

My whole existence has been nothing more than a discordant melody, carried through time and space at the whim of the wind, and is now played into total exhaustion.

Chapter 38 - Therapist's Story

The call came around one in the afternoon. It was Ruth. "Becka isn't doing very well. She came for her appointment this morning and said she is going to kill herself tonight. She's really low and seems resigned to do it. I don't know what to do. I suggested we call and talk to you."

I sighed deeply and took some time to think. The news was shocking, and yet it wasn't. Becka's recovery was going so fast that it had been almost too difficult to believe it was true. Staying alive was a constant struggle for her. Nobody can know what it is like in the blackest, darkest of places that seem to be the jurisdiction of people with unrelenting clinical depression. Oh, yes, I've been depressed and even wanted to die at times. But being with her through these dark years had taught me respect for the endurance required to sustain life in the face of such enduring depression.

"But she has been doing so incredibly well," I said. "This was just a temporary reprieve, I guess; and who knows what effect all the changes in medication have been causing. She must have crashed. Or, maybe she was planning to kill herself all along, was making her final arrangements and goodbyes, and had it planned for as soon as she got out of the hospital. That could account for her apparent relief and high spirits. Maybe she has been disguising her real intentions for days, stringing us along. What if this was all a huge plan she concocted— maybe even before she went in the hospital?" I was musing out loud. "Is she just not able to try any more?"

Ruth answered, "I don't think she will try any longer. Her body is almost without any spark of life, even now. The work I did with her on the table seems to have produced no change. I really tried. Will you talk to her? I have another client coming soon, but this is important. What should I do?"

"Of course I'll talk to her. If I can't get her to change her mind, you know what I have to do, don't you?"

"What do you mean?" Ruth asked with uncertainty.

"I have to let her go. I gave her my word. I told her I wouldn't stand in her way another time."

Ruth spoke very quietly now, "That's a tough one. But what about me?"

"Well, you have no such commitment with her, do you?" "Not in so many words. But I have felt the pain through her body— her whole being— for so long I can understand her desire to leave. Perhaps I should do something, though."

"Absolutely. You must do what will make you feel right about it within yourself, whatever that is. I just know that I must release her if I cannot persuade her one last time to stay. But you can call Dr. Feinberg, Chris, and the police, although I don't know what they can do."

"She told me she's going go to sleep in her car in a garage she rented. She also said she has put in a call to Dr. Feinberg, but it's to say goodbye. She absolutely insists that her saying goodbye to us is not a plea for help to stop her."

"I know," I said. "I've been over that many times before with her. Why would somebody who doesn't want intervention tell people she is going to kill herself? It makes no sense, and yet she claims she just doesn't want to leave without saying goodbye to the people she loves. What about Chris? She would try to stop her."

Ruth replied, "I tried to call the house but got the answering machine. It's sort of messed up and not answering properly. Maybe it took a message, but it seems Chris isn't home."

"Well, Ruth, I can't tell you what to do, or even advise you, other than to say you must do what you need to do so you can live with your decision. It's a damned hard one, to be sure. I've already given it a tremendous amount of thought. I'm sorry. I should talk to Becka now. Let's talk again after I speak with her."

"Yes, I'll see to it. Here's Becka."

Becka's voice was very small, lacking any energy at all, the way I had heard it many times before. But this time was somehow different. It was more like the period when she was a zombie. She wasn't offering anything herself, so I had to start.

"Becka . . . Ruth tells me you're going to take your life tonight. I don't want you to do that. You know that don't you?"

"I can't wait any longer. I've waited long enough."

"But you've been doing so well. You're almost there. We've
seen such a bright light ahead this last week . . ."

"There's only dull grey now. I don't see any light. Everything
is flat."

"You sure sound flat," I responded. "You sound terrible. It's
hard for me to believe that just yesterday you were doing so well, so
confident. What happened?"

"I don't know. It just came on last night, all of a sudden. I just
knew it was time to go. I've been totally calm about it, certain that it's
the right thing to do. I just started doing what needs to be done. It
took me most of the night, but I'm just about ready." Her voice was
devoid of emotion.

"I can't believe this!" I cried. "I just can't believe that things
could turn around so fast. Becka, I don't want you to go." I was crying silently, tears streaming down my cheeks.

"I know. But I have to. That's all."

I didn't know where to go next. I wanted more time, some
clever idea to pop into my head, some convincing words, some
glimmer of hope. Nothing came.

"Oh, my dear, dear Becka. I'm going to miss you so. This is
very hard for me. I knew it would be. Remember I asked you to convince me that telling me you are going to kill yourself is *not* a plea for
help? I need to be convinced now."

Becka's voice became stronger, and firm. "There isn't anything I can tell you except that I absolutely do not want you or anyone else to step in to stop me. I just wanted to hear your voice one
last time. I came to my appointment with Ruth because I wanted to
be touched, one last time. I am going."

"But what about calling Dr. Feinberg? Why did you call her?
You wouldn't tell her if you didn't want anyone to stop you."

"I feel like I owe it to her to call. She has tried, and I want her
to know it's not her fault. She really tried."

I wanted to ask Becka if she felt she herself had really tried,
but I knew she would be hurt by that, and angry. She had tried. I
could not say she hadn't. I just wanted her to try again.

"That decision is not rational, Becka. You don't go telling all
your therapists and doctor that you are going to kill yourself tonight if
you don't want them to intervene."

"I guess I'm not rational then," she said flatly.

I went on about it a while more, and she seemed content

228

just to let me talk. Finally I asked her what she was going to do next. She said she had to do some last errands, and then she would go home and leave her message for Chris, who was away from the house all day until evening. By then it would be too late for her to do anything. She assured me she had left no stone unturned this time, and it would work. She reminded me she could not afford another missed attempt.

"I know, Becka. And I haven't forgotten my promise to you. You clearly trust that I will keep it, even though it hurts so much I can barely stand it. I will remain bound by my word, because I can't bear for you to be in any more pain, either. But can't you please try one more time with a different medication to lift that depression?"

Becka answered, still without any emotion or change in tone, "I have to leave." It was so emphatically final, without expression.

I tried one more stall. "What time will you be home this afternoon?" "Can I call you then?"

"Yes. I'll be home by four." "Will you answer the phone?"

"Yes. At four o'clock. I can't lie to you."

I spoke to Ruth again, enough to summarize what we had said. Meanwhile, she had decided to put in an emergency call to Dr. Feinberg.

I hung up the phone and sat frozen in the chair, numb from my scalp to the soles of my feet, as if I had no body at all. But on the inside I burned. My mind churned erratic thoughts and memories. My family members, somewhat aware of what was happening, gathered around me one at a time to offer some comfort. I couldn't respond to them. I was groping for some way to deal with what was about to happen, the position in which I had put myself.

My compassion for Becka was so intense that I wept most for the suffering she was still having to endure, the outrageousness of her position, knowing she is going to take her own life . . . tonight. Tonight. This day. Becka gone. Forever. No more chances to help turn her life around. What life? What are her chances for quality of life? She is a woman who holds beliefs that she has nothing to live for— a woman who battles with severe depression, who fears facing every day the memories of her father having sex with her, demeaning and abusing her. A woman who weighs three hundred pounds, a lesbian obsessed by unrequited love who believes that life can't be any life at all without someone to cherish, to hold, to cuddle, to sleep next to, to talk to, to play with. A woman who is reclusive, a charming

conversationalist who is obviously excellent in her profession, yet
has lost sight of any goals or desires to continue with it. A woman
who was wrongfully treated and twisted into a nightmarish state of
undeserved guilt and worthlessness. A woman who believes that
everyone she loves leaves her. A woman who cannot find joy in life
just to listen to music, to read a book, to walk in the woods, or to eat
a piece of rich chocolate cake. A woman who will do none of these
anymore. Never. The words made no sense. They sounded very
strange to me. Gone. Dead. None of them made any sense.

Becka was choosing consciously about not living. It was her
life, her choice. She wasn't choosing dying, rather she was choosing
not living— in what she had experienced as hell on earth. And what
could I tell her to live for? That I truly cared for her, that I wished her
peace in this life, that I wished her a fulfilling relationship with a lover
meant nothing, because wishes are made of paper. Life is NOT fair.
No matter how undeserving of suffering any person can be, no one
is so special as to be exempt. Suffering strikes randomly and everywhere on the planet.

The shock and my denial made it difficult to think clearly. I
would try one more time to persuade Becka to stay when I called her
at four o'clock. I had never said I wouldn't try as long as she was still
alive. But what could I say to her that I hadn't already tried?

The four o'clock conversation was the last one we had. I
begged her again, and then once more. I sobbed and let her feel my
grief because it was real; it was who I really am. I reminded her of
the book we were to write, that I needed her to write her part, that it
would sustain our friendship between the miles. When the answer
came again, "I have to leave," I just wept into the phone. Now I was
the one not letting go.

"I'll still write it, Becka. I promise to tell your story and to see
that people read it." I sputtered and sobbed as I continued talking to
her. "This afternoon I found myself having morbid thoughts of my
own. Thoughts that came out of the anger I have toward your father."

I had no idea what effect my words were having on Becka,
but it didn't seem to matter. Her psychological self was soon to
leave. It only mattered to me to be honest with her, very real. I owed
her that much, given what was about to happen. When I could think
of nothing more to say, and Becka would offer nothing, I ended
with,"Goodbye, Becka. I love you. I will always love you."

Goodbye was said, but it still wasn't over. I had to wait

through the next unknown number of hours, not knowing what was happening, or whether I would get a call from anyone, or how I would find out what had happened. No calls came. All that night I couldn't sleep. The time dragged on.

I went out early in the morning, exhausted from the stress and feeling cowardly, to hike alone in the mountains near my home. When I got back, I wanted to call Chris, but had no idea what to say, or ask. The problem was solved: there were several messages on my answering machine, two from Chris. Her first message had come at 7:30 a.m.; she said she had spent the night trying to find Becka because she found a note from her stating she was going to kill herself. I felt a terrible pang of guilt and pain for Chris. The next message from Chris had come at 9:15 a.m., that she had found Becka's body in her car that morning. She was still alive and in the emergency room. She had rented a garage and tried to gas herself.

Oh, God, no! She can't be alive. Please let her be dead. Oh, please, God, don't make her suffer anymore. She has to be dead. It's been at least sixteen to twenty hours. Why is this happening? How is this possible? It can't be. It must not.

The last message was a Dr. Chu from the emergency unit, wanting me to call him. I identified myself as Becka's therapist and answered a few of his questions. He explained: "This woman was found in her automobile by her roommate. She was showing minimal vital signs and arrived in the emergency room already on oxygen. When a patient comes in already on life supports, I am obliged to continue treatment, even though her roommate had shown me the document that was found in the car with the patient, stating that she does not wish any support systems. It is my belief that she will not make it without life support. I believe that she has suffered massive brain damage, due to the length of time she apparently has had little oxygen. But I cannot take her off the oxygen. It just isn't the policy of this hospital."

I was outraged. "Are you telling me that Becka's legal document, after all the trouble she went to to make it, is meaningless—that her Living Will has no validity in this context?"

"We have legalities to follow, too. Can you accept the responsibility for asking the medical staff to take her off oxygen?" It seemed that he was stranded with a moral and legal dilemma and wanted me to be culpable. The shock that I was really having this conversation was starting to take effect. My anger kept me focused.

"All I can tell you, Dr. Chu, is that I think you should respect that poor woman's wishes as stated in her legal document and let her rest in peace."

I was in agony, now even greater than before, fantasizing that Becka's spirit was hovering over her racked, pathetic body on a sterile hospital gurney, in utter dismay that she still could not get escape out the window. What more did she have to do? Dear Becka had had so much difficulty with living, and now was having just as much difficulty dying. Dr. Chu tried to be patient with me. He knew this situation was as hard for me as it was for him. He asked if I knew how to contact her mother. He would ask her mother what she wanted him to do, so I readily gave him her phone number.

The next phone call came two stressful hours later. It was Chris again, this time with news that Becka had just been taken off oxygen. It took only a few moments for her to leave her suffering the final time.

She's free! At last, she has finally escaped.

Epilogue

Thirty years ago this saga was an actual part of my life and practice. It was not the only thing going on, but I have shown it was a time of tremendous upheaval for me personally in many ways. I sought to have it published, but the letters I mailed out (no internet yet for doing it electronically) met with resistance, and just no reply at all. It wasn't unusual then for the unknown writer to encounter mostly rejections, but I knew part of it was subject matter. It never gets easier to hear the details of what all people, women, men, and children suffer at the hands of other humans in the form of physical and sexual abuse.

What was needed, is still needed: awareness, compassion, mental health care, legal assistance, openness, education and most important:
END THE BLAMING OF THE VICTIMS.

It is never a matter for joking, even though it relieves one's conscience to laugh. After the laughter of discomfort, get serious; take responsibility to be attuned; help someone; or get help yourself.
Parents: don't just educate your daughters … educate your sons, too. We all need to help with the solution and not be part of the problem. We need to remember that it is not really that difficult to respect other humans, in every context.

To contact the author send email to

klyn864@gmail.com